Inside INTERNAL AFFAIRS

An In-Depth Look at the People, Process & Politics

JOHN F. HEIN, CPP

43-08 162nd Street
Flushing, NY 11358
www.LooseleafLaw.com
800-647-5547

1st Printing 2012
2nd Printing 2013

Library of Congress – In Publication Data

Hein, John F.
Inside internal affairs : an in-depth look at the people, process & politics / by John F. Hein.
p. cm.
Includes bibliographical references and index.
ISBN 978-1-60885-052-5
1. Police corruption--United States. 2. Police misconduct--United States. 3. Police internal investigation--United States. 4. Police--Complaints against--United States. 5. Police administration--United States. I. Title.
HV7936.C85H45 2013
363.25'9323--dc23

2012035492

Cover by *Sans Serif,* Saline, Michigan

TABLE OF CONTENTS

DEDICATION

Dedicated
to
Margaret Hein Myers

About the Author

John F. Hein is an adjunct instructor for American Public University System with 35 years military and civilian security and law enforcement experience. He earned a Bachelor of Arts in Business Administration and a Master of Arts in Public Service with an emphasis in law enforcement. He has taken numerous courses offered by the Federal Law Enforcement Training Center and the Air Force Office of Special Investigations (AFOSI) Academy, Brunswick, GA. He is a member of ASIS International, an association of security professionals, and has been a Certified Protection Professional (CPP) since 2001.

He began his military career in 1968, as an active duty Special Agent with U.S. Army Military Intelligence (MI) and was assigned to the 902d MI Group, Pentagon Counterintelligence Force and also the 502d MI Battalion, Seoul, South Korea. As a member of the U.S. Coast Guard Reserve, he was assigned to port security duties for six years before joining AFOSI as a reserve special agent. Immediately after the September 11th attacks, he was recalled to active duty and spent 2½ years with AFOSI in various positions at HQ, AFOSI, Andrews AFB, MD; the Counterintelligence Field Activity, Arlington, VA, and the Criminal Investigation Task Force, Ft. Belvoir, VA. He retired from the Air Force Reserve in August 2005, with 35 years military service.

His civilian law enforcement career began in 1973 as a deputy sheriff for the Will County Sheriff's Police, Joliet, IL. He spent 27 years as a federal special agent in three federal agencies; Internal Revenue Service, Criminal Investigations Division, U.S. Department of Transportation, Office of Inspector General, and the U.S. Customs Service, Office of Investigations, Office of Internal Affairs and Office of International Affairs; stationed in Chicago, Miami, Washington, DC, and New York City. While stationed in Miami for U.S. Customs, he was assigned for 2½ years to the Florida Joint Task Group, a joint Drug Enforcement Administration/U.S. Customs Interagency Unit.

In November 2001, he retired from U.S. Customs as an Area Director, Foreign Operations, Office of International Affairs, after being activated by the Air Force Reserve.

He has been an adjunct instructor of criminal justice for the American Public University System since 2004.

ACKNOWLEDGMENTS

To the people who taught me that ethics, morals, and hard work will fulfill my dreams: Clarence J. Hein and Marjorie E. Cleaver Hein, Brother Leonard Stoffel, FSC (Joseph Stoffel) of De LaSalle High School, Chicago; George R. Price of the Walgreen Drug Co.; and Father John Fogarty, O. Carm., former Campus Minister, Lewis University, Romeoville, IL.

To the people who taught me how to live and enjoy life: Kathy Ann Pinter Hein, Jason Hein, Michael (Mike) Hein, Kathleen (Katie) Hein, and Vern Stemke of Commonwealth Edison, Joliet, IL.

To all the internal affairs investigators, past, present, and future, who believe fair play is best for the individual and the organization.

I thank the many law enforcement officers and administrators, city, county, township, state, and federal, identified and anonymous, who helped me with this book. Many officers from the states of Virginia, New York, Illinois, Indiana, Florida, Tennessee, Georgia, North Carolina, South Carolina, Michigan, Washington, Wisconsin, California, Pennsylvania, Ohio, Colorado, Texas, Massachusetts, Kentucky, and Maryland contributed to this work. I understand why many of you decided to stay anonymous.

I also thank a retired U.S. Customs Special Agent who will remain anonymous. I worked with her in Miami assigned to the Office of Investigations and again in Washington, DC, while we both were assigned to the Office of Internal Affairs. She gave me counsel and shared her knowledge when I needed it most. Thank you also goes to a very special federal official who gave me guidance and professional advice on the hiring process and pointed me in the right direction. I also thank Shelley Vance, a friend who spent many hours giving advice and encouragement and I needed lots of encouragement. Thanks go to my brother, Richard M. Hein, for the advice and counsel he always freely gives. Very special thanks to Marilyn A. McBride Freeman who so unselfishly gave her time when she had little time left to give.

I thank Milo Grasman and Wayne Roques of the Drug Enforcement Administration, and Donald Lucky Clark of the former U.S. Customs Service for taking a seasoned white collar crime investigator and transforming him into an acceptable narcotics smuggling investigator.

Thanks also go to numerous subject matter experts who reviewed a draft manuscript:

Raymond F. Connolly, former U.S. Air Force Air Policeman, Special Agent (retired), U.S. Air Force Office of Special Investigations. *John G. Shirley*, former Trooper, Florida Highway Patrol; Deputy Regional Special Agent in Charge (retired), Department of Homeland Security, Tampa, Fl; former instructor, Federal Law Enforcement Training Center, Brunswick, Ga. *Tim Hardiman*, Inspector (retired), New York City Police Department. *Michael F. Pavone*, Detective Lieutenant (retired), Massachusetts State Police, Internal Affairs Section; Recording Secretary, National Internal Affairs Investigators Association. *Edward J. Hagerty*, PhD, Lieutenant (retired) Philadelphia Police Department; Special Agent, U.S. Air Force (reserve) Office of Special Investigations. *Drexel T. Neal*, Assistant Chief/Commander of the Bureau of Internal Affairs (retired), Lexington, KY Division of Police; current Manager, Staff Services and Planning Office, Kentucky Department of Criminal Justice Training. *Joseph Gallazzi*, Captain (retired) New York City Police Department; Special Agent (retired) U.S. Air Force (reserve) Office of Special Investigations. *Constance St. Germain-Driscoll*, Associate Vice President and Dean, School of Public Service and Health, American Public University System. *Carl G. Freeman*, former Lansing, IL Police Officer, former U.S. Border Patrol Agent, Officer-in-Charge (retired), U.S. Immigration and Naturalization Service, Springfield, IL. *Ralph R. Smith*, President and CEO, FedSmith.com. *Susan McGuire Smith*, General Counsel, FedSmith.com. *Berle Littmann*, Supervisory Special Agent (retired), Internal Revenue Service, Criminal Investigations Division; Special Agent (retired) U.S. Army Intelligence Command; former Chief Investigator, Special Investigative Counsel's Office, Committee on the Judiciary, U.S. House of Representatives.

I also express appreciation to many individuals who gave much time and effort to contribute to this publication. Thanks goes to *Dr. Jeffery T. Walker*, Professor and Chair, Department of Criminal Justice, University of Arkansas at Little Rock, Special Agent (retired), U.S. Air Force (reserve) Office of Special Investigations. *Robert R. Fuesel*, Supervisory Special

Agent (retired), Internal Revenue Service, Criminal Investigation Division; Special Agent (retired), U.S. Air Force (reserve) Office of Special Investigations, former Executive Director, Chicago Crime Commission. *Steve Marks*, former Special Agent U.S. Army Intelligence Command, former Arizona Republic law enforcement beat reporter. *Raymond J. McGury*, former Chief, Bolingbrook, IL Police Department. *Dr. Stephen M. Hennessy*, Associate Professor of Criminal Justice, St. Cloud State University, St. Cloud, Minnesota. *Wayne W. Schmidt*, Executive Director, Americans for Effective Law Enforcement. *Homer J. Williams*, former Assistant Commissioner, U.S. Customs Service, Office of Internal Affairs. *Bruce Mercer*, Program Director (retired), International Anti-Corruption and Integrity Awareness Program, Department of Homeland Security, Immigration and Customs Enforcement. *Adrian Van Brussel*, Investigator (retired), Cook County (IL) Sheriff's Police Department. *Jeffrey M. Vargo*, Deputy Chief, Susquehanna Township Police Department, Harrisburg, PA. *K.M. Castelloe*, Captain, North Carolina State Highway Patrol. *Willard "Neal" White*, Chief, department will remain anonymous. *Gary Hillberry*, Special Agent in Charge (retired), U.S. Customs Service. Corporate executive (retired) who will remain anonymous, Johnson & Johnson. *Lon Eilders, Sr.*, Lieutenant (retired), Manager, Accreditation and Planning, Chattanooga, TN Police Department. *Kevin Anderson*, Anderson Software. *Richard W. Carter*, Judge (retired), Director of Legal Service, Crime Stoppers of the United States of America, Inc. *Detective James Howe*, department will remain anonymous. *Randy Rider*, Lieutenant (retired), Douglasville, GA, Police Department, former President, National Internal Affairs Investigators Association. *Dr. Gilbert Peterson*, PhD, Associate Professor, U.S. Air Force Institute of Technology, *Robert W. Weber,* former Director, Office of Professional Responsibility, Immigration and Customs Enforcement; Deputy Assistant Director (retired), Homeland Security Investigations, Department of Homeland Security; President, Robert Weber Consulting; *Tom Cowper. Frank Serpico.*

Introduction

I was in county, federal, and military law enforcement for more than 30 years. I worked with many fine dedicated officers who worked hard and exhibited a professional command presence and respect for the citizens they served. However, there is a minority of officers who, because of hasty action or conscious choice, make poor decisions that negatively affect citizens, other officers, and entire departments.

Police misconduct is as old as the profession itself. Misconduct of the eighteenth, nineteenth, and twentieth centuries still happens today. Poor leadership, little or no supervision, political influence, and the acceptance of bribes as a way to supplement salaries all have added to a long history of police dishonesty and bad acts. Over time, police science has made many changes to improve service and professionalism, from call boxes to dash-mounted computers, from walking a beat to police vehicles with state-of-the-art communications systems. What has not entered the twenty-first century, as did updated police technology and techniques, is sufficient ethical reform of police corruption.

Modern policing has transformed the days of on-the-job training to months of classroom instruction, role playing, problem-solving, and group discussions. Job requirements in many departments and agencies have gone from little if any formal education to a high school diploma, two years of college, or a four-year degree. What heightened training and increased requirements have not done is stimulate total ethical reform. As modernization has evolved in police discipline, ethics reform has had only a limited effect on the law enforcement profession. Ethical changes have taken place from the "outside" because of citizen pressure in reaction to civil rights demonstrations and so-called police "riots." The media have played a role in reform by reporting police misconduct and to a lesser extent by airing "feel good" T.V. programs like *Adam-12.* Internal ethical reforms, however, have had a lesser impact. Generally, reforms from the "inside," unless prodded by scandal, have had limited impact because of the narrow self interest of police leaders and a clear lack of actionable concern from elected officials.

While historically there have been periodic calls for higher ethical standards, scandals continue in some of the same police departments receiving these very calls for higher standards. These troubling recurrent incidents suggest modern ethical standards are not as stringently enforced as the requirement to wear a clean uniform.

It is evident that true change will continue to come from "outside" sources that will obligate the "inside" to raise ethical standards by enforcing already accepted principles. Many elected officials and to a lesser extent law enforcement leadership will take drastic steps to enforce ethical standards only when compelled by public opinion.

Human nature makes ethics a difficult sell to some officers. For various sociological and psychological reasons some officers never rise to the standards demanded of them. In addition, some would argue that organizations representing the rank and file are more concerned with protecting officers from department management and the citizenry than fostering high ethical standards among their membership.

As law enforcement officers protect the social order, police culture must be of a higher caliber than the culture of the citizens the officers protect, even if the officers are a product of the same citizen culture. Police discipline must be a stable system that maintains acceptable behavior by citizens while, at the same time, maintaining their own ethical conduct.

As the emerging twenty-first century becomes more complex law enforcement must be proactive and stay ahead of a changing society, not reactionary as was typical, especially in the mid- to late-twentieth century. The divide between the haves and have-nots is widening. The separation between political parties is widening. It seems compromise and crossing party lines is a thing of the past, which has created more distance between those for and against social change. The law enforcement community must stay above the fray and continue to protect the acknowledged social order.

Many will find the following pages controversial as are most aspects of an investigation of a law enforcement officer. My ethics, beliefs, and experiences formed the opinions given in this book. I speak to The Lord every day, but am not outwardly religious. I was accused of being righteous twice in my life, both while working for the U.S. Customs Service; however, I consider myself just someone who, when the need arises, stands up for what is right. Being called righteous made me think I had absolute ethics; that there is only right or wrong and no gray areas to consider. I realize, however, that ethics are to some degree relative. I understand everything is not black or white, and there is room for discretion.

I still can hear my father telling me to be honest and not cheat. (I also vividly remember him telling me that no son of his was going to be a "copper.") I believe in giving back to society by volunteering, supporting worthy causes, and protecting those who cannot protect themselves.

Why Write a Book About Internal Affairs?

For a period of time during my years as a law enforcement officer, I served with a federal Office of Inspector General. Although the vast majority of the investigations I conducted were related to contract fraud and bid rigging, I also investigated departmental employees for wrongdoing. Notwithstanding the fact I was an occasional internal affairs (IA) type, I was the recipient of insulting comments while investigating programs managed by department employees that apparently gave them a feeling of "big brother is watching." I also was a reservist for the Air Force Office of Special Investigations for 23 years. Calling AFOSI an internal affairs organization might cause an argument, but as a reservist I did conduct internal investigations of Air Force members. Snide comments by U.S. Air Force members were infrequent, but there were many stories of an occasional high-ranking officer's dislike for AFOSI. But the reason that led me to write about employee investigations and internal affairs investigators was my experience inside and out of the Office of Internal Affairs while a special agent with the United States Customs Service.

My father told me many years ago that I would make three memorable mistakes in my life and three great choices I would never forget. I will not go into my memorable mistakes, but I did make three great choices not necessarily listed in order of importance. At the age of 21, I joined the U.S. Army; at 29 I married my wife Kathy; and at 39 I transferred federal agencies and joined the U.S. Customs Service.

Starting in the late 1970s, the Customs Service began a metamorphosis from a small agency of about 500 special agents along with other professionals, to well over 3,000 special agents by the late 1980s. By then U.S. Customs totaled more than 20,000 employees, including Customs

Inspectors, Import Specialists, and others. During this mass hiring of special agents, I and others questioned why some of the new employees were hired. Along with questionable backgrounds or associations of some new hires, it appeared that some special agents were promoted to senior agent status merely to fill a position before it was lost. Added to poor hiring practices and promotional decisions was the U.S. Customs' culture. I can speak only for the culture of the Office of Enforcement, later called the Office of Investigations, to which I was assigned for more than ten years.

A joke circulated that the Customs Service had over 200 years of tradition unimpeded by progress. The Customs Service was an uncomplicated organization. While training at the Federal Law Enforcement Training Center in Brunswick, GA, an instructor questioned why he was distributing Special Agent Handbooks (policies and procedures) in front of a class of new special agents. He stated that no one ever looked at it. I later found that if you wanted to determine how to draft an official request for, say, operational funds, you shouted down the hall until someone said they had a "go by," a recently approved document making the same or similar request. As loose as its policies and procedures were, the U.S. Customs Service was a great place to work, conducted many sophisticated investigations, and had many successes.

Along with little acknowledged or ignored policy other than what was required in the Federal Rules of Evidence, the "good old boy" network was alive and well. The network established and promoted a culture of playing hard, fast, and loose with few rules. Certain agents could do no wrong while others were castigated for minor infractions or for merely disagreeing with a member of an informal group of agents with powerful senior leaders. Certain allegations or suspicions of wrongdoing were never reviewed or investigated because they were kept quiet and never reported to the Office of Internal Affairs. If someone did not go along with the status quo, he was in danger of professional and personal attack.

With a "cowboy" attitude and culture of unaccountability, the Office of Internal Affairs was considered by many to be a mandated nuisance. Many leaders in the Office of Investigations had only contempt for the Office of Internal Affairs and its investigators. This, along with the fact that internal affairs investigators were often portrayed in the media as cut-throats, led me to wonder "What creates the culture of *laissez faire* and distrust?" In the Customs Service it might have been the lack of management support of the internal affairs function. When I transferred from the Office of Investigations to the Office of Internal Affairs, I found a well-organized and managed ethical program despite little support from the parent organization, the U.S. Customs Service.

I realize now that U.S. Customs management did not put forth a command presence that showed support for the IA function. The negative command presence exhibited resistance, dislike, and an expression of disapproval and encouraged the same attitude from the rank and file. What U.S. Customs management failed to understand was that the internal affairs function is a tool to better manage an organization.

I wrote this book out of frustration because of the attitudes I encountered when I was involved in internal investigations; attitudes that may have narrowly benefited the officers and leaders who expressed them, but were not necessarily best for the department or the citizens served.

My intention is to bring to the surface many misunderstandings and misconceptions about the internal affairs function even though much of what I have to say is subjective. From my perspective, I will show how an internal affairs organization works or does not work, and how it should and should not work. In addition, I believe the function I describe, including ethics, should be part of mainstream education in law enforcement academia. Further, my hope is that investigators new to employee investigations, as well as employees, leaders, managers, and others will develop a better understanding of the IA function and become more accepting of a mechanism designed to protect, not antagonize.

In discussing my efforts with coworkers, I was asked if my work would be fiction or nonfiction. I answered affirmative to both. At the time I was unsure whether I could gather enough, little discussed factual information to make my case. I can now say fiction has been overwhelmed by reality. But many believe the IA function is too sensitive to discuss openly. While conducting inquires for this project, several contacts suggested I discontinue my efforts. Others simply ignored my request for information. Many friends believed I would reveal "secrets" everyone knows, but no one talks about. Others did not want to rehash old, embarrassing news. There is enough controversy in law enforcement without uncovering more close to home.

I believe my years of conducting, supporting, or supervising employee investigations give me the requisite knowledge to write this work. I have witnessed it, experienced it, and discussed it as it happened; I did not just read about it. Some may say there is insufficient research to back up what I have written, but I believe in the Dirty Harry theory: "When a naked man is chasing a woman through an alley with a butcher knife and a hard-on, I figure he isn't out collecting for the Red Cross."[1] I do not condone Harry's well-known noble cause corruption, but use the quote as an illustration.

Not all people have had the same experiences I have had. Reportedly, there are more than 15,000 law enforcement organizations in the United States, which makes generalizations difficult. Relationships and perceptions can be different in large and small organizations and in local and statewide departments and federal agencies. It can be better or worse because of organizational culture; because of management support or the lack of it; and because of local public values. Many things I have written here may be controversial within the internal affairs community, to leaders, managers, employees, and to the reader. It would be naïve for me to believe others embrace the same thoughts or express the same opinions. I invite readers to present their experiences, opinions, comments or rebuttals to insideinternalaffairs@gmail.com

Notes

Sinyard, Neil. (1995). *Clint Eastwood.* Crescent Books. Pages 29–30.

Gender-Neutral References

Since the passage of amended civil rights legislation in the early 1970s, a diverse workforce has become the norm. Female law enforcement officers have added notable value to community relations, the enforcement of law, the investigation of crime, the protection of citizens, and to many other aspects of the criminal justice system. Throughout this book, references to an officer or other individual, where I use the terms "he," "him," and "his," also refers to female officers or individuals. Until the English language adopts a *singular*, gender-neutral referent, I have chosen to use the terms "he," "him," and "his," which have traditionally referred to either a man or a woman rather than the gender-neutral, but plural, "they," "them," and "their."

End of Chapter Questions

At the end of each chapter the reader will find case study and discussion questions. For the law enforcement student the case study and questions are presented to encourage further thought on the subject matter. There are not necessarily right or wrong responses. Outside resources may be necessary to fully answer a question.

Instructors of Criminal Justice

The content of this non-fiction publication can be used to present instruction on the internal affairs function, the internal affairs process and ethics in law enforcement. An Instructor CD is available to criminal justice instructors to assist in the presentation of this subject matter. The CD, which includes more than 400 multiple choice, fill-in-the-blank and true/false questions and an instructor's guide, is available upon request.

Chapter One
The Beginning

In most organizations, an employee investigation is a sensitive issue. The employee being investigated can become unsettled, many times agitated, and mentally and emotionally exhausted. Employees directly or indirectly involved can also become emotionally excited or disturbed.

I was a county, federal, and military law enforcement officer for more than 30 years. Many times during my career, even after joining the internal affairs community, I experienced the uncomfortable feeling of knowing that someone, other than my supervisor, had the authority to review my actions. In my mind I sometimes doubted a statement, an action or inaction that could cause me to be investigated. A complaint by a subject under investigation could cause a dreaded review of my investigative techniques, adherence to policy, or, even worse, adherence to the rules of evidence. An inadvertent mistake could be deemed willful. A mistake could cause a dedicated investigator, including an internal affairs investigator, to be investigated.

The internal affairs function of investigating officer misconduct and the internal investigators themselves are many times viewed as unfair. Both are part of the management structure in any organization, which can be the cause of distrust. Officers under investigation feel vulnerable, threatened, and sometimes defenseless against baseless allegations. For much of my career, I disliked internal investigators as did most of my friends and coworkers.

In 1979 the tables were turned; I moved to the dark side. People who had nothing to fear feared me or at least did not want to be around me. Once when I walked into a bustling lunchroom, conversation stopped and all heads went down. This might be an unusual reaction to an internal investigator's presence in a lunchroom, but it happened. In my next agency the relationship between employees and internal investigators was worse because of the lack of support from management. Such is life in the public sector for an internal affairs investigator.

An investigator must deal with resentment due to fact, difference of opinion, or merely because of the perception of inequity. If an employee is exonerated, the resentment does not go away: "See, I told you so!" Resentment and fear can also be caused by the fact that, given enough time, an investigator can almost always find wrongdoing on the part of any individual, but a witch hunt by internal affairs is always wrong. An allegation may be anything from coming in late to work and leaving early, the egregious mismanagement of a program, or an affair with a coworker to more serious criminal violations like excessive use of force, bribery, or theft. Almost everyone has done things they regret, such as, violated departmental policy, committed a criminal act, or disrespected a citizen.

Over time, my confusion about the relationship between employees and the internal affairs function made me look beyond my experience; although while researching this work, I looked at the caliber of people with knowledge well above mine and felt like a meter maid among chiefs. But it became a passion because of frustration due to continuing negative attitudes toward the IA function. Some employees showed their hatred for internal affairs even when they had nothing to fear. They listened to others, to rumors, and innuendo.

Many fiction and nonfiction books have been written about the many facets of law enforcement, but less is found on the relationship among management, employees, and the internal affairs function. Books and articles have been written and studies have been conducted on patrol, criminal investigations, ethics, use of force, probation, parole, the prosecutor, and the courts. However, less information is found on internal employee investigations even though the internal affairs function is as important as other facets of law enforcement. I found organizations, notably the Charlotte-Mecklenburg Police Department, to have an outstanding publication explaining the relationship between all four elements; *employees* and *the internal affairs function*; with the addition of the relationship *the department* has or wishes to have *with citizens the department serves*. Yet, few departments place the development of interrelationships and ethics training on the same level as officer protection. I also found that the focus on ethics changes as often as a department's leadership.

Scattered information on employee investigations might be due to their secretive nature. Privacy laws have something to do with the secrecy, but how many managers want to discuss the fact that a rapist, thief, or wrongdoer is part of their organization? Poorly conducted and led internal investigations, the lack of ethics, and conflict among officers, citizen complaints, and leadership failures result in many departments and agencies turning a blind eye.

Read a newspaper or watch the nightly news and you will see why any organization needs an employee investigations section. A difference in, or lack of ethics, a misunderstanding, a fit of anger, a dumb mistake, a misconception, or a willful act can be cause to investigate the action or inaction of an employee. Internal investigations of policy or of a criminal violation protect the public, the organization, and the people within it.

Without a strong internal affairs function supported by management, an organization can lose focus and public support; eventually it can even lose control of itself. No chief, mayor, or agency head wants to lose control of an internal investigation to the Federal Bureau of Investigation. The phrase: "play it close to the vest" and the word "secrecy" both characterize J. Edgar Hoover. Across the country there continues to be a move, arguably a limited move, by civic organizations and others to establish citizen review boards. Some boards are created by legislation while others are created by police departments, city governments, or independent government agencies. Many are established because of emotionally charged citizen demands in response to misconduct by officers. Having a citizen review board can give a department a sense of transparency. I will not debate the need for citizen review, but departments can lose management control [proponents will debate that] when an outside organization begins to examine conduct.

A leader always is responsible for the actions of his subordinates. Many chiefs of police have lost their positions because of employee wrongdoing, or more appropriately said, because of the chief's apparent ignorance of it. Plausible deniability was first coined in the 1970s during a Senate investigation of Central Intelligence Agency operations conducted in the early 1960s. The term represents undocumented information known to government officials, but knowledge of which can be denied if the information is made public and found to be scandalous. In a police organization plausible deniability might involve undocumented, but reliable information that an officer is accepting bribes or assaulting motorists during traffic stops. Because of politics or the desire to avoid public scrutiny the undocumented information is never acted upon. One reason for the establishment of citizen review boards is that some governmental agencies have failed to have or support a strong internal affairs function and the ethics it represents.

The media is replete with examples of public misconduct by law enforcement officers: officers of all ranks, from local, county, and state-wide departments, and from federal agencies. Misconduct can be anything from sexually assaulting females, dealing drugs, stealing property, to doing stupid things like seemingly assaulting rather than subduing Rodney King while trying to arrest him. The list is long and wide.

Corruption by public officials, including law enforcement officers, is not a new phenomenon. "The 'lawlessness' of the police—their systematic corruption and nonenforcement of the laws—became one of the paramount issues in municipal politics during the nineteenth century."[1] The Lexow Committee investigation in 1894 discovered the "miracles" New York City Detective Thomas Brynes could work when his expertise was needed. "If a particularly valuable piece of property was stolen, Brynes could arrange for its return through his contacts in the underworld."[2] It was discovered that Brynes' wealth was enormous as a result of his relationship with professional thieves and prominent figures. "The findings, however, were drearily repetitious and were not untypical of conditions in other large city police departments."[3]

Corruption in the United States became so outrageous in the 1920s that the National Committee on Law Observance and Enforcement was created in 1929 by President Herbert Hoover. The committee, commonly called the Wickersham Commission, focused on the widespread disregard for alcohol prohibition. However, of the 14 published volumes, two concentrated on American police. Report 11, *Lawlessness in Law Enforcement*, authored by August Vollmer "found a widespread pattern of police abuse ... police could be expected to deny accusations ... the inflicting of pain, physical or mental ... is widespread throughout the country ... Other abuses included protracted questioning, the use of threats (usually physical harm), illegal detention, and the use of physical brutality to make arrests."[4]

In the early 1970s The Knapp Commission publicized the New York Police Department's "institutionalized corruption and made Frank Serpico a household name."[5]

In 1993, *The New York Times* reported, "In a harshly critical report, a special mayoral panel asserted yesterday that the New York City Police Department had failed at every level to uproot corruption and had instead tolerated a culture that fostered misconduct and concealed lawlessness by police officers."[6]

In 2000, the Report of the Rampart Independent Review Panel was issued regarding a specialized unit assigned to the Los Angeles Police Department Rampart Area. The unit, Community Resources Against Street Hoodlums (CRASH), had many successes. "The 'success' of CRASH, however, came at a great price. Rampart CRASH officers developed an independent subculture that embodied a 'war on gangs' mentality where the ends justified the means. They resisted supervision and control and ignored LAPD's procedures and policies. The misconduct of the CRASH officers went undetected because the Department's managers ignored warning signs and failed to provide the leadership, oversight, management, and supervision necessary to control this specialized unit. The ultimate result is a police corruption scandal of historic proportions, involving allegations not just of widespread perjury and corruption, but of routine evidence-planting, and incidents of attempted murder and the beating of suspects."[7]

In 2007, the City of Chicago "agreed to pay nearly $20 million to settle lawsuits filed by four former death row inmates who claimed they were tortured by Chicago police and wrongly convicted ...two special prosecutors released a 300-page report that nearly 200 black men were tortured in police interrogation rooms in the 1970s and 1980s." Police Lt. [retired] Jon Burge and others were accused of torturing suspects by punching, kicking, burning, and shocking them to obtain confessions.[8] The actions of the CRASH unit and Lt. [retired] Jon Burge are examples of noble cause corruption; officers ignoring constitutional protections to protect society.

In October 2007, *The New York Post* reported that police corruption in New York City increased sharply in 2006. The corruption included everything from accepting sexual favors to stealing property of the dead. It was reported that arrests of corrupt New York City police officers increased 25% over those in 2005.[9]

In December 2008, the FBI arrested 15 officers who used their authority to protect drug operations, provide security for poker games and assist other criminal activities. The sting operation was conducted pursuant to reports of corruption in southern Cook County, Illinois. Charged were a Chicago officer, four officers from Harvey, Illinois, and ten Cook County Sheriff's correctional officers.[10]

Then there is the legacy of J. Edgar Hoover. Reportedly, Mr. Hoover was not the tower of justice he portrayed himself to be. If all the facts are correct, Hoover regularly violated the constitutional rights of many, used government funds for personal gain, and failed to file accurate federal tax returns. All are examples of misconduct at the highest level.

There are more than 800,000 sworn law enforcement officers in the United States. The vast majority are ethical, have a desire to serve, and have little direct contact with internal affairs. Even with direct contact, some investigations are conducted because of disagreements and mistakes, not corruption or misconduct. A law enforcement officer may enforce unpopular laws or ordinances. But public appreciation is further tempered and good officers condemned and placed under suspicion when the news media often report stories of officers' misconduct, especially the brutalization of citizens without placing the same focus on the honorable service provided.

Unquestionably any department or agency needs to support its employee investigations unit in order to dispel misconceptions, to create a better understanding of what an internal affairs unit does, and why it does it. It is important to emphasize the necessity of management support and the consequences if support is not firm and ongoing. A culture must be fostered that encourages a law enforcement officer to understand it is acceptable to disclose the actions or inactions of others, whether they are friends, family, or fellow officers, who betray the public trust.

Case Study

An officer, well known as a hothead, is accused of verbally abusing a woman during a traffic stop. You and other patrol officers have heard the officer complaining about how women are poor drivers, are stupid, and need someone to take care of them. You have personally seen the officer verbally assault other motorists. None of the other verbal assaults have generated a complaint. You have also personally seen the officer violate use of force standards and physically assault others while making arrests.

The internal affairs office in your department is not well liked by the rank and file. It is considered a management tool to harass officers by investigating minor policy violations. Management's attitude is to punish officers for minor violations and ignore or mitigate serious violations of law. The department is known for poor service to citizens, is underfunded, and has an overall failing reputation.

Community activists are mounting a campaign to force the city to replace department leadership. The ongoing controversy has caused department morale to fall and several outstanding officers are considering leaving the department.

Case Study Questions

Answer the following questions in one narrative response.

- *What is the "blue wall of silence"? Do you believe in it?*
- *If you saw another officer assault a citizen, would you report the incident to internal affairs?*
- *Why or why not?*

Questions for Discussion

Answer each of the following questions in a separate response.

- As a student of law enforcement, what is your personal perception of the internal affairs function? Discuss how you developed this perception, i.e., through personal experience, from media reports, from TV programs, from discussion with others.

- Respond to the following questions about a chosen department in one narrative response from personal experience or interview a law enforcement officer from a department of your choice.

    - *How many sworn and civilian employees are in the department?*

    - *How does the department address policy and law violations?*

    - *Does the department have a dedicated internal affairs section?*

    - *What is the relationship between employees and the internal affairs function?*

    - *How can the department's internal affairs function be improved?*

Notes

1. Walker, Samuel. (1977). *A Critical History of Police Reform, The Emergence of Professionalism.* Lexington Books, D.C. Heath & Co. Page 25.
2. Ibid., p. 22.
3. Ibid., p. 44.
4. Ibid., pp. 131 – 133.
5. Bratton, William, & Knobler, Perter. (1998). *Turnaround—How America's Top Cop Reversed the Crime Epidemic.* Random House, New York. Page 217.
6. Raab, Selwyn. (29 Dec. 1993). New York's Police allow corruption, Mollen Panel Says. New York Times Archives. Retrieved from

http://www.nytimes.com/1993/12/29/nyregion/new-york-s-police-allow-corruption-mollen-panel-says.html

7. Rampart Independent Review Panel, Report of. (16 Nov 2000). Executive Summary. Page 1.
8. Babwin, Don. (7 Dec 2007). Chicago to pay $20M in torture case. USA Today. Retrieved from http://www.usatoday.com/news/nation/2007-12-07-134317093_x.htm
9. Weiss, Murray. (22 Oct 2007). Crooked-Cop Cases Surge: NYPD's Top-Secret Corruption Report Offers A Look Inside the Rank and File. New York Post.
Retrieved from http://www.nypost.com/p/news/item_oMzS4gu8fR8W20gTJ3sRRL
10. Robinson, Mike. (3 Dec 2008) FBI Agents Staged Stings on Corrupt Illinois Officers. Associated Press. Retrieved from http://www.foxnews.com/wires/2008Dec03/0,4670,IllinoisPoliceCorruption,00.html

Suggested Reading

Bratton, William & Knobler, Peter. (1998). *Turnaround: How America's Top Cop Reversed the Crime Epidemic.* New York: Random House.

Stamper, Norm. (2005). *Breaking Rank: A Top Cop's Exposé of the Dark side of American Policing.* New York: Nation Books.

Wadman, Robert, C., & Allison, William, Thomas. (2004). *To Protect and to Serve: A History of Police in America.* Upper Saddle River, New Jersey: Pearson–Prentice Hall.

CHAPTER TWO
Internal Affairs and the People Served

Expectations

Everyone who enters the work force is entitled to certain expectations in the work environment: that it be a well-managed organization and free from any form of corruption.

Being part of a well-managed and respected organization can bring a sense of pride to many people. Most public service employees are caring, community-focused people who are proud of the service they provide to the citizens they serve. Employees, along with the citizens they serve, are entitled to and expect public service organizations known for integrity, accountability and freedom from corruption and dishonest practices.

Internal Affairs Function

"The internal affairs function is important for the maintenance of professional conduct in a law enforcement agency. The integrity of the agency depends on the personal integrity and discipline of each employee. To a large degree, the public image of the agency is determined by the quality of the internal affairs function in responding to allegations of misconduct by the agency or its employees."[1]

It must be understood that the internal affairs function is a key part of departmental management. It is not an enforcement function that seeks compliance with policy and laws, but a policing function that works with employees and supervisors to address issues. It does not make management decisions, but reports issues to management for determination. The internal affairs function reports; it does not suspend or adjudicate.

Within most law enforcement organizations, there is a unit or individual that provides oversight to ensure ethical conduct by employees. However, the definition of an internal affairs unit is broad. Although there is a basic theme of employee investigation, each unit is unique. An internal affairs unit in the public sector is a section or individual within a parent organization that investigates administrative and/or criminal violations by employees. A parent organization could be a city, township, county, state police department, or federal department or agency. Like any IA unit, there is no typical agency or department and many generalizations are made. Many parent organizations do not have internal investigative units or will not investigate sensitive issues and use county, state or federal authorities to investigate complaints.

A local, county, state, or federal internal affairs unit focuses on wrongdoing by law enforcement officers because of the officers' frequent contact with the public and resultant complaints. Units also can investigate misconduct by non-enforcement personnel in their parent organization when the need arises. State police units may be called upon to support smaller city or county departments to conduct internal investigations where no internal affairs units exist. An outside agency may also be called on when the allegations are so significant or politically charged that an outside, impartial investigation is warranted.

The unit also may take part in ethics training. It may conduct background clearance investigations and administrative and operational inspections, or it may focus solely on the investigation of criminal and policy violations by employees. A unit also could investigate security violations or the dissemination of proprietary data to unauthorized persons. Others may focus solely on policy violations and forward criminal violations to criminal investigators. Some units, especially federal Offices of Inspector General, may investigate fraud by grant recipients on several levels or outside vendors doing business with the parent organization. These offices also investigate parent organization employees when the need arises. My definition of an internal affairs unit includes both police and federal units and, arguably, military organizations as well.

An internal affairs unit must mirror both the department and community it serves. The investigator is usually part of a parent organization and most often the investigator is employed, trained by, part of, and loyal to that organization. Some organizations make it a practice to hire experienced investigators from other agencies. Some federal agencies, but not all, operate this way. However, when possible, the unit should have diversity in gender and race. A diverse internal affairs unit will foster greater cooperation by gender and racial minorities. Depending upon department culture or personal attitude, a minority officer may be more disposed to be candid to an internal affairs investigator of the same sex or race. Just as a female rape victim may feel more comfortable discussing the crime with another woman, a female victim of sexual harassment also may be more inclined to give more details to a female internal affairs investigator.

The Effect of Command Presence

The Function and the Process

The Commission on Accreditation for Law Enforcement (CALEA) defines the IA function as an action in response to allegations of misconduct, but the function is only a part of the overall process. The internal affairs process is much broader and includes much more than the function of an internal affairs unit. The process includes the command presence of many players. Each player in the process through his desires, actions, and interactions creates his own command presence. Command presence is an attitude that conveys an air of authority, but could also convey respect, like or dislike, support or disapproval. The combination of multiple attitudes creates a perception, either positive or negative, one of biased injustice, or one of fair and ethical treatment by the internal affairs function.

A command presence exhibits the desires, actions, and interactions of leaders, internal affairs investigators, political leaders, rank and file, union representatives, the media, community leaders, and citizens served. An individual or group command presence has a great affect on a law enforcement officer's ethical behavior by either presenting a strong ethical message, or showing a lack of ethical commitment. The process made up of people with divergent opinions and goals can work together to maintain or raise the ethical behavior of officers. The process not only plays a direct role in building trust in the internal affairs function, but also trust between the community and the department. However, in reality, one or more of the players may have agendas that serve their purpose, do not positively affect police ethics, and in fact, create a negative perception of the internal affairs function.

Department Size Matters

Personalities and gender can play a large part in who would best be an internal affairs investigator, but the size of the department can also play a role. Randy Rider, former President of the National Internal Affairs Investigators Association, believes many people may have the expertise to conduct an internal investigation, but their position in a small department may not allow them to become involved.[2]

In small departments, having the organization's leader as the investigator is problematic. The duties of a chief or sheriff are often such that they would not allow the time needed to conduct a thorough investigation in a timely manner. Furthermore, the department head most likely will be involved in the penalty process that would cause a conflict of interest. In addition, an image of unfairness may also be presented if the same, high-ranking person conducts an investigation, comes to a conclusion, adjudicates, and imposes a penalty.[3]

The officer's supervisor as an internal affairs investigator is also problematic because of negative bias or friendship. Although a supervisor should handle minor violations of policy and make a recommendation for punishment if warranted, the investigation of a significant violation of policy or of criminal law would be inappropriate.[4]

In smaller departments the decision of who to appoint to conduct an internal investigation may not rest within the department, but with someone in a position to make an unbiased and rational decision. This will not only help to eliminate the possibility of the perception of unfairness, but may avoid unwanted media attention. As previously stated, serious violations committed in a small department may not be conducted by personnel in that department, but by others in a county, state, or federal agency.

A Rocky Road to Professionalism

Historically, some type of internal affairs function or at least oversight became part of law enforcement agencies in the United States even prior to their official creation. In the

1700s, because of corruption and the negligence of duty, special effort was made to recruit "watchmen" who were responsible and would take the position seriously. Prior to the Civil War, police boards were created in cities around the United States in an effort to better administer young police departments. In the late 1800s the State of New York created the Lexow Committee, which recommended and caused the implementation of a short-lived, bipartisan police commission to weed out police corruption and malfeasance in New York City. Other cities around the country came under the control of some type of state-run or politically appointed oversight board. However, efforts to reform were transitory, as political "machines" and their agendas were more powerful than any rehabilitation attempt. At the turn of the twentieth century, many departments followed civil service standards. New testing, hiring, fitness, and training criteria were established to recruit, hire, and train better qualified officers. Despite continued efforts by reform-minded citizens, politics continued to circumvent or frustrate many improvements to further personal agendas.[5]

Continuing in the twentieth century, two world wars, the creation of professional associations, crime commissions, race relations and civil rights legislation, the GI Bill, and a continued push for higher education influenced society, which then demanded better and more professional police services. The media's appetite to report controversy rightfully added to reform efforts. The Summerdale corruption scandal and so-called police riot in Chicago in the 1960s, and the numerous corruption and misconduct revelations in New York City, Los Angeles, and other U.S. cities added to concerted, sometimes contrived and disjointed efforts of reform.[6]

The Basis for Internal Affairs

Office of Internal Affairs (IA), Internal Affairs Bureau (IAB), Office of Professional Responsibility (OPR), Office of Inspector General (OIG)—operate in various ways, some more specialized than others, but all have one basic theme: conducting investigations of employee corruption and misconduct.

Corruption, along with misconduct, can be any dishonest act or a failure to act by a public official. A public official can be anyone who is employed by a government organization to include competitive civil servants as well as appointed or elected individuals. The words "corruption" and "misconduct" are catchalls or generic terms for wrongdoing of numerous types: some criminal, some not. Both can be for personal gain or for the public good; the ends justify the means.

I define corruption as a deep-seated, intentional dishonesty that can be attributed to either an individual or an organization. Misconduct is attributed to an individual and can be as serious as corruption, but it can also be a mistake, not necessarily done purposely and where the individual has no intention of doing it again. Either can be a criminal offense or a policy violation.

There are some who will differentiate between when and where a law enforcement officer commits a crime to determine whether it is a corrupt act by an officer as a public servant, or by an officer acting as a private citizen. If an officer commits a crime off-duty using information not obtained while on duty or using information from civilians rather than from other officers, some would argue it is not police corruption. That is a naïve definition and should be rejected. When a mayor, county commissioner, sheriff, or police chief is approached by a news reporter followed by TV cameras, it would be laughable for any of them to say, "Yes, my officer is a burglar, but it has nothing to do with this department."

Whether on duty or off, law enforcement officers who commit crimes are held to a higher standard and viewed differently than members of the general public who commit crimes. When a criminal is caught burglarizing homes, he is identified as a burglar. When a law enforcement officer is caught burglarizing homes, he is identified as a law enforcement officer who is a burglar. In March 2007, an off-duty Chicago police officer, now former officer, beat a female bartender, and the beating was videotaped. The headlines did not say, "Drunken Man Beats Bartender." The headlines stated, "Chicago Police Officer Beats Barmaid." Even the gender was reported, apparently to make the situation sound worse.

Raymond J. McGury, the former Chief of the Bolingbrook, Illinois, Police Department stated that police officers are held to a different, higher standard than an average citizen. McGury was the chief when the news broke that (then) Sgt Drew Peterson was under suspicion of murdering his fourth wife and then under more suspicion of murdering his third wife. "To make a mistake is human nature, although some might believe at times, a human mistake by a police officer is corruption. But to use the knowledge gained while in a public office to commit a crime is corruption. To use knowledge of the criminal justice system to commit a felony or to gain privilege is an act of corruption that may also bring the perception of corruption to anyone close to the violator. The perception is as destructive as the real thing."[7]

The Many Faces of Corruption

There are many types of corruption. Some corruption is an outright criminal act easily seen as reported by the media, while some, arguably most, are not widely known and not reported by the media, but known to many officers.

Controlled, bilateral, or wanted corruption is accepted by the criminal element, by businessmen furthering their interests, by politicians, and by citizens who are resigned to the fact that corruption is the only way to be safe in a neighborhood. It may also be favored by some in the media because when this usually unknown corruption is uncovered, it offers a great story. A law enforcement officer can get caught up in this type of corruption willingly to keep a job or get a promotion or might be unwillingly involved with seemingly no way to get out.

Unwanted corruption, or inconvenient corruption, is that which is not controlled by those in power. It is unilateral corruption on the part of individuals and used as a means to an end. It adds no value, if any corruption does, other than to one's psyche or wallet. Examples of unwanted corruption are violations like excessive use of force or the theft of seized narcotics. This unilateral corruption gets the most frequent media attention and causes problems for those in power.

For purposes of discussion here, corruption includes: bribery, perjury, conflict of interest, favoritism, and disloyalty, but could also include theft, assault/excessive use of force, homicide, or other violation of law or policy.

Bribery is the acceptance of something of value by a public official. The benefit most often is monetary but could also be a vacation, sports tickets, a vehicle, home renovations, or anything else of value to include sexual favors. The purpose of bribery may be to curry favor on an issue or to cause the public official to favor one individual or group over another. The purpose can also be to overlook an illegal act by failing to enforce a law or by intentionally being absent at a post of duty when an illegal act takes place. Bribery is a form of theft of services.

My father was born and raised in Chicago as was I. I wanted to become a police officer since I was 14 years old. My father and I had many arguments about my career goal from the time I told him until I became a deputy sheriff in 1973 when I was 26 years old. I never knew why he was against my entering the law enforcement career field until I asked him in 1980. I was studying for my master's degree and was conducting research for a paper titled, *Education: A Way of Changing the Police Image.* After some discussion, he told me several stories, three of which I relate here.

My father told me his first contact with the police came in 1927 when he was ten years old and delivering newspapers. He delivered an afternoon paper to a tavern on the corner of 59th and Bishop in Chicago. "There were always one or two paddy wagons parked on the side and six or eight policemen inside the tavern at the bar. They were always pretty well loaded, and it seemed they always had food slopped all over their uniforms." He told me he always wondered how they managed to drive the wagons back to the station without having an accident.[8]

In the early 1950s, my father attempted to become a postal inspector for the then U.S. Post Office Department (now called the U.S. Postal Service). He told me he passed the written test with flying colors but had to pass one other test. He had to convince his city alderman that he was qualified to become an inspector. To pass this test my father was required to pay the alderman $2,000. He did not agree to the request and retired 20 years later as the superintendent of a suburban Chicago post office.[9]

Later in the 1950s, my father was driving to work very early in the morning and made a rolling stop at 66th and Ashland. He was a mailman and had to be at work at 5 a.m. "One morning he was stopped by a police officer on a motorcycle and the officer asked if my father was going to buy his breakfast. My father told the officer he only had a pocket full of change. The officer said that's OK and my father handed the officer about 75 cents in pennies, nickels, and dimes. My father continued by telling me that he saw the police hit all the neighborhood taverns around Christmas time for bottles of liquor, although he told me he still kept a respect for policemen but felt that about 75% of them were dishonest. He said it seemed to go with the job."[10]

Author's Note

> On the other hand, I saw little corruption until I was an adult. I had three memorable encounters with the Chicago police while in elementary and high school. I personally interacted with three black officers and one white officer between about 1959 and 1965 during minor adolescent behavior. All four officers were professional and appeared to have one thing in mind: the safety and well being of my friends and me.

Berle Littmann described his encounter with a bribery attempt. A man he slightly knew from a social event asked for help with an Internal Revenue Service audit. At the time, Littmann was a Special Agent for the Internal Revenue Service (IRS) and well trained in ethically responding to a bribery attempt. The man wanted Littmann's help in reducing a $4,000 tax bill. Littmann was offered one-half of any savings the man obtained. Over several weeks through monitored telephone conversations and the use of a body recorder, Littmann, along with the IRS Inspection Service (Internal Affairs), gathered evidence to convict the individual of 18 United States Code, section 201, bribery of public officials.[11]

In 2005, I became an employee of a former Washington, DC–based company: a company whose only business was fulfilling federal government contracts. The company was one of thousands of companies in the Washington, DC area whose mainstay was the federal government. They are commonly referred to as "beltway bandits." Calling the company a beltway bandit could be an understatement.

My assignment as a contract employee was as a Desk Officer in the Operations Center of the U.S. Department of Homeland Security (DHS); I coordinated message traffic between DHS and state and local emergency managers, police and fire departments. My first day on the job, prior to reporting to DHS, I was introduced to the president and owner of the company and had a short but cordial meeting. Several months later I discovered, while reading the *Washington Post*, the corporate president was indicted by a federal grand jury and eventually pled guilty to various federal charges. The charges involved "illegally influencing Defense Department contracting officials and [trying] to curry favor with two House [U.S. Congress] members, in addition to lavishing more the $1 million in cash, cars, a boat, antiques and other bribes on convicted Rep. Randy "Duke" Cunningham (R-Calif.)."[12]

Perjury is willfully giving false testimony after swearing to an oath to tell the truth. For any law enforcement officer perjury is usually committed in court at a hearing or trial before a judge. However, perjured testimony could also be giving false information under oath in a report of investigation or traffic ticket. Any false testimony violates an officer's oath of office or duty to serve responsibly and honestly. In federal purview an offending officer could be charged through several statutes: 18 United States Code (USC) 1001 for making false statements; 18 USC 1621 for lying under oath, or 28 USC 1746 for making a false unsworn declaration.

During my years in law enforcement I never considered committing perjury; but while a deputy sheriff, I did hear other officers discussing how to fill-in-the-blanks by making plausible, but fabricated statements of how something happened. An officer would testify that he saw or heard something he did not, or testify to something another officer heard or saw but the officer was not available for testimony. I have also heard of a number of federal agents—two or three over 30 years—who would "curbstone" a report. To curbstone is to fabricate all or some of a report usually because of laziness or just stupidity.

A way to commit noble cause corruption is to perjure oneself during a court proceeding. Some officers will use extreme means to support a noble, but illegal end. Violations of constitutional rights, lying in court, falsifying reports, and planting evidence to sustain a successful prosecution without factual evidence are all efforts to remove known criminals from society through a noble cause effort resulting in a corrupt result.

Conflict of interest is an action or inaction by a public official that personally benefits the public official or others with whom the public official has a special relationship.

While a deputy sheriff I saw some conflicts of interest, but most were quickly resolved. A deputy I slightly knew owned a tow truck that he operated off duty. One day I was told he no longer worked for the sheriff's police. Apparently he was not contacted often enough to make his towing service worthwhile so he began to tow disabled vehicles off the interstate without permission, charging the owners for his service. One complaint and he was gone.

While I was a federal criminal investigator another agent was investigated for a conflict because as a deciding official he caused a contract to be entered into with a close relative. It was alleged his association with the purchaser was not "arms length" and, therefore, the possibility of corruption was present. I never knew the outcome.

Favoritism, also known as discrimination or preferential treatment, can take many forms, ethically or criminally. Criminal favoritism can include the act of bribery but is the act of favoring one person, group, or thing over another. Favoritism can also be an act of prejudice or unfair treatment of a person or group of people. Favoritism can be the unfair treatment of a person or group because of beliefs, family ties or friendships. Favoritism and many other forms of misconduct can be a violation of various civil rights statutes enforced civilly by 42 United States Code [U.S.C.] 1983 and criminally by 18 U.S.C., 242, Deprivation of Rights under Color of Law and other federal civil rights statutes.

While a deputy sheriff, I was the recipient of many discounted meals. I believe the unofficial benefit of being a law enforcement officer is not a universal practice, but is widespread in the profession. I interacted with several local departments whose policy specifically excluded discounts, but most departments looked the other way. I know of at least one federal agency that readily solicits and accepts discounts in the business world.

Usually on a Friday or Saturday night before the dispatcher lit up my patrol car radio, I would stop for a beef sandwich dripping with au jus at a local shop whose owner was only too happy to give police officers a heavy discount. One Saturday night another deputy gave chase to a speeding car but lost the vehicle in traffic. I and another officer responded to the area where the vehicle was last seen. With three cars now on the lookout, we thought we could find and stop the violator. After several minutes I got a glimpse of the speeding driver at a cross street, just enough time to make identification: the delivery man and son of the owner of the sandwich shop. No arrest was made because of the relationship with the restaurateur, but the revelation caused some embarrassment for the other deputies and me. The shop was never frequented again.

Loyalty is faithfulness, adherence, and steady devotion to your employer. Being disloyal is a violation of your duty as an employee. Disloyalty is usually not criminal unless it is in the federal realm, but can lead to criminal behavior in other governmental domains. Loyalty issues include the above violations (bribery, conflict of interest, perjury, and favoritism), but could also be the disclosure of employer proprietary information or the disclosure of information of others kept in confidence by the employer, such as the National Crime Information Center (NCIC) or warrant information. The information could be personnel records, payroll figures, or disciplinary action taken on others. An even more serious loyalty issue would include not only disloyalty to a government organization but to the city, county, or state government itself. Disloyalty to a local or state government could include disclosure of plans for land annexation or proprietary purchase price offers (secret bid among competitors). Disloyalty also includes any willful act of misconduct or corruption. Ultimate disloyalty is disloyalty to the United States government. This involves conduct unknown to others or secret behavior that usually causes harm to the security of the United States. Disloyalty to the U.S. government could involve espionage or sabotage. Espionage is the act of spying to obtain proprietary political or military information of one government for another government. Sabotage is undermining or interfering with a cause or work product or destroying property or obstructing an integral operation of a government.

A recent example of disloyalty and espionage is the case of Robert Philip Hanssen. For decades Hanssen was a respected special agent of the Federal Bureau of Investigation but known as one with a strange personality. He was a top counterintelligence agent and expert on Russian affairs. He was a religious family man who collected hundreds of thousands of dollars from Russian spies who subverted U.S efforts and caused the deaths of Russian agents friendly to the United States. In February 2001, Hanssen was arrested for his treachery after a long and complicated undercover internal, counterintelligence investigation. He eventually pled to espionage charges and was sentenced to life without parole.[13]

A New Age

The twenty-first century and the increased threat of terrorism on U.S. soil have brought a new responsibility into the internal affairs realm. This new obligation not only brings added responsibility but a new relationship between the smallest police department and many federal agencies. Since September 11, 2001, each state and many cities created fusion/intelligence centers staffed by intelligence analysts and many sworn police officers. The U.S. government shares sensitive national security information with these centers. As time passes, coordination between federal, state, and city internal affairs units may increase because of this sharing of information.

No police officer who belonged to or helped a terrorist organization has yet been identified with fraudulently gaining employment. However, the federal government identified an individual who reportedly was fraudulently employed by two of the most sensitive federal organizations. On November 13, 2007, "Nada Nadim Prouty, a 37-year-old Lebanese national and resident of Vienna, Va., pleaded guilty ...in the Eastern District of Michigan to charges of fraudulently obtaining U.S. citizenship, which she later used to gain employment at the FBI and CIA; accessing a federal computer system to unlawfully query information about her relatives and the terrorist organization Hizballah; and conspiracy to defraud the United States."[14] A *60 Minutes* telecast minimized the severity of the allegations, but Prouty did plead guilty to federal charges.

It is already known that terrorist organizations are making attempts to infiltrate American society. Introducing a covert terrorist member into a large police department or even the smallest with a power plant in its jurisdiction is not outside the realm of possibility. Therefore, the internal affairs responsibilities are not the same as they were just a few years ago.

There is now much more to the function than the maintenance of professional conduct in a law enforcement agency.

Disloyalty to the United States is as much employee misconduct as a police officer assaulting a citizen. A terrorist action by a police officer is employee misconduct but on a grander scale with compound consequences. Since the attacks of September 11, 2001, subversion by a public employee whether local, federal, or military can be a reality. Federal, military, and civilian law enforcement agencies and their internal affairs units must increasingly work together to safeguard U.S. soil against terrorist acts.

Federal Government Internal Investigative Units

As do police departments, federal departments and agencies have internal affairs units, more frequently identified as an Office of Professional Responsibility, Professional Standards, or Office of Inspector General.

Numerous Offices of Inspector General (OIG) were created by the passage of the Inspector General Act of 1978. The investigation of employees is only a small part of an OIG's role to review, audit, and investigate the funding and use of federal grant monies. The Inspector General Act of 1978, as amended, established the responsibilities and duties of an OIG. The OIG Act was amended various times during the 1980s to increase the number of agencies with statutory OIGs, culminating in 1988 with the establishment of offices in smaller, independent agencies. At last count there were 57 statutory Offices of Inspector General.[15]

> The establishment of Offices of Inspector General created independent and objective units:
>
> 1. To conduct and supervise audits and investigations relating to the programs and operations of various federal departments and agencies;
>
> 2. To provide leadership and recommend policies for activities designed to promote economy, efficiency, and effectiveness in the administration of various federal departments and agencies and to prevent and detect fraud and abuse in various federal programs and operations; and

3. To keep the head of various federal departments and agencies and the Congress fully informed of problems and deficiencies relating to programs and operations and the progress and result of corrective action.[16]

Military Internal Affairs Organizations

Although some law enforcement and military professionals would argue that military units are not part of the internal affairs community, there are military units that do conduct investigations of the same type as civilian internal affairs units. Certainly military internal affairs organizations may have many more duties than a civilian internal affairs organization; in fact, many military units conduct a combination of internal employee investigations and criminal and administrative investigations of all types along with counterintelligence matters to neutralize threats to national security.

Military units include the Air Force Office of Special Investigations (AFOSI), Naval Criminal Investigative Service (NCIS), U.S. Coast Guard Intelligence and Criminal Investigations, U.S. Army Criminal Investigations Command (CID), and U.S. Army Intelligence and Security Command (INSCOM).

Also included in the Department of Defense is the Defense Criminal Investigative Service (DCIS), a civilian arm of the Defense Department's Office of Inspector General staffed with civilian personnel.

U.S. Justice Department

An internal affairs unit, whether local, state, federal, or military, can be supplemented, collaboratively or independently, by outside entities such as the Federal Bureau of Investigation. According to FBI-published information, "Public corruption is one of the FBI's top investigative priorities—behind only terrorism, espionage, and cyber crimes. Why? Because our democracy and national security depend on a healthy, efficient, and ethical government. Public corruption can impact everything from how well our borders are secured and our neighborhoods protected ...to verdicts handed down in courts of law ...to the quality of our roads and schools."[17]

Along with investigations conducted by the FBI, prosecution can be implemented under federal law by the U.S.

Department of Justice. "The Public Integrity Section oversees the federal effort to combat corruption through the prosecution of elected and appointed public officials at all levels of government. The Section has exclusive jurisdiction over allegations of criminal misconduct on the part of federal judges and also monitors the investigation and prosecution of election and conflict of interest crimes. Section attorneys prosecute selected cases against federal, state, and local officials, and are available as a source of advice and expertise to other prosecutors and investigators. Since 1978, the Section has supervised the administration of the Independent Counsel provisions of the Ethics in Government Act."[18]

Case Study

You are the commander of the Internal Affairs Bureau of a large police department. Your department chief has asked you to meet with a community leader, Richard O'Shay, an ordained minister, who is a constant thorn in the department's side. Continuous criticism from him and other community leaders is the norm. Reverend O'Shay is an unofficial chaplain of several police districts and he has many friends who are police officers. It seems no matter what the chief does to satisfy him it is not good enough. Allegations of wrongdoing by department personnel are always quickly acted upon. However, the reverend constantly complains about the way internal affairs makes allegations against good officers and how some officers told him internal affairs places officers on suspension. Reverend O'Shay does not seem to understand how the internal affairs function works. You feel this may be an opportunity to educate the good reverend.

Case Study Question

What would you say to Reverend Richard O'Shay to give him a better understanding of the responsibilities of the Internal Affairs Bureau and the difficulties faced while performing its function?

Questions for Discussion

Answer each of the following questions in a separate response.

- From your research what is *your* definition of corruption?
- What is *your* definition of misconduct? Is there any instance of policy or law violations that would be accepted and sanctioned by citizens served by a department?
- Some departments are large enough to staff an in-house internal affairs function. Others of limited size assign complaints for investigation to supervisory officers, while others may ask for assistance from outside sources. On occasion department leadership will find that an officer is under investigation by the federal government. Discuss the advantages and disadvantages of an investigation conducted in-house as compared to an investigation conducted by an external entity.

Notes

1. Commission on Accreditation for Law Enforcement Agencies, Inc. (2006). Standards for Law Enforcement Agencies. Retrieved from http://www.calea.org/
2. Rider, Randy. (25 Mar 2007). The Internal Affairs Investigator. Officer. Com. Retrieved from http://www.officer.com/article/10250041/the-internal-affairs-investigator?page=1
3. Ibid.
4. Ibid.
5. Wadman, Robert, C. & Allison, William Thomas. (2004). *To Protect and to Serve: A History of Police in America.* Pearson Education.
6. Ibid.
7. McGury, Raymond, J. (20 Oct 2008). Telephonic interview.

8. Hein, John, F. (28 Apr 1980). Education: A Way of Changing the Police Image. Governor's State University.
9. Ibid.
10. Ibid.
11. Littmann, Berle. (27 Apr 2011). Electronic interview.
12. Babcock, Charles, R. (25 Feb 2006). *Contractor Pleads Guilty to Corruption: Probe Extends Beyond Bribes to Congressman.* Washington Post. Retrieved from http://www.washingtonpost.com/wp-dyn/content/article/2006/02/24/AR2006022401737.html
13. Havill, Adrian. (2001). *The Spy Who Stayed Out in the Cold: The Secret Life of FBI Double Agent Robert Hanssen.* St. Martin's Press.
14. U.S. Department of Justice. (13 Nov 2007). News Release. Detroit, Michigan.
15. Council of the Inspectors General on Integrity and Efficiency. (2011). The Inspector General Act of 1978, as amended. Retrieved from http://www.ignet.gov/
16. Title 5, Government Organization and Employees, Title 5—Appendix: Inspector General Act of 1978. Retrieved from http://www.ignet.gov/pande/leg/igactasof0609.pdf
17. Federal Bureau of Investigation. Public Corruption. Retrieved from http://www.fbi.gov/hq/cid/pubcorrupt/pubcorrupt.htm
18. U.S. Department of Justice, Public Integrity Section. Retrieved from http://www.usdoj.gov/criminal/pin.html

Suggested Reading

Havill, Adrian. (2001). *The Spy Who Stayed Out in the Cold: The Secret Life of FBI Double Agent Robert Hanssen.* New York: St. Martin's Press

CHAPTER THREE
It's the Process

"If you tell the truth, you don't have to remember anything."
— Mark Twain
Twainquotes.com

Often in the media citizens see why an internal affairs function must be part of a law enforcement agency. Law enforcement officers make mistakes, get into disagreements, consciously violate a department policy, or commit criminal acts.

Because of a difference of opinion, enforcement of an unpopular law, an abundance of testosterone, a willful act, or a false allegation, a complaint is filed and the investigative function begins. However, even before the investigation begins, the internal affairs function is often misunderstood by the employees the unit serves. An internal affairs unit serves employees as a law enforcement agency serves the public. Employees served may have a bias against the function for many reasons. Depending on the culture in the department or agency, the bias generally holds that the investigative function is unfair.

Anyone can have a negative bias and be resentful because an internal affairs function has the authority to compel them to answer for alleged inappropriate conduct. The function holds officers accountable for their actions. In addition, the investigation of a false or unfounded allegation can have the same devastating effect as confirmed misconduct. It can be said that the involvement of internal affairs is not welcome because no one wants to be investigated whether innocent or guilty, for obvious reasons. Of course, some individuals would never admit they have done anything wrong.

The Mix Includes Many

The causes of negative perception of internal affairs spring from many sources. The internal affairs function is perceived as unfair because the internal affairs process makes it so. It can be caused by politicians attaining their goals or failing to meet promises, by businessmen looking after their own interests, or by community leaders who dramatize police-citizen interactions before the facts are known. The worst perception is created by department leadership when it does not give ethical standards and the internal affairs function the same level of attention as firearms and defensive training; corruption among law enforcement officers is overlooked and tolerated. A perception of unfairness can be further enhanced by the media reporting sensational, negative items that portray the entire department as corrupt even when only one officer or a small portion of the department may be liable. At the same time, the media fail to report positive actions by officers who place their lives on the line. A positive story may last one newspaper edition or TV news cast while a negative story may last days, weeks, and sometimes months; some never go away.

The cause of a negative bias can also be shared with citizens who live in high crime areas with frequent police contact. Citizen complaints of police actions can be unclear, controversial, and disputed, resulting in investigative conclusions by the internal affairs unit that cause more controversy. The negative bias can be shared by citizens who dislike police officers, who complain when force is used, even when that force is used to protect the complainant. The relationship between a citizen and a law enforcement officer can be somewhat the same as the relationship between an internal affairs investigator and the investigated: a vicious cycle of recriminations.

In any police department, a sworn officer has frequent interaction with the public, which is sometimes an emotionally charged confrontation. A federal officer investigating allegations of criminal fraud in a federal program or enforcing federal rules and regulations can be an unwelcome addition to anyone's day. A uniformed officer makes split-second, sometimes controversial, decisions that cause considerable consternation. In addition, a citizen seeing a patrol car in the rearview mirror and subsequently receiving a traffic summons can also lead to a difference of opinion that can instigate an internal investigation. An ordinary citizen may fail to understand an officer's duty to maintain order, the subtleties of traffic laws or the importance of traffic enforcement mandates used to reduce auto accidents. In a national survey conducted in 2005,[1] it was found that:

- Although most drivers believe they were stopped by a police officer for a legitimate reason, in a research group of more than 17,000,000 drivers stopped by the police in 2005, 13.8%, or more than 2,300,000 drivers believed they were stopped for an illegitimate reason.
- In 2005, 43.5 million people had face-to-face contact with the police. Of that 43.5 million, an estimated 1.6%, or more than 700,000 people reported they had force or threatened force used against them. Of the approximately 700,000 people, an estimated 83%, or more than 580,000, who had force used against them believed the force used was excessive.

Whether fact or fiction, reality or belief, all are perception. The almost always negative bias starts somewhere, or maybe it starts everywhere.

Inside and Out

A positive or negative perception of the internal affairs function comes from both inside and outside a department or agency. It is created outside by political posturing, citizen demands, the business community protecting illegal excesses, community leaders protecting their turf, unions pointing a finger, and the media creating a story. The perception is created inside by the actions of management, officers, civilian employees, and internal affairs investigators. A negative bias can be created just by the fact that an officer does not take responsibility for his actions.

The perception of internal affairs is also influenced by the perception of the department or agency itself. The perceptions of both influence the other: the department is corrupt because the internal affairs function is weak; the internal affairs function is weak because the department is corrupt. A department cannot totally succeed or adequately serve citizens if the organization or any of its parts is corrupt or is perceived to be corrupt.

Therefore, the perception of the internal affairs function cannot be discussed without addressing the corruption or the perception of corruption of a department or agency. Because of human nature or, more accurately, human weakness, there will always be corruption or misconduct. Either can be a criminal offense, a policy violation, or a lapse in proper conduct. To simplify the issue I will use the word "corruption" as an umbrella for this discussion.

Individual corruption can be ongoing or occasional. Corruption of an entity can be systemic to the department or to any one of many divisions or sections. Some might say agency management is corrupt because of a lack of integrity or a lack of honesty dealing with employees. Whether individual or systemic, corruption can be real or imagined, wanted or unwanted, easily seen or unknown, or at least hard to detect and caused by self-interest or mistake.

The causes that create a perception are so interwoven there often seems to be no starting point. However, the earliest point that creates a negative bias by a citizen might be the service given or treatment offered by a law enforcement officer.

> *"I needed to create an atmosphere in which both sides could be heard and understood. So I ordered Street Crime Unit cops to attend community meetings in their neighborhoods. To fight the insidious arrogance and condescension that can often be mistaken for racism among cops, I instructed beat cops and commanders to be more polite and responsive. I demanded that station houses be more businesslike and that officers greet people respectfully as they enter the building."*[2]

What I believe Bernard B. Kerik, the (then) New York City Police Commissioner, was saying is that a police officer not only must respect the citizens served, but it is OK to be nice to people. "To be nice" may sound simplistic, but I have seen officers who appeared to be too busy to bother with a citizen who was merely asking a question. A law enforcement officer must reserve his game face, his attitude, and face of authority—a certain strict command presence—for select clientele, not for the average citizen. Arrogance, aloofness, or being overbearing at the wrong time can add to a negative perception of a department and cause citizen complaints, many of which will cause officer aggravation and a further negative perception of the internal affairs function. Having the right command presence at the right time does not show weakness, but rather strength exhibited by a professional.

Author's Note

Bernard B. Kerik is a highly decorated former law enforcement officer. I use his expertise here to illustrate a point. In 2006, Kerik admitted guilt to a New York City ethics code misdemeanor. In 2009, he pled guilty to federal tax and perjury violations. Kerik was sentenced to federal prison.

I have seen officers who appeared to be "detached," almost disinterested or unconcerned with a victim's plight in minor situations like asking for directions or help with a flat tire. "I can't help you with that lady, call a tow!" I have seen and heard officers shouting at citizens, calling them names, and demeaning them while directing vehicular and foot traffic. The command presence exhibited was one of disrespect and dislike. Officers must understand they are public servants and should show respect and be sensitive to the needs of the citizens served, and reserve authoritarian, overbearing, or arrogant attitudes for a chosen few. Citizens must understand they are due respect by public servants and know the process for filing a complaint.

Adding to a real or imagined dispute may be a complaint process difficult or not easily understood or accessed. "Procedures for registering complaints should be made available to the community through the media or the agency's community relations programs. This information should also be disseminated to all agency employees." The agency should also compile "annual statistical summaries based upon records of internal affairs investigations" which should be "made available to the public and agency employees."[3]

The Needy Politician

But the beginning of a negative perception might also be in the political arena. Politicians can use an enforcement agency as a football on the political playing field. Many politicians are happy to make use of corruption to further their own agenda. An officer in a choice assignment can see what others do not, politicians at their best or at their worst. Some may see how politics work in the so-called smoke-filled backrooms. Deals are made, some for the good of the department or the citizens served. Other deals are not so good for citizens and the department is blamed. Then there are the deals made for the benefit of those making them. Politicians make promises to officers like: increased salaries and benefits if the right ballot is cast; support in racially charged community disputes over an officer's action; or supporting an adequate budget to fund a woefully equipped department. But promises are not kept. Officers see how the "system" works and the internal affairs function is part of the "system."

It Always Starts at the Top

Whether the starting point is a law enforcement officer's behavior or a political agenda, a lack of leadership is what lets a negative perception take hold. A lack of leadership support or sustained attention allows others to perceive that the internal affairs function is unfair. The function along with ethics training is not a priority for some leaders. Furthermore, denying a problem exists allows leadership, whether political or departmental, to avoid difficult situations, challenging explanations, or a media-induced crisis. Just like the saying by investigators "big cases, big problems; little cases, little problems," some leaders say, "no information, no investigation" to avoid public scrutiny.

Worse than inattention to the function is interference by leadership with investigations and the investigators who conduct them. Some may also use the function for their own purposes, debasing the mechanism to the point of unfairness. I have seen how a leader intent on minimizing fallout of investigative results will diminish evidentiary value or demonstrate how a witness or complainant has blown things out of proportion. I have seen how threats to an internal affairs investigator can affect the function. I was approached by a special agent involved in internal investigations who confided in me how, for the good of his family and career, he was leaving an agency because of threats made by a departmental executive. The executive was outspoken, brazen, and sometimes thoughtless and frequently voiced his disapproval of the intrusion of an internal affairs investigator into his or a friend's actions. This well-known intimidation caused numerous investigations to be neglected until supervisors took steps to transfer investigations to other investigators not close to the controversy. Intimidation of employees as witnesses, or at least a "caution" not to cooperate with an internal affairs investigator was also common in this agency. This situation existed only because of a negative command presence shown by many executives who are part of the internal affairs process.

The Officers

Officers may have the strongest bias toward internal affairs because they have a unique responsibility and identity. They may feel above reproach because of their responsibilities. Some may also have a sense of superiority and believe the internal affairs function is beneath them. Law enforcement officers maintain a high sense of self-esteem because they are in a position of trust and authority. Officers have powerful authority over people they encounter. It may be difficult for an officer to accept the higher authority of an internal affairs investigation over which the officer has little or no control. The officer resents that authority, which also enforces the same laws and regulations the officer does, but in a different way. Like the "them and us" attitude developed while dealing with citizens, an officer can also have a "them and us" feeling when interacting with internal affairs.

An officer who has stretched the rules or lied to convict someone may now believe that the deck is stacked against him. Some officers may cheat and steal, while others straddle a line between good and unethical. Officers are trained that lying to a suspect is ethical to obtain the truth, but some cross a line from good to evil. They know from personal experience the system is corrupt because that is how they acted. "There exists a serious threat to law enforcement, which can compromise the high ethical standards and values our profession has achieved during the past several decades. This threat is typically referred to as 'Noble Cause Corruption.' ... a mindset or sub-culture which fosters a belief that the ends justify the means ... law enforcement is engaged in a mission to make our streets and communities safe, and if that requires suspending the constitution or violating laws ourselves in order to accomplish our mission, then for the greater good of society, so be it."[4] An example of noble cause corruption is Jon Burge, a retired lieutenant from the Chicago Police Department. In June 2010, Burge was convicted of perjury and obstruction of justice in connection with the alleged torture of hundreds of suspects to force confessions.[5]

Officers may also realize what being under investigation can do to them. They investigate; now they are investigated. An investigation can affect an officer's life, his health, and the lives of his family, certainly his employment, and his financial situation. It can affect his reputation. Because he knows the system, he does not trust it.

Failed trust because of management, politicians, the media, citizens, and internal affairs: all of this helps to cause what is called the "blue wall of silence." The unspoken code: "I saw nothing, I heard nothing, I did nothing illegal," us against everyone else. The question, "Why should I expose a bad act, bring an act of corruption to light when management will not stand behind me, my fellow officers will not support me, the politicians will deny any corruption occurred, and I will be portrayed as a disgruntled employee?" The code of silence is an ingrained feature of some cultures in the law enforcement arena. The cynicism continues to multiply.

Look What You've Done to Me!

Another reason for negative bias is anger and misdirected blame. "I'm a good guy. I have been in law enforcement all my adult life. It is all I have ever done and all I know. How could you do this to me? I stole, I lied, but I am a good guy. I only stole from criminals, not good people." Therein lies the rub: a corrupt officer is not a "true" law enforcement officer, a corrupt officer does not know how to be a law enforcement officer, a corrupt officer rationalizes that he is still an officer when, in fact, he is a criminal, a rogue.

Most corrupt officers did not start out to be that way; some do, but most do not. Over time corruption is rationalized because of the criminal environment and because "everyone else is doing it." Most officers are not corrupt, but the "everyone" in "everyone else" includes other corrupt officers. In addition, many political leaders are corrupt, or at least unethical, so rationalization continues with the "system." Family and friends help in the misdirected blame. Instead of a corrupt officer taking responsibility, family and friends will help deflect the blame to internal affairs, honest officers, supervisors, or anyone else directly or indirectly involved in bringing the corrupt officer to justice. It is all part of the internal affairs process. As a result, much of what causes the internal affairs function to be viewed as unfair is caused by the officers and those close to them. Many citizen complaints are caused by the misguided, even thoughtless actions of officers. I have also known several federal officers and civilian employees investigated for a minor offense only to compound the violation by lying to a supervisor or internal investigator.

"A recent decision by the federal appeals court underscores the perils of lying to government investigators when they are investigating possible misconduct—if the offense doesn't trip an employee up, the lie most likely will. (*Delapenia v. Merit Systems Protection Board*, C.A.F.C. No. 2010-3116 (nonprecedential), 11/9/10)."[6] A federal police officer was charged with the misuse of a government vehicle by using it to drive to a Denny's restaurant. The officer lied about the misuse and signed a sworn statement attesting to the fact. He ran into a problem when federal investigators uncovered a video tape clearly showing the misuse. The officer was allowed to resign voluntarily prior to a forced removal. On appeal, a federal court stated, "By answering untruthfully, he now has to face the consequences."[7] His appeal was denied.

Over time I have been aware of several federal agents stonewalling or falsifying reports of investigation. Stonewalling in this sense means fabricating information. Others have been either accused of or charged with making false statements. Whether a policy or criminal violation, lying has far-ranging consequences for the individual and the department for which he works. Past court testimony and sworn statements as an affiant are now suspect and open to question for court appeal. Future testimony is out of the question and offenders, if still employed, must be given a position where they will never be placed in a situation where testimony is required.

It's the Leadership—Again

It is no surprise that law enforcement officers work in a hostile environment and many times will look for support from management. If that support does not materialize, distrust can replace idealism. Receiving a complaint of an alleged action, a first line supervisor might be more inclined to show support for an accused officer. However, upper management may be more inclined to distance itself from any allegation. In fact, it may be more expedient for leadership to apologize for an officer's actions giving the impression the officer is guilty before the wheels of justice turn rather than show support until all facts are known. A lack of management support along with media pot shots before all the evidence is known adds to the distrust. It does not take long for a local officer or federal agent to become a cynic. It is the "system" again; an officer may have a negative bias regarding internal affairs because of a cynical or distrustful opinion of the system in which the officer works. "In short, cynicism is the antithesis of idealism, truth, and justice—the very virtues that law enforcement officers swear to uphold."[8]

Along with cynicism of the "system" caused by management from the "inside," the cynicism can also be caused by realities on the "outside." Even if an officer is an idealist when first on the job, his professional life may change that idealism to realism. In some departments this transformation may never happen or if it does, it may take longer in some departments than in others. Some officers see mayhem, death, child abuse, and other horrific sights on a daily basis, while others see it infrequently. Some federal agents, like those assigned to the Drug Enforcement Agency, certainly see street reality more frequently than a federal agent assigned to investigate contract fraud. When added to having little trust in department management, street realities augment the cynicism.

The Union and Internal Affairs

While a Headquarters Desk Officer (field support) and Supervisory Special Agent for U.S. Customs, Office of Internal Affairs, I had limited contact with employee union representatives. I did hear many complaints, however, about union representatives from field agents who conducted employee investigations. The union representing some U.S. Customs personnel labored to influence working conditions and protect employee rights.

I heard complaints that many union representatives were confrontational and difficult to deal with. However, I spoke to investigators who I believe were unsympathetic and insensitive to employees; they may also have had a "headhunter" attitude; an approach where the ends justify the means. I believe this caused an apparent vicious cycle where attitudes of the employee and union representative aggravated the internal affairs investigator whose attitude aggravated the employee and the union representative.

I did have two notable encounters with union representatives. The first was merely a union official representing an employee, questioning me in front of an administrative judge. I gave testimony during an informal hearing in a conference room. However, the second was an official with an attitude, for which I was prepared. I interviewed an employee regarding a policy violation. A union representative was present. The interview went well until the conclusion when I informed the employee that I wanted to interview him again at a certain, later date. The representative suddenly became agitated and aggressive, stood up and announced that he would decide when and where the employee would be available. I recall the representative looked surprised when I asked him, "What's with the attitude?" Our contact had been cordial until then. The vicious cycle could have started, but I stated that there was no need to be difficult and the encounter became cordial again. The union representative's showboating also added to the perception of unfairness.

Citizens, Prosecutors, and the Courts

At times there is a conflict between controlling crime/ maintaining order and due process. The vast majority of law enforcement officers, wherever they work, are ones who want to help people. They want to help people the ethical way and control crime while maintaining order. They want to make a difference. They see things in life that should not be: rape, robbery, suffering, people who cannot help themselves, and people who take advantage of others. This is how idealistic officers become cynical. They know the citizens they serve want to be safe, but at the same time, the same citizens criticize "the police" when an injustice is perceived. Further along in the criminal justice system, officers begin to believe the court system is unjust. Prosecuting attorneys make pre-trial deals, which sometimes quickly put criminals back on the streets; law enforcement officers must then deal with the same criminal again. An officer may not care that the court system is clogged with cases, overburdened because of inadequate funding and demanding crime rate. An officer may have only one point of view, make arrests, and get convictions.

Defense attorneys assemble a plausible, but seemingly misleading defense to show reasonable doubt, and then there are the juries of peers, most times chosen by manipulation called voir dire. I watched voir dire many times. A prosecutor and defense attorney questioning prospective jurors to determine their backgrounds (Do they have a criminal record? Were they ever a victim? Do they know a victim of a like crime?), likes, dislikes, and most especially their prejudices. They are juries of peers, many uneducated, many not aware of the truths of the street; people who only see the defendant clean shaven, hair well combed, not with the weapon of choice in hand. The officer may see uneducated jurors who do not understand what is placed before them. Then there are jurors who are streetwise and know how "the system" works. For an accused officer, a streetwise juror is a tie breaker: which way does the bias go?

Officers may believe the court system is unjust, citizen jurors may side with other citizens who are defendants, and like employees with perceptions of internal affairs, a citizen juror may have a set perception of an enforcement officer caused by a grievance from one interaction. The bias cycle continues.

The Media Make It So

I believe the media are a special case and the effect the media have on the perception of law enforcement in general, and the internal affairs function in particular, needs special attention. The media includes many electronic sources, many of which show the professional along with the corrupt realities of law enforcement. However, for this discussion, I include in the media television programs, movies, and newsprint because of the historical and ongoing dramatization of the internal affairs function.

The media have changed law enforcement, some for the good, and some for the bad. Television has arguably shown professionalism in shows like *Dragnet*. It has also arguably shown professionalism in more recent programs like *NYPD Blue* and *Law and Order*. I say this even though the media have also shown some inappropriate, ill-advised, or unwise ways of performing basic law enforcement tasks to add drama.

Admittedly, I was trained as a deputy sheriff and federal agent some 35 years ago. Training has evolved for the better and expanded greatly. The six-week training I received as a newly hired deputy sheriff at the Police Training Institute in Champaign, IL, has been expanded greatly with the inclusion of many advanced subjects. Likewise, the training I received as a federal agent has also been improved. But there are still basics that have not changed. The basics may have been enhanced, but the basic principle is still there. For interviews: who, what, where, when, why, and how. Get all the facts, get the facts on record, and obtain a signed sworn statement when appropriate. I believe the media have changed that to some extent. Watch a law enforcement program on TV and you will often see an interview where a suspect admits a crime. After the admission, the officer conducting the interview will throw a pad and pencil on the table and tell the suspect to write a statement. Yes, it is best to obtain a statement in the handwriting of the affiant. However, throwing a pad on the table may enhance the drama but does not do much for the investigation. In 35 years I tried this pad-throwing stunt twice with poor results. I have taken close to 100 signed sworn affidavits, all with my active assistance. The two times I got lazy were both with law enforcement officers who were witnesses in an internal investigation. Who better to write their own statement than a law enforcement officer? But a person who writes his own statement may not know the investigative focus or scope or may not know how to express himself in writing. The officer may not understand the element of proof the investigator is seeking. The suspects you see on TV who are supposedly writing their own statement are ones who appear to have fewer qualities than a trained officer. Will the suspect write the statement and document the evidence needed without help from the investigator? In most instances, I doubt it.

TV has also had an effect on the way arrests are made. When trained by the State of Illinois and the U.S. government, I was trained that an arrest can be made in numerous ways depending upon the situation. If arresting a violent felon, an officer is more likely to have a weapon drawn and place the suspect on the ground with his hands behind his back. If obligated to arrest an 89-year-old woman for shoplifting, I suggest the arrest techniques would be less aggressive. No matter who I was arresting, I was taught to be in control and to be vigilant. I recall a video (I suppose a movie back in the mid-'70s) I was shown at the Federal Law Enforcement Training Center (FLETC). While being placed under arrest, an elderly man shot both agents who were portrayed as being inattentive and careless. Training made me understand that each situation and person must be quickly assessed and appropriate action taken. The media, on the other hand, has shown that all arrests are drama opportunities. There is a program that is broadcast periodically. I describe it as sensational journalism. An alleged pedophile arrives at a home where he believes he is meeting with a child, only to be confronted by a journalist and camera. A discussion ensues where the adult is embarrassed, or admits guilt, or tells a story, or all of the above. The pedophile then exits the home to be met by several law enforcement officers who, on camera, arrest the suspect, with weapons drawn, by shouting orders to hit the ground. As portrayed on the TV program, I have never seen the accused in a rage or being violent. The ones I have seen while watching the program come out of the house with their tail between their legs. Some officers may find this interpretation controversial, but off camera the arrest would be less dramatic and more matter of fact.

The media must report the news. That's their job. If there is no "news," a reporter will find some, anything that will make a story and, hopefully at least for the reporter, evolve into "*The* Story." With the proliferation of cable news outlets, stories are at a premium. Twenty-four hour news channels report the same stories over and over again until a new story arises: news that reports controversy with excitement; dramatic news with conflict, sensation and emotion with lots of embellishment and poetic license.

The media have portrayed internal affairs investigators for decades as tough and insensitive people who have no understanding of the officers they are dealing with when they are accused of wrongdoing. The investigator is depicted with a focus limited to making a case against the accused with no regard to mitigating factors. An internal affairs investigator is characterized as a renegade actor rather than a team player, a hostile person with a vendetta to find the accused guilty without regard to innocence. "A bad government agency or a corrupt police officer can make good television, but reports on such topics too often exaggerate the problems."[9] Likewise a hostile internal affairs investigator makes good television, but too often exaggerates the problems and inflames an already delicate balance. Therefore, the media as part of the internal affairs process taints the IA function as being unfair.

Do What Is Fair for the Employee and Best for the Citizens Served

If it is negative, the perception of internal affairs boils down to the understanding of fairness: "If I am accused of misconduct, will I get a fair shake?"

Fairness in the internal affairs function means honestly validating or disproving a complaint by gathering all evidence, all evidence including mitigating evidence, commonly called Brady material. In 1963 the Supreme Court ruled in *Brady v. Maryland* 373 U.S.83 that any evidence favorable to the defendant, which may point to innocence, must be disclosed. Fairness continues with the resulting totality of data being adjudicated impartially. Fairness also means timely and appropriate discipline, if any. But from my experience, innuendo, a false accusation, and an extended investigation are all informal types of discipline—at least that is how an accused will describe it. Discipline must be swift and must be appropriate for the violation.

Although the IA process might make the IA function look unfair, in reality "the system" gives an officer many avenues of protection.

The Non-right of the Garrity Rule

Garrity v. New Jersey, 385 U.S. 493 was a 1967 Supreme Court decision that held public employees are free from compulsory self-incrimination. Many law enforcement officers may not think of *Garrity* as a protection but a threat. Although the Garrity decision resulted from an investigation of police officers, I read *Garrity* rights to many federal employees, not one of whom was a law enforcement officer. Under *Garrity* a public employee can be compelled to give testimony and if testimony is not given, the employee can be disciplined or fired. The *Garrity* decision, however, prohibits coercion of an accused by an investigator, where coerced statements can later be used for criminal prosecution; hence the protection. If testimony is given, the employee cannot be prosecuted if it is found to be self-incriminating. Although in some departments the Garrity rights must be asserted by the employee, in my experience –

Garrity rights are openly given when:

- the investigation is administrative in nature
- no criminal violations are known at the time
- no criminal violations, if known, will likely be addressed, or
- no criminal prosecution will be made against the person given the Garrity warning.

Once *Garrity* is asserted, the employee must answer questions, but the questions must be specific to the employee's employment: no fishing expeditions or witch hunts. *Garrity* then guarantees that answers to compelled questions cannot be used against the employee in a criminal proceeding. However, the answers can be used against the employee if administrative discipline is warranted. The *Garrity* decision was reinforced by *Gardner v. Broderick*, 392 U.S. 273 in 1968.

The *Garrity* warning is controversial and considered by some as unfair because the ruling places an officer between a rock and a hard place. *Garrity* guarantees an officer cannot be coerced into incriminating himself, but the testimony can be used, if found to violate departmental policy or criminal law, for disciplinary action that can mean termination. Do not testify and be fired because department policy is violated; testify and be fired because criminal law was violated.

The accused has the right to the best and most competent defense, but the government has the duty to prosecute corruption. A good defense from the standpoint of the internal affairs function does not include the effort by the accused to stymie an investigation. The *Garrity* decision prevents officers from obstructing an investigation, but from the standpoint of the accused the perception of "unfairness" is alive and well.

The Unfairness of the Grand Jury

As a federal criminal investigator I testified before a grand jury numerous times in various cities. A grand jury is a group of people appointed by a United States district court to hear testimony to determine if probable cause exists to indict or accuse a person of a crime. The Fifth Amendment of the Constitution mandates that a person will not answer for a capital crime unless indicted by a grand jury. The purpose of a grand jury is to safeguard the rights of innocent people. It is the duty of the grand jurors to determine if probable cause exists that the accused actually committed a crime. If it is determined probable cause does exist, the grand jury will formally accuse or indict the person in question by returning a "true bill" of indictment. During grand jury testimony hearsay evidence and evidence collected in violation of law is admissible. Neither a suspect nor a witness has the right to have an attorney present while giving testimony. Grand jury procedures at the state or county level may be different from those at the federal level.

During a conversation regarding grand jury testimony of a witness, a defense attorney, while I was present, told an Assistant United States Attorney a grand jury in the U.S. judicial system has too much power and is unfair. What I believe the defense attorney really meant was that he perceived grand jury power to be unfair because he had little power over what the grand jury did, was a tool of the prosecution, and his client was up against the same rock Garrity placed police officers: tell the truth or risk being prosecuted.

Miranda Rights—You Must Invoke

Any law enforcement officer is thoroughly familiar with rights guaranteed by Article 5 of the U.S. Constitution, more commonly known as Miranda or Fifth Amendment Rights. However, many officers may not be so familiar with a Supreme Court decision that affirms that questions in a criminal investigation can continue until the suspect ***invokes*** (emphasis added by author) the right against self-incrimination.

Some might say the 2010 Supreme Court ruling in *Berghuis v. Thompkins*, 130 S.Ct. 2250, Supreme Court 2010, has, to some extent, eroded the right against self-incrimination. The court held that after a rights advisement police could begin to or continue to interview a suspect until the suspect invokes his Miranda rights. The ruling validated how I and others interacted with narcotics smugglers at Miami International Airport in the 1980s. As a U.S. Customs Special Agent assigned to a Drug Enforcement Administration task force I arrested dozens of individuals from the Caribbean and South America smuggling cocaine, marijuana, and hashish. After rights advisement the arrestee was asked "Do you understand your rights?" After an affirmative response, the questioning began. I never once asked, "Do you want to talk to me?" To some the "system" is again unfair.

Seeking the Truth

In many states there is legislation providing added protection for a law enforcement officer when the officer is subjected to an internal investigation or contentious managerial questioning. Many more factors are in play that make an officer feel that the internal investigations function is unfair. Some departments allegedly use intimidation and threats of firing to obtain testimony from a reluctant officer. In California the added protection is the Public Safety Officers Procedural Bill of Rights Act passed in 1977.

"The Legislature hereby finds and declares that the rights and protections provided to peace officers under this chapter constitute a matter of statewide concern. The Legislature further finds and declares that effective law enforcement depends upon the maintenance of stable employer-employee relations, between public safety employees and their employers. In order to assure that stable relations are continued throughout the state and to further assure that effective services are provided to all people of the state, it is necessary that this chapter be applicable to all public safety officers, as defined in this section, wherever situated within the State of California."[10] The California legislation is similar to a Fraternal Order of Police (FOP) initiative that was a priority for a number of years.

According to the FOP National Lodge website, the top priority in 2009/2010 on the national level was H.R. 1972, the "Law Enforcement Officer's Procedural Bill of Rights Act of 2009." In 2012, the legislation sought is titled, H.R. 1789, the "State and Local Law Enforcement Discipline, Accountability, and Due Process Act." According to the FOP, "rank-and-file police officers are sometimes subjected to abusive and improper procedures and conduct on the part of the very departments or agencies they serve." Many times an officer is dismissed without an explanation. "The need for a minimal level of procedural protections for police officers accused of administrative wrongdoing, the gravity of the potential harm to officers created by the lack of uniform safeguards, and the patently unfair disparity in rights afforded criminal suspects *but not police officers* are compelling reasons to enact this legislation."[11]

Author's Note

This legislation has been proposed in various forms and designations for many years.

In many departments hiring and firing are not in the authority of the leadership or department administration but in the purview of the city council or county board. It may be the sole responsibility of the county sheriff. In some departments an officer can lose a job in the morning because of a traffic ticket written the night before. It may not be just, but anyone hired with a wink and a nod can be fired in the same manner. From my viewpoint the FOP is making an attempt to professionalize the departments controlled by patronage rather than a merit system.

On the one hand, the FOP is doing a service for its members and others; the organization is standing up for those who, because of location or other circumstances, cannot or do not work for a department where minimum rights, usually guaranteed by a merit commission or labor agreement, are afforded its employees. On the other hand, I see language used by the FOP as misleading; to an uninformed reader it may incite alarm, fear, wonder, and concern: "...rights afforded criminal suspects but not police officers..." The FOP is mixing apples and oranges by comparing rights associated with an administrative investigation or personnel issue with one associated with a criminal violation.[12]

The apple is a criminal trial, which is a proceeding where entities and personnel from outside a department, with no personal interest in the process, would take overall control.

The orange is an administrative hearing that, depending on legal maneuvering, would most likely be set in motion, managed, and controlled by the very department in which the officer is in disagreement. A hearing offers fewer "rights" than does a criminal trial. The FOP focus is controlling an internal investigation to limit evidence in an administrative proceeding where less deference would be given to legal bravado.

According to the FOP, "Federal legislation would establish a minimum level of procedural protections available while at the same time making the law on this issue unambiguous." [13]

> The FOP-supported legislation would guarantee law enforcement officers the following "basic" rights:
>
> 1. "Law enforcement officers shall, if disciplinary action is expected, be notified of the investigation, the nature of the alleged violation, and be notified of the outcome of the investigation and the recommendations made to superiors by the investigators;
>
> 2. Questioning of a law enforcement officer should be conducted for a reasonable length of time and preferably while the officer is on duty unless exigent circumstances apply;
>
> 3. Questioning of the law enforcement officer should take place at the offices of those conducting the investigation or at the place where the officer reports to work, unless the officer consents to another location;
>
> 4. Law enforcement officers will be questioned by no more than two investigators, and he or she shall be informed of the name, rank and command of the officers conducting the investigation;
>
> 5. Law enforcement officers under investigation are entitled to have counsel or any other individual of their choice present at the interrogation;
>
> 6. Law enforcement officers cannot be threatened, harassed or promised rewards to induce the answering of any question;

7. Law enforcement officers are entitled to a hearing, with notification in advance of the date, access to transcripts and other relevant documents and evidence generated by the hearing and to representation by counsel or another non-attorney representative at the hearing;

8. Law enforcement officers shall have the opportunity to comment in writing on any adverse materials placed in his or her personnel file; and

9. Law enforcement officers cannot be subject to retaliation for the exercise of these or any other rights under Federal, State or local law."[14]

Not all departments can be put in the same evidence bag, but the sought-after criteria above certainly question the fairness of "management" and its role in the creation of the perception of unfairness. Any officer is entitled to counsel during an interview, notice of a hearing and access to information, the opportunity to comment on personnel issues, and not be subject to retaliation. However, the bill itself also continues a sense of unfairness, not only by asking for protection from management but by providing more "rights" than afforded a citizen. An argument could be made that a citizen would never face an internal investigation. However, the FOP does not make that distinction and the reader is left to ponder what rights are afforded criminal suspects but not police officers?

From the standpoint of the internal affairs function certain criteria would control or manipulate to the point of interference. This interference would affect any internal investigation whether conducted by a department with or without civil service protections. Of course that is the intent of any defense team. Notifying a suspect of an investigation (#1) would, in many instances, negate any hope of confirming an allegation. Questioning "for a reasonable amount of time" (#2); allowing a suspect to identify a place to conduct an interview (#3), limiting the number of interviewers (#4), and having the ability to influence the demeanor of an investigator (#6) would allow a suspect or defense team to control and manipulate an internal investigation. From an internal affairs standpoint, FOP-supported legislation would give more "rights" to an officer than afforded to the citizens they serve.[15]

The pressure of union-sponsored legislation caused the International Association of Chiefs of Police (IACP) to take a pre-emptive step in 1996. The entire legislative effort is surrounded with such controversy that the "Rights and Responsibilities of Law Enforcement Personnel in Disciplinary Investigations" authored by the IACP Subcommittee on Internal Affairs Legislation was never adopted. However, the IACP did share the document with its members to address union demands in various states.

Among numerous criteria in response to those supported by the FOP, the IACP stated:

1. An interview should be conducted at a reasonable time before, during, or immediately after a tour of duty, unless the seriousness of the allegation requires immediate action, with overtime paid if conducted during off-duty;

2. The place of interview will take place at the choosing of the person in charge of the interview or of the "investigating parties";

3. All persons who ask questions would be identified;

4. The identification of complainants should be known to the accused, although the identity of a confidential informant would not be made public;

5. No more than two persons could be present during questioning, although rotating more than two persons is permissible; and,

6. Officers interviewed in non-criminal matters shall be treated with respect, should not be subjected to unlawful threats, harassment, or be improperly offered a "reward" for information.

An interesting supplement to the IACP's opposition to the FOP-supported legislation is the additional requirement that it is the duty of officers and civilian employees to report serious misconduct.[16]

To advocate the legislation, the FOP asserts that, "This measure does not afford police officers any greater rights than those possessed by other citizens; it simply reaffirms the existence of those rights in the unique context of the law enforcement community."[17]

I would argue the FOP tactic to sway the debate is fraught with innuendo, mixed messages, and intimidation. The tactic creates a feeling that the sky is falling, the world is coming to an end and disaster is imminent. Close to 20 states have taken the step to pass some form of a peace officers' bill of rights; it is said others are still contemplating the legislation. Federal legislators have not taken the bait and a discussion is still ongoing but the pressure is on. The search for the truth continues with the perception of unfairness fueled by competing values, constituents, and focus.

It's Not Always the Way It Seems

In the early 1990s, The Mollen Commission studied the New York City Police Department and the way it addressed police corruption. The Mollen Commission was named after Judge Milton Mollen, who was appointed by New York City Mayor David N. Dinkins. The formal name of the commission was the City of New York Commission to Investigate Allegations of Police Corruption and the Anti-Corruption Procedures of the Police Department. Created in 1992, the commission issued a report in 1994 regarding the nature and extent of police corruption and the procedures for preventing and detecting corruption and recommended changes. The commission issued a report that indicated "that many members of the Department viewed Internal Affairs Division as a 'white socks' operation, i.e., an operation that harassed hardworking members for petty transgressions rather than an investigative body interested in the investigation of those committing serious misconduct and crimes." The commission also "found that many members of the department were distrustful of IAD (Internal Affairs Division) personnel, believing them to be incompetent investigators who were out of touch with the realities of 'real' police work."[18] But it is important to know what officers assigned to IAD had to say.

Author's Note

Sometime after the issuance of the Mollen Commission Report the title "Internal Affairs Division" (IAD) was changed to "Internal Affairs Bureau" (IAB).

Over half of the individuals interviewed by the commission indicated their assignment to IAD was not one that they would have chosen for themselves. They were chosen by IAD because of Internal Order #39 (IO) giving IAD first choice over other bureaus. After being assigned to IAD, most of the officers had feelings of anger, shock, discontent, and dismay. Many thought involvement in the investigation of a high-ranking officer would have a negative impact on their career. The officers were reluctant to work with IAD because of their "perception that IAD investigators were lazy, incompetent or incapable of carrying out 'real' police work." The officers also thought that "IAB had limited ability to do sophisticated police work such as undercover operations, would be conducting many investigations of insignificant allegations, and had a general sense that working with IAB branded one as a 'rat'."[19]

In hindsight however, all the officers interviewed found satisfaction "with their IAB experiences and believed themselves to be better officers because of their IAB tenure." Their fears of incompetence, "the lack of interesting work, and the notion of being branded a 'rat' were, for the most part, unfounded." Many of the officers found IAB's investigative methods and resources to be sophisticated compared to other bureaus where they had worked. They also found that most of the people working in IAB were skilled members of the department rather than outcasts that they had been expecting to encounter.[20]

IAB management felt that the IO improved the quality of IAB recruits. Because of the order, new IAB personnel were some of the department's most skilled and proactive investigators. Admittedly there are some departmental personnel who still may characterize IAB investigators as "rats," but the commission reported that, in general, the attitude was slowly being eroded because the IO enabled IAB to recruit outstanding individuals. Many former IAB officers interviewed believed the IO actually removed much of the negative perception previously held by department personnel. When assignment to IAB was mainly voluntary, the perception was that those who volunteered were incompetent officers who were uncomfortable in other areas of police work, lacked street knowledge and experience, and were unequal to others in the department. Volunteers to IAB were therefore viewed with suspicion by many in the department.[21]

However, since the issuance of the IO, department personnel no longer view IAB investigators with suspicion and contempt. In addition, because the non-volunteers in IAB are viewed as those seeking highly regarded positions prior to being drafted, they are also viewed as investigators who raised the competence of the bureau.[22]

Case Study

You are the commander of an internal affairs bureau in a large police department. In the 3rd police district there have always been sporadic rumors and anonymous complaints from rank and file officers about personal property being stolen in the station locker room. The thefts always take place when the officers are on patrol. While attending the funeral of a retired officer you heard others joking about a lieutenant in the 3rd district who uses department gasoline to fuel his personal car. Reportedly this has been happening for a long period, but no officer wants to be the one known to have "informed" on another officer. Asking other officers about the lieutenant you only received blank stares, but one officer did say he "wouldn't leave a nickel where the lieutenant could find it."

A recent audit of fuel consumption revealed a shortage of almost 100 gallons of fuel a month in the last 12 months.

You suspect the district commander knows the lieutenant is responsible for the thefts but is little help when you question him. Officers have complained to the commander several times about the locker room thefts, but all were told to make sure to lock up their property or call internal affairs. District personnel are in an uproar.

Case Study Questions

Answer the following questions in one narrative response.

1. *Would you open an investigation?*

2. *What would you say, if anything, to the district commander?*

3. *What would you say, if anything, to the officers affected?*

4. *What could you do to ensure a situation like this does not happen again?*

5. *How can the perception of the department and the internal affairs function be improved?*

Questions for Discussion

Answer each of the following questions in a separate response.

1. Discuss the Law Enforcement Officer's Procedural Bill of Rights Act supported by the Fraternal Order of Police. What does the act propose to do? What exactly is being protected? If again put before Congress and passed, will the act interfere with the internal affairs function?

2. Discuss "the need for corruption" and "inconvenient corruption." Explain why you agree or disagree with the author's interpretation.

Notes

1. Department of Justice—Office of Justice Programs Bureau of Justice Statistics—State & Local Law Enforcement Statistics. (2005). National survey. Retrieved from http://www.ojp.usdoj.gov/bjs/sandlle.htm. Accessed October 7, 2009.
2. Kerik, Bernard, B. (2001). *The Lost Son: A Life in Pursuit of Justice.* HarperCollins Publisher. Page 303.
3. Commission on Accreditation for Law Enforcement Agencies, Inc. (2006). Standards for Law Enforcement Agencies. Part 52.
4. Rothlein, Steve. (2008). Noble Cause Corruption. Legal & Liability Risk Management Institute, Public Agency Training Council. PATC

E-Newsletter. Retrieved from http://www.srassociatesinc.org/files/noble-cause-corruption.pdf.

5. Walberg, Matthew, Lee, William, & Mack, Kristen. (28 Jun 2010). Burge Found Guilty of Lying about Torture. Chicago Breaking News Center. Retrieved from http://www.chicagobreakingnews.com/search/dispatcher.front?Query=lt+jon+burge&target=adv_article.
6. Smith, Susan. (8 Dec 2010). Lying to a Government Investigator Can Create More Problems than Possible Misconduct. FedSmith Inc. Retrieved from http://www.fedsmith.com/article/2646/lying-government-investigator-can-create-more.html.
7. Ibid.
8. Graves, Wallace. (Jun 1996). Police Cynicism: causes and cures. FBI Law Enforcement Bulletin. 65(6), pg. 16-20. Retrieved from http://proquest.umi.com.ezproxy2.apus.edu/pqdweb?index=0&did=9724801&SrchMode=2&sid=1&Fmt=3&VInst=PROD&VType=PQD&RQT=309&VName=PQD&TS=1306185404&clientId=62546.
9. Pew Research Center's Project for Excellence in Journalism. (1 Mar 1999). Local TV News Project 1998. What Works, What Flops, and Why - Approaches that Work. Retrieved from http://www.journalism.org/node/382.
10. Peace Officers Research Association of California. (1977). Public Safety Officers Procedural Bill of Rights Act. Retrieved from http://www.porac.org/POBOR.html.
11. Fraternal Order of Police National Ledge. Steve Young Law Enforcement Legislative Advocacy Center. Retrieved from http://www.fop.net/legislative/issues/leobr/index.shtml. Accessed 15 Jul 2010; 16 May 2011; 23 May 2011.
12. Ibid.
13. Ibid.
14. Ibid.
15. Ibid.
16. Schmidt, Wayne, W. (Mar 2005). Illinois Law Enforcement Training and Standards Board—Law Enforcement Executive Forum. Peace Officers Bill of Rights Guarantees: Responding to Union Demands with a Sanctioned Version. Retrieved from http://www.aele.org/pobr-iacp.pdf. Accessed, July 16, 2010.
17. Ibid.
18. City of New York Commission to Investigate Allegations of Police Corruption and the Anti-Corruption Procedures of the Police Department. (July 1994).
19. Ibid.
20. Ibid.
21. Ibid.
22. Ibid.

Suggested Reading

Kerik, Bernard, B. (2001). *The Lost Son: A Life In Pursuit of Justice.* New York: Regan Books.

U.S. Department of Justice, Office of Community Oriented Policing Services. (2010). Building Trust Between the Police and the Citizens They Serve: an Internal Affairs Promising Practices Guide for Local Law Enforcement.

Rothlein, Steve. (2008). *Noble Cause Corruption.* Indianapolis, IN: Public Agency Training Council.

CHAPTER FOUR
More on Leadership

"Leadership and learning are indispensable to each other."
— John F. Kennedy

Just as senior leadership can affect the creation, training, and operation of the internal affairs function; it can also play a role in the creation or continuation of negative bias through the IA process. Leadership, which does not fully support the internal affairs function, or uses the function for self-serving goals, can create an overall negative perception, a perception of unfairness as one of the players in the process. An internal affairs unit limited by management to minimize its value can be a detriment to morale. Organizational culture may control a unit to a point where it is only minimally effective. What is the probability that an act of wrongdoing will be reported if the employees know that a properly conducted investigation is doubtful?

Ways to Interfere

Interference in internal investigations can come in many forms. While a special agent with U.S. Customs, I lived through periods of consternation between the Office of Internal Affairs and other staff offices, especially the Office of Investigations. In the late 1990s, there was open discussion within the Customs Service concerning the Office of Internal Affairs becoming too independent and being too tenacious while conducting investigations. Several special agents in the Office of Investigations were at the forefront in a quest to limit the effectiveness of the Office of Internal Affairs.

At about the same time internal affairs was being accused of being too independent, the Office of the U.S. Attorney in San Diego, CA, requested that all employee investigations, both criminal and administrative, with venue in the Southern District of CA, be referred to the Office for management control purposes. It is unclear why the request was made, but I suspect information from the Office of Investigations, derogatory of the investigations conducted by the Office of Internal Affairs, was given to the Office of the U.S. Attorney.

The Assistant Commissioner, Office of Internal Affairs, refused to comply with the U.S. Attorney's request.

About June 2000, Homer J. Williams, Assistant Commissioner (AC), Office of Internal Affairs, U.S. Customs Service, was indicted by a federal grand jury by the very same Office of the U.S. Attorney in San Diego, CA, for alleged false statements and perjury during a Merit Systems Protection Board proceeding. As the AC, Mr. Williams was the head of internal affairs and actually was employed in Washington, DC at the time of the indictment. This is the same Homer Williams who was the AC during the late 1990s when internal affairs was rumored to be too independent, too tenacious. The indictments had to do with alleged false statements made by Mr. Williams about a relationship with a woman who was under investigation by the very office he supervised.

The transcript of trial deliberations, dated March 9, 2001, tells an interesting story of how investigations can be manipulated and how a high-ranking law enforcement officer can be indicted for disputed or questionable statements. Mr. Williams was accused of informing a female friend, a U.S. Customs Special Agent, that she was under investigation by the Office of Internal Affairs and that he influenced the investigation of her. While under investigation, Mr. Williams was deposed, twice, regarding whether he made a disclosure and influenced the investigation of his female friend and about his personal relationship with the agent. It could not be proven he informed her of the investigation or influenced it, so the prosecutor focused on Mr. Williams' sworn testimony regarding the personal relationship. In the transcript, the trial judge, the Honorable Marilyn L. Huff, stated, "You don't do an end around and then say that this is a false statement ... whether this is material or not is a significant issue that I've got major concerns about."[1] During their deliberations, the trial jury also asked about the materiality of Williams' statements. The trial judge also stated "I don't think that you ...should be able to nitpick one or two words without taking into consideration the entire context of the whole of the statement and the circumstances under which it was made ... I have significant reservations about the proof, the level of proof on the case."[2] In the trial transcript the court also questioned how to determine the absolute truth, what is a mistake, and what is real. What followed was an analysis of what constituted Mr. Williams immediately removing himself from supervision of the investigation of his female friend. "Should he be convicted of a felony because of that word 'immediately'? I thought that that was interesting."[3] Homer J. Williams was found not guilty by a trial jury on March 9, 2001.

The trial judge stated to the jury, "Had I been a juror, I would have voted not guilty ...and also we've seen the history of **politics in America** [emphasis added by author] and other factors. And so sometimes one wonders why is [sic] this case brought, but there might have been other—other things that are not known to you ..."[4] I contend if additional prosecutorial evidence was known, it would have been presented.

More Interference

Another example of interference through retaliation occurred in April 2003.

Detroit Police Officer, Harold Nelthrope forwarded information to the internal affairs unit of the Detroit Police Department alleging officers assigned to Detroit Mayor Kwame Kilpatrick's protection unit were, among other things, falsifying time sheets and drinking while on duty. The allegations also included sexual exploits at the mayoral mansion and extramarital affairs by Kilpatrick.

Several officers, including Nelthrope, reportedly were retaliated against for conducting an investigation or cooperating with investigators. Gary A. Brown, Deputy Chief of the internal affairs unit was removed from the position. Other officers were criticized for investigating the mayor and the mayor's friends. It was reported that officers were transferred or resigned their positions to protect themselves and their families. It was similarly reported that the mayor's agenda was to interfere by discouraging the reporting of wrongdoing and the conduct of investigations into his activities or the actions of his friends.[5] On September 4, 2008, Kwame Kilpatrick, pursuant to a plea agreement, resigned as the mayor of Detroit. He pled guilty to two counts of obstruction of justice and no contest to assaulting or obstructing a public officer. He served four months in a county jail, was fined $1 million, lost his law license and was given five-years probation, and forfeited his pension.[6]

Another Way to Interfere

Another way to interfere in an internal investigation is to limit the scope of the investigation. There are numerous professionals in responsible positions to supervise or adjudicate investigations of Chicago Police Officers accused of wrongdoing. The Chicago Police Board is staffed with an abundance of prominent professionals. The police board is a civilian body that has the responsibility, among others, to decide disciplinary cases. In 2004, then Chicago Police Superintendent Philip Cline appointed Tisa Morris, a seasoned prosecutor from the Cook County Prosecutor's Office, as the head of the Office of Professional Standards. But a contradiction presented itself when the conduct of employee investigations was reviewed. As reported by the *Chicago Tribune* in December 2007, internal investigations are not only underfunded, but internal investigations by the Chicago Police Department are cursory and incomplete, with interference by roundtables informally chaired by high-ranking officers to adjudicate allegations on the scene.[7] *The Chicago Sun-Times* reported in 2006 that a defense attorney confirmed the cursory investigations by stating, "a lot of times [the Office of Professional Responsibility] brings cases to the police board without all the facts."[8]

The City of Chicago is now taking misconduct more seriously. "In 2007, in response to concerns about how allegations of police misconduct were being investigated by the Chicago Police Department, the Independent Police Review Authority (IPRA) was created and approved by the City Council. Headed by a civilian Chief Administrator and staffed entirely with civilian investigators, IPRA is an independent agency of the City of Chicago, separate from the Chicago Police Department. IPRA replaced the former Office of Professional Standards ...IPRA exists for EVERY member of the community and the members of the Chicago Police Department. Its service is structured to promote cooperative relationships of trust and responsibility between citizens and the police."[9]

The Rat Squad

Tim Dees, former Editor-in-Chief, Officer.com, published an editorial titled, "The Rat Squad." He described how he believes internal affairs investigators are portrayed on television programs: "shifty, malevolent-looking guys whom no one spoke to willingly, and whom you just knew spent their weekends wetting the bed and twisting the heads off of baby ducks." It would be hard to offer a more offensive description. He goes on to say, "There are some police executives that use IA as their own administrative death squad. The IA investigators aren't sent out to kill people, but rather careers."[10] I agree with Mr. Dees with reservations.

Dees' editorial was answered by Randy Rider, then President, National Internal Affairs Investigators Association. Rider agreed that Hollywood has unfairly branded internal affairs investigators. He described real-life IA investigators as professional, honest, and fair. They "are dispatched to find the truth."[11] I also agree with Mr. Rider with reservations. During my research I uncovered three departments where variations of Mr. Dees' allegations proved true. Three out of thousands of departments and agencies, but three is three too many.

Dees responded to Rider's letter with another editorial. Dees did not shrink from his original statements, but did report a better understanding of internal affairs types. He personally met with hundreds of internal affairs investigators in 2006, at their annual training conference in Gatlinburg, TN. He was not dissuaded from his claim that "Internal Affairs is used to retaliate against officers that have fallen into disfavor with their bosses."[12] Dees went on to say, "As someone who always thought of himself as an honest cop, I had no fear of someone who was going to inspect my work and determine if I had acted properly. I did have significant fear of anyone that was going to investigate me with a pre-determined disposition in mind."[13]

True Leadership

Strong leadership is the first factor in fostering a professional internal affairs function. Confidence in internal affairs must be exhibited by leaders and its influence must be felt at all levels in the organization. It is human nature to be threatened by a function that can look into records and question others to evaluate one's actions. It is also human nature to resent and criticize that authority. Through strong leadership a course of action is directed to establish a greater understanding of the entire function. A picture of fairness must be demonstrated in all aspects, which can only be displayed by leadership with a strong foundation of ethics. Ethics is instilled in the workplace by supporting a strong employee integrity program and by sponsoring an office of internal affairs recognized as fair and unbiased. "Police leaders must demonstrate their commitment to the ideals of honesty, fairness, justice, courage, integrity, loyalty, and compassion. Leaders who fail to prove themselves trustworthy help spread the seeds of cynicism ...Police leaders must exhibit appropriate conduct by example, not just by words ... confidence can help officers respect the judicial system rather than feel manipulated by it. Most important, leaders need to build a culture of integrity with their agencies, so that officers have something to believe in when all else seems to fail." [14]

To instill confidence, understanding, and a sense of fairness in the internal affairs function, leadership must exhibit a strong command presence. To demonstrate a strong command presence leadership should display an enthusiastic, ongoing desire for policy, regulation and law compliance. Command presence by leadership would encourage ethical behavior by all officers to include internal affairs investigators. Ethical behavior will ensure confidence and a perception of fairness in the internal affairs function.

Parent Organization Operational Leaders

An expert in personnel management may identify several levels of management in an organization, but for this explanation management is divided into senior leaders (staff function) and operational supervisors (line function) in the parent organization and in internal affairs.

Senior leaders in a successful organization support ethics in all they do, give full support to internal affairs operations, and maintain a positive attitude in all internal affairs investigations. They create performance expectations, which foster high ethics in the entire workforce and support continuing ethics education.

Operational supervisors are the link between the workforce and senior leaders. Operational supervisors turn senior leadership directives into action and ensure all directives are followed. Although senior leadership is focused on strategic plans, operational supervisors are focused on tactical issues. They foster the environment that is created by senior leadership. They ensure a continuous learning process in theory and practice in the classroom and field operations. An operational supervisor must be in charge as a leader, not just as a manager.

According to Frederick F. Reichheld, "Loyalty remains the hallmark of great leadership ...and must begin with leaders who recognize the enormous value of building and maintaining mutually beneficial relationships."[15] In law enforcement that beneficial relationship from the chief to the street officer protects citizens from assault by officers and protects good officers who want to do the right thing from officers like the ones who assault citizens rather than protect them. The right relationship will protect the managers and leadership from bad officers and from constitutional violations.

The character played by S. Epatha Merkerson, Lt Anita Van Buren, on the television show *Law & Order* is a good example of an operational supervisor as a strong leader. Nothing seems to get by her. When Detectives Green, Briscoe, or others cross the line of legality, Lt. Van Buren steps in to put them in their place. The operational supervisor must know their subordinates well; they must be present not only in spirit but also in body and mind.

Although the fictional character Van Buren plays is a lieutenant, another very important operational supervisor in a police department is the sergeant or the senior special agent or group supervisor in a federal agency. That supervisor must know which subordinate needs more supervision than others. On August 9, 1997, Abner Louima was arrested outside a New York City nightclub for, among other things, disorderly conduct. On the ride to the police station officers beat Louima with their fists and batons. Upon arriving at the station, Louima was sexually assaulted with a toilet plunger. If the facts are reported correctly, the NYPD officers who beat Abner Louima on that August night did not wake up one morning and decide to beat people they arrest. Previous misconduct was accepted and ignored. The officers learned from others that the actions were acceptable or at least would be overlooked. The officer who sodomized Mr. Louima with a toilet plunger did not suddenly decide to assault someone. All these officers were free to act the way they did because, over time, others disregarded their actions, which led to the assault.

Operational supervisors must understand they are part of the internal affairs process. Their desires, actions, and interactions with others are part of the process to protect the organization, themselves, their subordinates, and the citizens they serve. In a heated situation where tempers are hot, such as the capture of an individual after a high-speed chase, the on-scene supervisor must step back and manage the situation, not be part of it. In many situations, thinking takes a back seat to action. The on-scene supervisor must be engaged and in charge and show the correct way. The supervisor must step back and control the tempers, the testosterone, the impatience, and the anger and foster compromise. The on-scene supervisor must slow down officers' actions and control the adrenaline factor.

The egregious and illegal behavior of police officers in many cases demonstrates a behavior called regressive pull. In a law enforcement sense, regressive pull is when an officer spends a great deal of time with the criminal element and begins to act like a criminal. More accurately said, an officer will disregard policy directives, common sense, and the law and commit criminal acts while enforcing the law. This is when an effective on-scene supervisor is essential. The supervisor must not only be engaged, but must fight the influence of regressive pull on him and on the officers supervised. The effects of associating with criminal elements to which all enforcement officers are exposed must be resisted. A supervisor is not a player, not a direct participant in the enforcement action, but a referee who shows the flag when the conduct is not according to the rules. Regressive pull qualifies for inclusion in early warning systems and supervisors and managers should be alert to its effects. This theory places supervisors on stage; they are looked up to, but some do not want the responsibility.

Lesson #1 of Colin Powell's 18 Gems states, "Being responsible sometimes means pissing people off ... Leadership is not a popularity contest." [16] Yes, being well-liked does come second to the good of an organization, but I have seen few leaders who could follow this advice. Actually, it is more about the supervisors' feelings rather than the employees'. Many supervisors are apprehensive about telling subordinates that they are wrong or out of bounds or that their actions are not appropriate. Law enforcement officers get into trouble because some may have the propensity to do wrong, or others just do dumb mistakes for various reasons. Officers most often get into trouble because their leaders are not prepared to anger them by telling them they are doing something wrong.

Some operational supervisors are just uneasy or afraid to supervise. They may be there physically, but not in spirit. They do not lead or even manage in difficult situations: neither in enforcement actions nor in personnel situations. Other operational supervisors can lead an enforcement operation, but cannot deal with people issues. People issues damage an organization when certain situations are not addressed: issues like drinking or drunk on the job and conscious neglect of duty, or heavier issues like assaulting citizens and accepting bribes.

As a supervisor, many times I found personnel issues difficult to deal with because of a lack of support from my supervisor, the second line supervisor. How do you deal with an investigator who arrives at the office drunk and your supervisor feigns ignorance or says, "handle it," and walks in the opposite direction? Making things even more difficult is a personnel issue that has grown from infancy to adulthood while more than one supervisor has watched it grow without an iota of recognition. I did not see a single one of my contemporaries begin the job as a drunk or a problem child, but I have seen ones grow to become employees that many supervisors did not want to handle.

Some issues will never go away. Some people will always be an issue no matter who supervises them or in what unit they work. Others may cause problems because they have been assigned to the same unit too long and are bored, burned out, or have become stale and just need a change. Still others will continually be a problem because they know they can get away with misconduct because the supervisor is more absent than present.

In an acting capacity, I once supervised an individual who was nowhere to be found most of the day. After two days on the job, I began wondering aloud and questioning others where this individual was. No one seemed to know, and I never found out. Being a temporary supervisor placed me in a difficult situation. However, to combat the problem, I began giving the individual short due dates for assignments. The situation improved somewhat, but not before retaliation. Leaving my building pass on my desk one day gave someone the opportunity to put "devil's horns" on my picture. Although appearing "foolish" I present the access card as a badge of honor; I did my job even though it was unpopular if only to one person.

The individual I suspected of wayward artistry was later transferred to another location. The individual flourished and was promoted.

On occasion, a law enforcement officer and other adults can be compared to children. From experience, I believe many adults, whether enforcement officers, or other professionals can act like children unless told otherwise. Some adults need to be told no. (Adults may act like children but should never be treated as such.) That is where the first line supervisor takes a deep breath and actually takes control and does the right thing for the organization, the people supervised, and for himself. Some adults I have worked with or supervised have behaved badly until they were told their actions were unacceptable and must be corrected. Because of my experience and opinions many officers may think of me as a "shoofly": a supervisor who takes responsibility for those he supervises and is not reluctant to tell others how to act, how to do the right thing, how to do a good job, and a supervisor willing to say stop! Being called a "shoofly" is not a complimentary title.

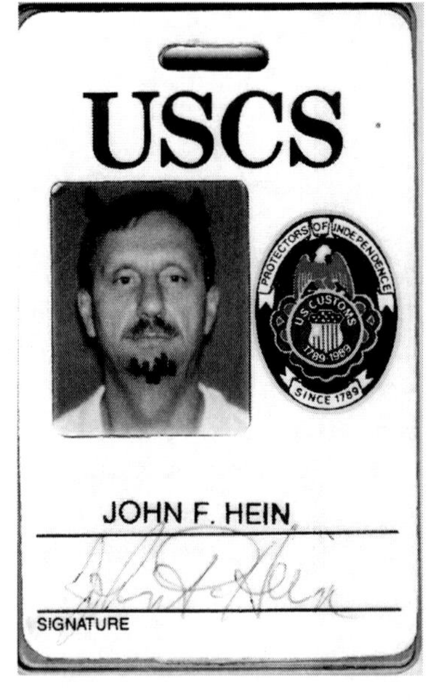

Although they have different focal points, public agencies and private industry are on the same path when discussing and implementing strategies to prevent misconduct. In a document on workplace dishonesty in the business community, Dr. Read Hayes stated, “Employees can be a company’s greatest asset and, unfortunately, its worst enemy. Counterproductive workplace behavior, or employee deviance, can be defined as intentional behaviors or omissions that not only violate company or public rules but also harm the organization or others. These behaviors and omissions are a pervasive problem for any type of organization and must be controlled.” Dr. Hayes also referenced various studies when he stated, “Another personal issue involves the perception by employees of a low or non-existent risk of detection and sanction. This attitude may account for much of the variance in the probability that an offending action will occur.” In relation to absent or uncaring supervision, Dr. Hayes stated, “They [Employees] know when alert, caring managers and colleagues are present as well as when naïve or apathetic associates are in charge.”[17]

A parent or anyone familiar with children has heard the phrases, “everyone is doing it,” or, “why didn’t you tell me not to do it” after the child is caught doing a forbidden action in school. Some adults act the same and must be told the same. Children need boundaries. When rules are not well-defined, children tend to get into trouble. On the other hand, in families that set clear boundaries, children have less trouble knowing right from wrong. Some adults need the same well-defined rules with clear boundaries, so they, like children, have less difficulty doing the right thing and knowing right from wrong.

Department Culture

Each department or agency for which I have worked has had its own culture. By culture I mean the beliefs, attitudes, and values held by the majority of the people in an organization. Not all people will have the same attributes, but what the leadership exhibits or allows, and what the majority of people express, shape the culture of the organization.

As a deputy sheriff in the early 1970s, I worked for a small, easygoing department with few problems of which I was aware. Later, as a special agent for the Internal Revenue Service, Criminal Investigation Division, I worked in an oppressive culture excessively concerned with the privacy of taxpayers to the point that suspected crimes, not the purview of the IRS, were ignored rather than brought to the attention of other enforcement agencies. Policy and regulations were to be followed exactly. Supervisors were constantly looking for the failure to follow directions. I worked in a "gotcha" climate where if a mistake was made, someone had to be blamed with dire consequences. The Inspection Division [internal affairs] was another worry and was not well-liked by anyone.

Transferring to the U.S. Department of Transportation, Office of Inspector General (OIG) was a breath of fresh air. OIG management was firm but fair, and unintentional mistakes were something to learn from. Department management supported the OIG but there was controversy on occasion, when investigative operations were withheld from department managers. As a special agent with the OIG, it was my first experience with employees looking at me critically.

When I transferred to the United States Customs Service, I found that the Office of Internal Affairs was tolerated by management and minimally supported. Many times IA investigators were insulted by executive managers and threatened with reprisal.

An organizational culture may be hard to define because it may be many things; there may be many cultures in one department. The department or agency culture can be determined by the chief or director. Some departments may have pseudo-leadership, which may be better or worse than the genuine thing and may create another culture. Other cultures may be portrayed by street officers, by investigators, by different divisions and districts, by "desk officers" and others who may never have been part of the street culture even if they did work the street. There may be other cultures if there are large contingents of gender or racial components.

Within these many cultures, there are supervisors who manage an existing condition and there are supervisors who lead by change: change for the good of the department. How does a leader change the attitude of a person who does not "get it," a person who does not understand, or a person who does not want to understand the life of an ethical law enforcement officer? How does a leader change a culture when the leader may be perceived as "righteous," or a "goody-two-shoes," or a leader who wants an officer to abide by the law no matter what the outcome? How does a leader entice officers to buy into something that may be perceived as too corny and virtuous and that is not practical in the real world? How do you present ethics to officers who are insulted by the insinuation that they could be anything less than an ethical, outstanding officer? How do you tell an officer that something is now wrong that has been done on the street longer than anyone can remember?

Shortly after the creation of the Office of Inspector General (OIG), U.S. Department of Transportation, the then-inspector general spoke to a group of construction contractors at a conference. The inspector general discussed the various programs, projects and contract stipulations that would be audited and investigated. Someone in the audience wanted to know why, just because the OIG was created, certain things he and others had been doing for years were now improper or illegal. There are many cultures in any organization, profession, or skill knowledge.

It Is Difficult to Admit

To combat personnel problems, a lack of ethics, or any wrongdoing, the department leadership must first admit there is a problem and the department culture must be changed. Many departments or agencies today cannot bring themselves to admit a wrong. Renunciation of abuses is nothing new. Allegations and denials of police misconduct have come in ebbs and swells over time. The 1910 International Association of Chiefs of Police convention was overshadowed by the "unjust criticism of the police in the United States."[18] The chiefs first denied that interrogation abuses existed, suggesting that the third degree was a phrase "coined in a newspaper office; then they suggested that private detectives were the guilty parties. Finally, they argued that "all this belongs in the past ...and we hear of such things no more."[19] However, the third degree again raised its ugly head in 1931 in a report by the Wickersham Commission. In one of many volumes reporting wide-spread criminal activity in the United States, the Commission discussed many police abuses, one being the third-degree; the forced confessions of suspected criminals by police.[20]

Expectations

No one wants to be the bad guy. A supervisor can avoid being the bad guy by setting and enforcing standards. Most will rise to the expectations, and some will not. Setting standards or conveying expectations may initially make things worse, but knowing what is expected is the first step to change or to correct behavior.

A supervisor can make job or performance expectations known in several ways:

- By discussing in an open forum
- By giving individuals personal attention
- By posting in a conspicuous place
- By issuing a memorandum

Whatever manner used, correct conduct and inappropriate actions must be understood.

In any law enforcement organization there are plenty of issues that can get an officer into trouble. Talk about them. There is nothing better than knowing the rules of the road. What is tougher is discussing inappropriate action after it takes place. Many supervisors may have a problem discussing the situation with the offending officer. I have seen some supervisors blame everyone for the actions of one offender or publish a memo chastising the group. The hardest approach is a sit-down with the offender, especially when that person is difficult to supervise, is reluctant to take direction, or is just plain argumentative when confronted. Added to the difficulty is an offender who is part of a minority class who files a complaint when something does not go his way. I have experienced this type of complaint; I was placed on the defensive, which makes things difficult within a small group or shift of officers.

Years ago during a conversation with my supervisor, he told me that even when you present your expectations, out of a large group, few are highly motivated. Out of ten special agents, two will be underachievers, six will be average, and two will be hard chargers. He told me to make sure the hard charges are taken care of to satisfy their needs whatever they may be. You must compliment the average employees, and must tolerate the underachievers. He said a supervisor cannot make a person do something he does not want to do. To a point I disagree with the last statement. Dwight D. Eisenhower stated, "Leadership is the art of getting someone else to do something you want done because he wants to do it."[21]

I believe you can change a person, but change comes over time; it will not happen by memo or by statement. Over time, with the right leader, people and the culture will change. During the late 1990s, the District of Columbia changed for the better. Anthony Williams became mayor and Charles Ramsey was appointed chief of police. A lieutenant with the police department told me that Chief Ramsey was hated for changes he was making in the department. What I saw was a leader who demoted or transferred people for non-productivity, who made people work and who professionalized the department. Williams and Ramsey were leaders who took the city and the police department from mediocrity and lifted them up to better run, respected organizations. They had expectations, and they were to be followed whether department members liked it or not.

Ethics in Law Enforcement

The primary responsibility of any law enforcement officer is to serve the people under his jurisdiction by protecting life and property. In law enforcement property can be many things from a home to a business, from the U.S. border to federal funds. To serve successfully, a law enforcement officer must maintain the public trust. Frequently reported in the media is how that trust is broken by outrageous lapses of ethics. The already discussed assault of Abner Louima by New York City police officers, the Rodney King beating by Los Angeles police officers and other examples are a constant reminder that ethics among law enforcement officers are not always the highest. When ethics lapses occur, the public understands that "the police" did it. All law enforcement officers become suspect.

Honesty and fair dealing, or the lack of them, can make or break anyone or anything: an individual, a corporation, a CEO, a law enforcement officer, or any public official. U.S. Air Force General Robert H. "Doc" Foglesong wrote that "It's clear that to be successful as a leader—to take your organization to extraordinary heights—you must possess the moral and ethical underpinnings to make tough but fair decisions. Ethics are the foundation to doing the right thing, and those who follow you will immediately recognize when you are predisposed to doing the right thing—or not."[22] Whether in the public sector or the corporate arena, ethics in leadership, in employee actions, and in business decisions will not only portray the internal affairs function as fair and ethical but will ensure the function is truly ethical.

As reported by Frank J. Aguilar in *Managing Corporate Ethics*, James Burke, former chairman and executive officer of Johnson & Johnson stated he believed "there is a deep and intensely human need for trust, honesty, integrity, ethical behavior in the people we form important relationships with ... and those businesses who are the most consistently ethical in their behavior, will, on average, be more successful."[23] LRN, a consultant on corporate ethics and compliance issues, conducted a research study that exhibited how unethical behavior could lead to decreased employee productivity. Over 70% of full-time American workers saw unethical conduct at work and one employee in three reported they were "distracted" by it. "By engaging employees in shared values and educating them on the company's expectations for appropriate conduct, companies can inspire both principled and profitable performance from their workforce,"[24] says LRN's CEO and Chairman Dov Seidman. In the law enforcement profession, principled and profitable performance means serving citizens ethically and corruption-free.

Much has been written about police ethics. Less has been written on the connection between internal affairs and organizational leadership and the relationship with the employees and the citizens they both serve. Whether policing the public or its own employees, a law enforcement investigator must execute authority fairly. Edwin J. Delattre reported, "Reaching out to the public – listening and speaking openly, honestly, respectfully; seeking to understand the perceptions, fears, hopes, recommendations of the public in all its diversity—is indispensable to sound policing and fulfillment of the police mission." [25] Some citizens are suspects, some are witnesses, and some are neither a suspect nor witness. In the internal affairs arena some law enforcement officers are suspects, some are witnesses and some are neither a suspect nor witness. Everything that can be said about police-citizen interaction can also be said of the internal affairs function.

Whether in a business organization or government entity, ethics should play a major part in all employee actions. Department or individual substance is made up of many things: character, morals, integrity, and ethics are just a few.

Character being a strength that differentiates one person from another.
Morals being standards of what is right or wrong.
Integrity being a strong adherence, without deviation, to a strict ethical code.
Ethics being a set of principles of right conduct.

Bruce Mercer uses the terms ethics and integrity interchangeably and believes there are different types of integrity throughout the world depending on culture. However, "there is a certain ethical code that reaches all over the world which includes, among other things integrity, justice, truthfulness, responsibility, freedom, and accountability. These are all universal values embraced by people the world over. The bottom line is to define a set of values a person can live by. Strong values for senior leadership down to the newest employee; strong values for internal affairs. A culture of honest treatment must come from leadership."[26]

"One of the most striking characteristics common to the ethical firms studied [by Frank Aguilar] is senior management's deep and enduring commitment to the organizational achievement of high ethical standards. What is also evident is that such commitment, to be effective, requires more than just good intentions."[27]

Bruce Mercer believes the importance placed on ethics is the foundation that measures any organization. "An organization must stand for something and strong leadership is needed with firmly understood values. A poorly led organization will have unclear values leaving employees to their own devices to use their personal values. This may cause a conflict between organizational and personal values and the personal values between many employees. Some may do what is considered ethically right, while others may not. Without a clear policy, five employees will react to one situation in five different ways. Leaders are responsible for what happens in their organization. If the perception is the organization is corrupt, the leadership has caused the perception. 'The fish rots from the head down.' Any organization or elected official must use integrity to their advantage. Whatever is the public perception of an organization or elected official is the public's reality. Prioritizing ethics is a win-win situation. Integrity is good for business or public service and is the foundation for longevity in public office."[28] The public perception of a police function is the public's reality. Just as with the public, an employee's perception of the internal affairs function is the employee's reality.

Whether an elected official, a law enforcement officer, or "civilian" government employee, they all represent the government entity for which they work. Government employees must practice a high level of ethics whether professionally on duty or personally off duty. If government employees are unethical, even on their own time, the perception may be that the government entity must also be unethical. There is no difference between professional and personal behavior. But there are no absolutes in the world. No mortal has absolute ethics; nothing is clear cut; there are many shades of gray; there are different degrees of honesty and dishonesty. Ethics means different things to different people. People of different cultures or different religions have different definitions of honesty, ethics, and morals. Muslim terrorists believe they are right in what they do; they believe they are as right as what the free world does to fight them. The phrase "business is business" is known in the business world as an explanation for a breach of confidence. The phrase describes deceit and fraudulent actions to gain unfair advantage. These shades of gray, these degrees of honesty and dishonesty, must be viewed in each situation and a judgment made that is right for the specific circumstance. However, any leader knows there can be no shades of gray or hidden messages when it comes to the ethics policy presented.

Bait and Switch

I became associated with a law enforcement agency in which an officer was promoted to sergeant with some control over most officers. The sergeant had not been on the original promotion list and was not considered qualified by most contemporaries. The promotion was made for political reasons. The new sergeant was self-centered and indifferent to the feelings of others. He had superficial charm but was callous, insensitive, and unsympathetic. Deceit and repeated lying were common. Some might say he had no conscience. I became well-acquainted with the sergeant as did others. Anyone who knew him also knew that the organization and its management were short on ethics even though the organization had a highly visible ethics program.

There may have been a hidden message in the Los Angeles Police Department culture emanating from Sergeant Stacy C. Koon, the on-scene supervisor during the Rodney King arrest. In a *Los Angeles Times* editorial Koon stated Chief Daryl Gates, "prostituted the foundations upon which the LAPD has built its reputation."[29] Koon appeared bitter at the time because Gates fired a probationary officer and criticized others involved in the Rodney King beating.

Skolnick and Fyfe state, "the cops on the scene were responding to a code they believed in and considered to be moral. The code decrees that cops protect cops, no matter what, and that cops of higher rank back up working street cops—no matter what. From the perspective of the indicted cops, Daryl Gates betrayed the code. Sergeant Koon was, in effect, alleging that Chief Gates was changing the unwritten rules, and consequently the tradition of the organization."[30] In fact, the entire chain of command failed in projecting a strong ethical code throughout the LAPD; Gates' senior leadership failed to drive the code to the operational supervisors, and Sergeant Koon as one, if all information was reported correctly, failed to lead his subordinates in an ethical manner.

I have spoken to numerous active and retired police officers regarding the Rodney King incident. The consensus is that the officers did not beat King, but merely acted as they were trained to do on the job while attempting to subdue him. That is "ambiguous speak" because the officers' formal training was overtaken by what their leadership taught or accepted on the street. What I believe the officers failed to do in a timely manner was to subdue King, but "played" him too long creating more than a perception of wrongdoing. Leadership, through words, actions, or plausible deniability, gave the officers the authority to "play."

Case Study

You are a newly promoted group supervisor in a federal agency. Your group of seven special agents conducts criminal investigations of various violations of criminal law. One agent in your group, Lenny Brown, is a natural leader and everyone in the group seeks out his advice when you are not around. This natural leader causes you few problems and makes big cases. Because of Brown's informal leadership, the group and the former group supervisor have received many accolades. As a senior special agent, you were the only agent that came close to being as good as Brown. Lenny has no interest in being a group supervisor, and you were handpicked over several other candidates to take over the new group. Many others are envious of you.

You recently discovered Brown may be violating court instructions and ignoring directions from the Office of the U.S. Attorney, along with failing to follow department policy. The former group supervisor apparently overlooked Brown's indiscretions and lack of ethics because Brown makes everyone look good. You also determined that your supervisor may already know of Brown's imprudence.

Case Study Questions

Answer the following questions in one narrative response.

1. *As a group supervisor, what is your responsibility regarding Brown's actions?*

2. *Should you immediately call internal affairs?*

3. *What would you say to your group as a whole?*

4. *Would you approach your supervisor with the problem or go over his head?*

Questions for Discussion

Answer each of the following questions in a separate response.

1. Contact a law enforcement department or agency. To whom did you speak? What is their title? What ethics training is given to newly hired employees? How are ethical standards enforced? Is there ongoing ethics training? How is leadership involved in the ethical standards?

2. How can a chief affect the way an arrest is made by a patrol officer? What can a sergeant do to affect the way an arrest is made by a patrol officer?

Notes

1. Plaintiff vs. Homer J. Williams, Defendant. (9 Mar 2001). Transcript of Trial (Deliberations). Case No. 00CR1890-H United States District Court, Southern District of California, United States of America.
2. Ibid.
3. Ibid.
4. Ibid.
5. Curt Guyette. (26 MY 2004) Internal Affairs? Onetime cops allege they were ousted and harassed because they knew of Mayor Kilpatrick's "philandering." *Detroit Metro News.* Retrieved from www2.metrotimes.com/editorial/story.asp?id=6269.
6. Bonisteel, Sara. (4 Sep 2008). Detroit Mayor Kwame Kilpatrick Resigns in Plea Deal. Fox News.com. Retrieved from http://www.foxnews.com/story/0,2933,416543,00.html.
7. Roe, Sam, Heinzmann, David, & Mills, Steve. (5 Dec 2007). Shielded From The Truth, The rush to clear police in shootings, Part 1 of 2. Chicagotribune.com. Retrieved from http://www.chicagotribune.com/news/local/chi-071205cops-htmlstory,0,2906787.htmlstory.
8. Main, Frank. (3 Jun 2006). Chicago Police Board Clears 7 of 29 cops facing firings. Chicago Sun-Times. Retrieved from http://www.policeone.com/officer-misconduct-internal-affairs/articles/135784-Chicago-Police-Board-clears-7-of-29-cops-facing-firings/.
9. Independent Police Review Authority. City of Chicago. Retrieved from http://www.iprachicago.org/about.html. Accessed December 7, 2010.
10. Dees, Tim. (21 Jul 2006). Editorial: The Rat Squad. Officer.com. Retrieved from http://timdees.com/blog/?p=47. Accessed 23 May 2011.
11. Rider, Randy. (10 Aug 2006). Letter to Tim Dees, Editor-in-Chief, Officer.com
12. Dees, Tim. (4 Oct 2006). Editorial: Another Look at IA, Officer.com. Retrieved from http://www.officer.com/interactive/2006/10/04/niaia.
13. Ibid.

14. Graves, Wallace. (Jun 1996). Police Cynicism: causes and cures. FBI Law Enforcement Bulletin. 65(6), pg. 16-20. Retrieved from http://proquest.umi.com.ezproxy2.apus.edu/pqdweb?index=0&did=9724801&SrchMode=2&sid=1&Fmt=3&VInst=PROD&VType=PQD&RQT=309&VName=PQD&TS=1306185404&clientId=62546.
15. Reichheld, Frederick, F. (2001). Loyalty Rules—How Today's Leaders Build Lasting Relationships. Harvard Business School Press.
16. Harari, Oren. (2002). *The Leadership Secrets of Colin Powell.* McGraw-Hill. pp. 17 & 18.
17. Hayes, Read, Ph.D. (2008). Strategies to Detect and Prevent Workplace Dishonesty, ASIS Foundation.
18. Walker, Samuel. (1977). A Critical History of Police Reform: The Emergence of Professionalism. Lexington Books, D.C. Heath & Co. p. 58.
19. Ibid.
20. United States Wickersham Commission on Law Observance and Enforcement, Report of. (1928–1931). Research Collections in American Legal History. Retrieved from http://www.lexisnexis.com/documents/academic/upa_cis/1965_WickershamCommPt1.pdf.
21. Eisenhower, Dwight, D. Brainy Quote. Retrieved from http://www.brainyquote.com/quotes/authors/d/dwight_d_eisenhower_2.html. Assessed April 29, 2011.
22. Foglesong, Gen. Robert, H, "Doc." (Dec 2004). The High Road, American Legion Magazine. Vol. 157, No. 6.
23. Pomeroy, Ann. (Jul 2007). Corporate Ethics Affect Employee Productivity. HRMagazine. Alexandria, VA. Vol. 52, Iss. 7, p. 16, 1 pg.
24. Ibid.
25. Delattre, Edwin, J. (1996). Character and Cops: Ethics in Policing: 3rd Edition. The AEI Press.
26. Mercer, Bruce. (Oct 2006). Program Director (retired) International Anti-Corruption and Integrity Awareness Program, Immigration and Customs Enforcement (ICE). Interview.
27. Aguilar, Francis, J. (1994). Managing Corporate Ethics: Learning from America's Ethical Companies, How to Supercharge Business Performance. Oxford University Press, p. 23.
28. Mercer, Bruce. (Oct 2006). Program Director (retired) International Anti-Corruption and Integrity Awareness Program, Immigration and Customs Enforcement (ICE). Interview.
29. Berger, Leslie. (12 May 1991). Indicted Officer Says Gates Should Resign King beating: The chief has "prostituted" the department's principles to keep his job, Sgt. Koon writes in the Times' Opinion section. Los Angeles Times. Retrieved from http://pqasb.pqarchiver.com/latimes/access/61287676.html?dids=6.
30. Skolnick, Jerome, H. & Fyfe, James, J. (1993). Above the Law, Police and the Excessive Use of Force. The Free Press, pp. 7 & 8.

Suggested Reading

Harari, Oren. (2002). *The Leadership Secrets of Colin Powell.* New York: McGraw-Hill.

Aguilar, Francis, J. (1994). *Managing Corporate Ethics: Learning from America's Ethical Companies How to SuperCharge Business Performance.* New York: Oxford University Press.

Thompson, George, J. PhD, & Walker, Gregory A., USASF (Ret.). (2007). *The Verbal Judo Way of Leadership.* Flushing, NY: Looseleaf Law Publications, Inc.

Reichheld, Frederick, F. (2001). *Loyalty Rules: How today's Leaders Build Lasting Relationships.* Boston: Harvard Business School Press.

Delattre, Edwin, J. (1996). *Character and Cops: Ethics in Policing.* Washington, DC: The AEI Press.

CHAPTER FIVE
Don't Hire Problems

As stated previously, everyone is entitled to a safe workplace: safe from fear, from harassment, and from discrimination. Employees have the right to feel secure in their environment. A good officer or employee should not be afraid of a bad officer or employee. The first step in making the environment and the organization secure is to hire the right people. The right people are ones who are not only highly qualified for a position, but ones who have, among other things, no past actions of workplace violence, gender or race harassment, have a good work record, and who have demonstrated personal responsibility. The right new hire is one who is a team player, works well with others, and knows the difference between right and wrong.

The citizens the organization serves are also entitled to unequalled service by an organization staffed by the best available people. To ensure a safe workplace and the best service performance, employers are obligated to use sound judgment in selecting, supervising, and retaining employees. A good selection process allows for a good work environment for employees and less foreseeable liability on the part of the organization.

The New Generations

The first step in good hiring is to know the people who you are trying to reach to offer employment. The vast majority of individuals seeking law enforcement positions will be young, 21 to 40, but there are exceptions in every department. In the federal government, without a waiver, when a person reaches his 37th birthday, he is excluded, from being hired to fill traditional law enforcement positions. Over time, because of age differences, I have seen a divide that has developed between those who are doing the hiring and those who are being hired.

Adrian Van Brussel, a baby boomer, believes "young police officers are looking for instant gratification and do not want to pay their dues; they believe they have experience when none is present. Their attitude is they are here and want to know what others are going to do for them, instead of what they can do for the organization. They are not team players, they believe they have all the answers before they have the experience and many will not listen to older, more experienced officers." Van Brussel feels "the older, baby boomer generation was highly motivated to learn and listened to the experienced officers while the current younger generation talks instead of listens. They also do not know what rapport or compassion is; they would rather play the macho role; they do not cultivate interpersonal relationships with the citizens they serve, but are authoritarian without concern for the feelings of the people they serve. The baby boomer generation learned from their mistakes, they learned that constant, or extreme aggressiveness did not portray the law enforcement community in the best light and developing professional relationships is a more professional approach."[1]

A police lieutenant, who will remain anonymous, agrees with Van Brussel. "The young officer, typically, was raised playing computer games and has limited interpersonal skills. Play time was sitting in front of a computer screen, not communicating with others. Young officers do not want to talk their way out of a tough spot or reason with people; there is no compromise, just an escalation of force."[2]

Jeffrey Vargo believes that "many young officers consider police work as just another job, rather than a 'calling' as he and others in an older generation looked at it when newly hired. Officers from the new generation, however, are better educated and keep supervisors on their toes. Answering a question by simply answering them with 'because that's the way it's always been done' does not suffice. I had better be able to back up what I say with something concrete, or a young officer will not respect the decision or me. Young officers tend to ask more questions than I and my contemporaries did, but many young officers do not have military experience and have few real life experiences because of a sheltered life. There are some exceptions to my view, but many in the new generation seem to be more interested in pay and benefits and less interested in the 'job'."[3]

There is a perceived decline in work ethic between generations, but some sources do not support the claim. Although there is an understanding among many that young people do not work as hard as older workers, many factors other than generational influences affect employee work ethics. A person's work ethic can vary by education level or whether the work is full or part-time. Income level and marital status are also factors that can influence an employee's worth.[4]

Sources have reported that loyalty differs depending on the age of the employee. Younger employees are less loyal whereas older employees seek stability. Employee fidelity appears to differ depending on the generation examined, but generations share like reasons for continuing employment with one organization. Factors such as: salaries and benefits, promotion opportunities, a challenging job, and learning new skills.[5]

Equally shared by young and older employees is the complaint that there is a lack of respect toward them, although their understanding differs. The older generation wants their proper due because of their experience and the younger generation should do what they are told. The younger generation wants to be heard and their opinions valued. Some in the older generation believe age and experience deserves more respect than youth and inexperience. A true challenge is created by age and generational differences.[6]

However, my experience with younger federal agents is close to what others have said. When I was in my 40s with 20 years experience, agents in their 20s with less than five years on the job wanted my position along with my salary. Some younger agents left federal employment for better paying private security positions, although I believe many regretted their move.

Because most applicants may be passed over for sworn law enforcement positions after age 40, the greatest number of positions will be filled by "youngsters" of the newer generations. The hiring process must be structured to hire those individuals with solid values equal to what the department expects. Although an employer can make every effort to hire the right people, well rounded and grounded, there still is a chance a new hire may not have the ethical standards or temperament required to fill a position of trust. A manager or internal affairs investigator will find that some employees cannot stay out of trouble and do not understand ethical issues, whereas others do understand, but fall victim to weaknesses they find hard to control. Most are hardworking people who sometimes make the wrong decision; others may be wrongly accused. To minimize possible integrity lapses, a closer look must be made at the background of each applicant. Ethics training must also take a sizable role in academy and in-service training. Training is especially important for some large metropolitan departments, or any department for that matter, which has lowered the job qualifications because they cannot find enough highly qualified applicants or because of a judicial mandate.

Negligent Hiring Doctrine

Under the negligent hiring doctrine, a majority of states recognize that an employer can be held legally responsible for acts by an employee even if the employee goes beyond the range or description of his authorized duties. This is especially significant with public service personnel who have frequent contact with the public, sometimes personal, intimate contact. An employer has an obligation to take due care, to make every effort to be cognizant of an applicant's background in order to foresee, as much as practicable, whether an applicant has the propensity to provide a high level of recognized public service. During the hiring process, an employer has the obligation to obtain enough information about an applicant during pre-employment screening to determine if it is safe to employ the prospective applicant in a position of trust.

"Negligent hiring liability is defined as 'the failure to exercise reasonable care in the selection of an applicant, in view of the risk created by the position.' This means that employers must adequately screen individuals before hiring (Bates, 1988)."[7]

Liability on the part of an organization can run into the millions of dollars because of employee workplace actions or even actions on personal time: "there has been a proliferation of lawsuits against employers for negligent hiring, negligent retention, and negligent supervision."[8]

There is an obvious need to hire the best-qualified candidates for any position; the media are replete with examples of unethical practices, workplace crime, and violence. In the mid-1980s, a corruption scandal that became known as the Miami River Cops demonstrated how the screening process can play a role, among other factors, in fostering corruption. In 1985, over a dozen Miami police officers boarded a boat docked on the Miami River to steal illegal narcotics. Three of the drug dealers jumped into the river to escape the police and drowned, and a middleman involved in the illegal activity was murdered by the officers. A subsequent investigation revealed a pattern of corruption in the City of Miami Police Department that had systematically increased over years. Dozens of officers were convicted of various crimes and dozens more were disciplined for various degrees of association. The officers were part of a recruiting effort in the late 1970s and early 1980s when hiring standards were substantially lowered to quickly hire police officers to combat rising crime.

It was reported on February 11, 2007, in *The New York Times* that many city mayors routinely hire police officers as quickly as they can to reduce crime. The mayor of Jersey City, NJ, Jerramiah Healy, added 250 officers to bring the Jersey City force to over 900 personnel, but an incident gave a warning to other cities not to rush to hire police officers without carefully screening them.

In 2005, Jersey City hired Officer Kevin Freibott, a former Middletown, NJ, police officer using a program that allowed Freibott to move from one police force to another. This gave Jersey City an experienced officer without incurring the expense of training. However, it was found that after he was hired, Freibott had been suspended from his former department after an accident while driving with an expired license. He had had numerous accidents and moving violations; his license had been suspended three times and revoked once for failure to attend a drug and alcohol program.[9]

Soon after being hired by Jersey City, Freibott rear-ended a car while off duty, killing a two-year-old boy and critically injuring his mother [who has since died]. Freibott was charged with various violations including aggravated manslaughter. In February 2008, Freibott was sentenced to 11 years in prison.[10]

The New York Post reported in November 2008, that Madison Square Garden (MSG) settled a multi-million-dollar lawsuit that alleged MSG vendors "recklessly" provided beer to a drunken off-duty Officer Freibott. The undisclosed settlement is estimated to be at least $8 million. The estimated settlement is reportedly the amount owed for family medical costs.[11]

"Police departments in municipalities everywhere should learn from this painful lesson. It may be a good idea to hire more police officers, but it is essential that warning signs in their backgrounds be taken seriously."[12]

Along with ever-present misconduct, Korver suggests fraud on applicants' resumes is over 50%. This could include resume inflation or deflation: inflation to falsely increase qualifications or deflation to hide or misrepresent pertinent information on employment, residences, criminal record, or birthplace.[13]

In 2007, Milwaukee Police Officer Jose Morales was arrested when it was discovered his real name was Oscar Ayala-Cornejo and was an illegal alien. Ayala-Cornejo took the identity of his deceased cousin, Jose Morales, while in high school. Ayala-Cornejo pled guilty to a felony for falsely claiming he was a United States citizen. Kari Kydersen reported in *The Washington Post* that "John Balcerzak, president of the Milwaukee Police Association labor union, said the incident shows that the department should beef up its background-check process ...This is a wake-up call to our department and departments around the country ...Balcerzak said the department could suffer consequences ...This is going to mushroom and cause problems down the road because even when you issue a citation you're swearing everything in it is true and correct."[14]

Captain K. M. Castelloe of the North Carolina State Patrol believes "you cannot change the value system of most individuals; their values have been ingrained in their youth. An academy cannot instill integrity; a new recruit must have the values advocated by your department or agency when hired. A thorough background check must be conducted prior to the first day on the job. Once in the academy it is too late to instill a value system, but a set of expectations can be introduced and a preventive maintenance program initiated to create a mindset of ethical decision making. Expectations will help each officer to understand the boundaries of loyalty; loyalty to the department, fellow officers, and loyalty to the citizens they serve. Loyalty means creating an atmosphere that makes the officer who is prone to misconduct fear the many honest officers. The chain of command can also monitor complaint histories; an early warning system; to manage problems before they become unmanageable. Integrity is like virginity; once it is gone you can never get it back."[15]

The *Chicago Sun-Times* reported that dozens of applicants for the Chicago Police Department, many of whom sold cocaine, smoked pot, were thieves, or had been rejected by other police departments, were restored to the department's hiring list by the Human Resources Board (HRB) after they were initially found to be unfit to become officers. "Many of those returned to the hiring list are related to current or retired cops who spoke on their behalf. Three times, aldermen successfully went to bat for the rejected applicants." In the past the department fought unsuccessfully to remove the HRB from the hiring process. The HRB has overruled the department's efforts to bar the hiring of applicants with gang connections. Retired Chicago Police Commander Brad Woods stated "If you have a tendency to steal or commit a theft, there is a chance you will do that again. You are not honest ...I remember people that we did not want to hire ...Some of those officers did not do well at all."[16]

Business Week Online reported employee theft is another reason to be concerned during the hiring process. Almost half of the "$32 billion in total retail theft losses nationwide are due to employees helping themselves to the profits."[17] The Association of Certified Fraud Examiners reported that although business entities suffered the largest median losses, government agencies had median losses of $37,000 per scheme.[18]

Along with employer liability for employee bad acts, an employer must also consider that "[t]he direct economic cost of replacing a single bad-hiring decision can be very expensive. Staffing industry sources estimate the cost of a single bad hire can range from twice the yearly salary to a much higher multiplier depending upon the position. The time, money and energy spent recruiting, hiring, and training [are] wasted ... An employer must also consider costs that are hard to quantify, such as loss of productivity, knowledge, know how, and the disruption of the workflow."[19]

"Where there are many applicants, few positions, and intensive screening, it might cost up to $20,000 to hire each trainee. Then add approximately $22,000 in salary, tuition, fees and board to train each trainee for 16 weeks at an academy, and another $28,000 to mature the employee—counting part of the salary of field training officers."[20]

This Makes It Official

Bivens v. Six Unknown Named Agents of the Federal Bureau of Narcotics (FBN), 403 U.S. 388, is a Supreme Court case decided in 1971. FBN is one of several predecessors of the Drug Enforcement Administration. In 1965, the six FBN agents entered the apartment of Webster Bivens without a warrant, searched the apartment and eventually arrested Bivens. It was alleged that the officers used excessive force in arresting him and frightened family members by their demeanor. In 1971, the Supreme Court held that the agent's behavior breached their duty to others. Alleged violations of the fourth amendment (freedom from unreasonable search and seizure), fifth amendment (deprivation of liberty), or sixth amendment (right to a speedy and public trial) of the Constitution can result in a constitutional tort (lawsuit) against a law enforcement officer.[21]

> 42 United States Code Section 1983
> *"Every person who, under color of any statute, ordinance, regulation, custom, or usage, of any State or Territory or the District of Columbia, subjects, or causes to be subjected, any citizen of the United States or other person within the jurisdiction thereof to the deprivation of any rights, privileges, or immunities secured by the Constitution and laws, shall be liable to the party injured in an action at law, suit in equity, or other proper proceeding for redress, except that in any action brought against a judicial officer for an act or omission taken in such officer's judicial capacity, injunctive relief shall not be granted unless a declaratory decree was violated or declaratory relief was unavailable. For the purposes of this section, any Act of Congress applicable exclusively to the District of Columbia shall be considered to be a statute of the District of Columbia."*[22]

Not only can this statute be used against a police officer for misconduct and violations of federally protected rights, it can also be used in state courts for violations of state laws.

Furthermore, double jeopardy, the constitutional right prohibiting being prosecuted twice for the same crime and intended to control prosecutorial abuse by the government, has no standing in civil court.

Civil Rights and the Hiring Process

Civil rights legislation created a contradiction that put many managers in a quandary. "The Equal Employment Opportunity Commission was established to enforce Title VII of the Civil Rights Act of 1964 and has become the cornerstone of the anti-discrimination laws in the United States" (Wendover, 1989). "[P]ersonnel departments face a paradoxical situation in that the doctrine of negligent hiring dictates some specific responsibilities and retention of trustworthy, safe-minded employees, but the EEOC effectively inhibits the pre-employment screening process, and, essentially contradicts the theory of negligent hiring and retention." [23]

"Balancing the needs of the agency and the EEO rights of the individual is a line so razor sharp that no decision seems to be the only one made lately." [24]

"Perhaps the greatest contradiction to the negligent hiring doctrine is that the EEOC has certain restrictions regarding an employer's possible requirement that applicants or employees have no previous arrest record. It states that it is unlawful to reject an applicant on the basis of conviction of a crime unless the crime was substantially related to job responsibilities. While an applicant convicted of embezzlement could be refused employment as a bookkeeper, a convicted rapist would not necessarily be refused a position as a bookkeeper. (Wendover, 1989). In this situation, if the convicted rapist is hired as a bookkeeper and rapes again either committing the crime at the workplace or assaulting a fellow [employee] outside the workplace, it is possible that the employer may be held liable. However, the employer does not have the right to not hire the potential rapist as a bookkeeper." [25]

"There is no Federal law that clearly prohibits an employer from asking about arrest and conviction records. However, using such records as an absolute measure to prevent an individual from being hired could limit the employment opportunities of some protected groups and thus cannot be used in this way." [26]

"Since an arrest alone does not necessarily mean that an applicant has committed a crime the employer should not assume that the applicant committed the offense. Instead, the employer should allow him or her the opportunity to explain the circumstances of the arrest(s) and should make a reasonable effort to determine whether the explanation is reliable."[27]

"Even if the employer believes that the applicant did engage in the conduct for which he or she was arrested that information should prevent him or her from employment only to the extent that it is evident that the applicant cannot be trusted to perform the duties of the position when

- considering the nature of the job,
- the nature and seriousness of the offense,
- the length of time since it occurred.

This is also true for a conviction."[28]

"Several state laws limit the use of arrest and conviction records by prospective employers. These range from laws and rules prohibiting the employer from asking the applicant any questions about arrest records to those restricting the employer's use of conviction data in making an employment decision."[29]

The FBI changed its hiring policy concerning former drug use, which, in the past, precluded many from being hired. An FBI statement confirmed that the policy change is the acceptance of reality: as much as a third of the United States population has tried marijuana. The decreased standards were caused by difficulties of filling job vacancies. "Mark A. de Bernardo, executive director of the Institute for a Drug-Free Workplace, a nonprofit group, said he applauds the FBI for dropping its numerical measures, in part because such requirements could run afoul of disability discrimination laws. Someone who may have engaged in illicit drug use 20 years ago—to say that person can never work at the FBI, that they can never be rehabilitated, would be not only inappropriate but possibly illegal," de Bernardo said. "I don't think this is sending a weaker message; I think the message can be just as strong, which is that we expect you to be drug-free."[30]

Because the impact of lawsuits for employee transgressions can run into the millions of dollars, how can a public organization legally avoid hiring a person with a high probability of employer liability? Notwithstanding the Civil Rights Act of 1964, reasonable care must be used in the hiring process to avoid hiring undesirable employees. The employment screening process must be fair and consistent according to all federal and appropriate state laws. The hiring process is a complicated labyrinth of rules, laws, and regulations. Certain questions can be asked of the applicant, and other questions are not permissible. Questions that can be asked are things like: name, address, and past work record. Prohibited questions are things like: what is your religion, are you pregnant, what is your sexual orientation, and do you have a disability or any mental emotional disorder? Certain information can be legally obtained while some information is protected by privacy laws. However, the inclusion or exclusion of any applicant can be accomplished through a well-thought-out, solid, legitimate business reason. As a business necessity, job descriptions, along with job qualifications are published as part of the hiring process. Job qualifications are included in the selection process and are necessary for job performance. They can help include the best or exclude the worst applicants as determined by a background investigation, along with structured interviews, and personality screening. However, notwithstanding political considerations, the screening process must be strictly followed.

Alcohol, Tobacco and Firearms Special Agent Applicants[31] must among other things:

- → Be a U.S. citizen.
- → Be registered with the Selective Service System if not exempt.
- → Be between the ages of 21 and 37, at the time of appointment if no previous civilian federal law enforcement service.
- → Possess a current and valid automobile operator's license.
- → Complete ATF special agent applicant questionnaire.
- → Take and pass the Treasury Enforcement Agent (TEA) Examination.
- → Take and pass the ATF special agent applicant assessment test.

- → Appear for and successfully complete a field panel interview—a writing sample will be required.
- → Take and pass a medical examination by an authorized government physician and meet medical requirements.

  Medical requirements include:

  - → Comply with certain eye requirements.
  - → Pass a hearing test.
  - → Weight must be in proportion to height.
  - → Take and pass a drug test.

- → Take and successfully complete a polygraph examination.
- → Successfully complete a background investigation for a top secret security clearance.

Other federal criminal investigation positions have similar qualifications along with additional requirements that may include undergraduate and higher degrees and special skills like accounting, law, and engineering.

City, township, county, or state law enforcement departments have requirements similar to those for federal agencies but may also include physical agility and psychological testing. Some departments require a recruit be trained and state certified before being hired. Some departments require a two-year associates degree, while others require anything from a GED to four years of college. Military experience can take the place of some education requirements.

Structured Hiring Process

Whether in the public or private sector, organizations are obligated to comply with certain state and/or federal personnel rules, laws, and regulations. The Code of Federal Regulations (CFR) is used in this instance as an example of how these rules, laws, and regulations are used. However, many city, county, and state law enforcement and related positions are affected, especially since September 11, 2001, by the following CFR when non-federal personnel become involved in national security issues.

"The purpose of the Code of Federal Regulations (CFR) is to establish criteria and procedures for making determinations of suitability for employment in the federal service." The CFR deals with "determinations of 'suitability' based on an individual's character or conduct that may have an impact on the integrity or efficiency of the service ... To establish a person's suitability for employment, appointments to positions in the (Federal) competitive service require the person to undergo an investigation by OPM [Office of Personnel Management] or by an agency with delegated authority from OPM to conduct investigations ... Agency heads shall designate every competitive service position within the agency at a high, moderate, or low risk level as determined by the position's potential for adverse impact to the efficiency and integrity of the service ... Positions at the high or moderate risk levels would normally be designated as 'Public Trust' positions. Such positions may involve policy making, major program responsibility, public safety and health, law enforcement duties, fiduciary responsibilities, or other duties demanding a significant degree of public trust ... An applicant, appointee, or employee may be denied Federal employment or removed from a position only when the action will protect the integrity or promote the efficiency of the service." [32]

Specific factors considered are the following:

1. Misconduct or negligence in employment;
2. Criminal or dishonest conduct;
3. Material, intentional false statement or deception or fraud in examination or appointment;
4. Refusal to furnish testimony as required;
5. Alcohol abuse of a nature and duration that suggests that the applicant or appointee would be prevented from performing the duties of the position in question, or would constitute a direct threat to the property or safety of others;
6. Illegal use of narcotics, drugs, or other controlled substances, without evidence of substantial rehabilitation;
7. Knowing and willful engagement in acts or activities designed to overthrow the U.S. Government by force;
8. Any statutory or regulatory bar that prevents the lawful employment of the person involved in the position in question.[33]

In making a suitability determination, OPM and agencies shall consider the following additional considerations to the extent they deem them pertinent to the individual case:

1. The nature of the position for which the person is applying or in which the person is employed;
2. The nature and seriousness of the conduct;
3. The circumstances surrounding the conduct;
4. The recency of the conduct;
5. The age of the person involved at the time of the conduct;
6. Contributing societal conditions; and
7. The absence or presence of rehabilitation or efforts toward rehabilitation. [34]

After consideration of the above one or more of the following actions can be taken:

1. Cancellation of eligibility;
2. Denial of appointment;
3. Removal;
4. Cancellation of reinstatement eligibility;
5. Debarment.[35]

"Supervisors, managers, any hiring official have to walk a fine line in trying to make hiring decisions. The CFR regulations on conducting and adjudicating background investigations before someone is hired are valuable so that one does not have to go through the drawn out process of firing someone. However, in my organization there is an ongoing fight with human resources who at times are only interested in numbers rather than quality. I do understand that unions and EEO regulations have a role in the numbers game. Union demands and EEO regulations instill wariness in supervisors in having to undergo the process of not hiring someone or later firing a new hired employee no matter for whom they work: federal, state, or local. Unions and EEO regulations have their purpose in protecting those who need it. However, like most good things some protections are commonly abused. This abuse leads to mistrust of anyone involved in these protections. Hind-sight being what it is, hiring officials are the first to be asked "how did this problem get on board?" They must then justify why they made the decision to hire."[36]

National Security

There are additional procedures for law enforcement or related positions when national security is involved and when positions are concerned with the protection of the nation from foreign aggression or espionage, including development of defense plans or policies, intelligence or counterintelligence activities. Additional procedures also come into play with the preservation of the military strength of the United States; and when positions require regular use of, or access to, classified information. National security requires that all persons employed in the federal government be reliable and honest, of good conduct and high character, and have complete loyalty to the United States.

These positions are considered sensitive and are identified at one of three sensitivity levels: Special-Sensitive, Critical-Sensitive, or Non-critical-Sensitive.[37]

Since September 11, 2001, numerous federal agencies have begun sharing classified information with city, county, and state law enforcement officers under the "need to share" outlined by the National Commission on Terrorist Attacks Upon the United States discussed in, and more commonly known as the 9/11 Commission Report of July, 2002. Although not federal applicants or employees, many city, county, and state supervisory officers and intelligence analysts assigned to "fusion centers" must now comply with federal regulations in order to have access to classified national security information. In fact, a city, county, or state employee, although not seeking or holding a federal position could still hold a federally sanctioned security clearance because a clearance is not part of the hiring adjudication process.

"Although a federal applicant can be denied employment for numerous reasons, in the past there were reports of hesitation on the part of some Federal agencies to take certain cases to litigation because adjudication is a complicated issue. However, since September 11, 2001, there appears to be less hesitation because there is now more at stake. Arguably, there could still be some hesitation because of the extraordinary effort required of the agency, as a whole, when involved in litigation. There is extensive documentation required, legal depositions and wrangling, and finally a trial.

Executive leadership, not just the supervisors or middle managers, are required to travel to give testimony. The time and effort to deny employment to a prospective applicant can be tremendous. However, case law is replete with examples of negligent hiring by a department of an officer who was later deemed unfit for employment upon a later review of his background."[38]

Working for the Enemy

"Federal law enforcement officers of all types are being caught daily working for people who will stop at nothing to make a profit. There are even a few federal officers who were hired with the intent to help the enemy so to speak. I wish they could be prosecuted for treason because that is the way I see their crime. The old mafia trick of keeping a few law enforcement officers 'clean' and away from the family business, then getting them in law enforcement positions in order to supply information seems to have worked for some folks. They are very difficult to catch in the average background investigation."[39]

What this federal official describes is something that has been going on for over a century. Traditional organized crime has been paying local officers to do their business either overtly or covertly. A good example of this is described in *When Corruption Was King: How I Helped the Mob Rule Chicago, Then Brought the Outfit Down.* Chicago is known worldwide for being Al Capone's playground and has continued to be for his successors. Robert Cooley, a former Chicago Police Officer and corrupt defense attorney, describes how the mob not only ran the court system in Cook County, IL, but had the Chief of Detectives of the Chicago Police Department as one of its minions.[40]

Robert Fuesel stated, "In the twenty-first century traditional organized crime is still alive and well in major cities all over the United States. However, the days of Al Capone or John Gotti are over. A metamorphosis has taken place in crime families where most illegal business is kept out of the public eye. The boosting and bravado have been replaced with caution and concealment. The three ingredients to survive: well placed judges, politicians and law enforcement officers are still recruited for information and favors. They are on the payroll and the phrase; 'the fix is in' is not outdated. Adding to the strength and resiliency of organized crime is the steady dissolution or consolidation of U.S. Department of Justice Organized Crime Strike Forces. Since the 1980s Strike Forces around the country have been eliminated or marginalized. Without a concentrated effort of eradication, organize crime will remain viable and dangerous."[41]

"There are traitors among us. Some are wearing the uniform of American law enforcement. They are members of our federal defense force at the U.S. border; others are from local police departments in areas nearby. They are men and women who carry a badge and a gun and are supposed to make sure the bad guys stay out of our country. Instead they are taking bribes and lining their own pockets at the expense of our nation's safety ... The FBI admits it is currently investigating at least 100 of these active corruption cases because corrupt border officials willing to sell out their country for a price represent a real national security threat."[42]

"Far less widely reported [than drug-related violence] is the infiltration and corruption of American law enforcement, according to Robert Killebrew, a retired U.S. Army colonel and senior fellow at the Washington-based Center for a New American Security. "This is a national security problem that does not yet have a name," he wrote last fall in The National Strategy Forum Review ... Michael Hayden, director of the Central Intelligence Agency under President George W. Bush, called the prospect of a narco-state in Mexico one of the gravest threats to American national security, second only to al-Qaeda and on par with a nuclear-armed Iran. But the threat to American law enforcement is still often underestimated."[43]

As the reader can see, traditional organized crime is not the only organized criminal element to threaten our democracy. In recent history it has become evident that extremists who threaten U.S. security support their activities with illegal narcotic sales and have partnered with long-established drug traffickers from South, Central and North America. Terrorists or their supporters are, arguably, already in police departments and federal agencies.

Case Study

Officer Taylor is a 20-year, married veteran of a mid-size law enforcement agency. The hiring practices of the agency are strict, and only the best applicants are hired. A new hire, Officer Smith, a single man who recently graduated from a local university, has been assigned to the same shift as Taylor. During a late-night tour, Taylor had the opportunity to get to know Smith. Taylor initially thought Smith was a great guy and on the ball, but after several hours of shooting the breeze Taylor decided the new officer may not be the right fit for a law enforcement career. Because Smith graduated with a degree in criminal justice, he seems to "know it all." During a call for service, Officer Smith questioned the way Officer Taylor handled the situation. Smith believed Taylor was too "nice" to a suspicious person and should have told the man who's the boss. Taylor does not believe Smith is a team player but is a self-centered "individual of one." Smith plans on attending law school because the department will help pay the tuition and is already talking about becoming a sergeant.

Case Study Questions

Answer the following questions in one narrative response.

1. *Do you believe Officer Taylor is correct in saying that Officer Smith may not be the right fit for law enforcement?*

2. *Should Officer Taylor discuss his misgivings with the shift commander?*

3. *As the shift commander, what would your response be to Officer Taylor?*

4. *As the shift commander, what, if anything, would you discuss with Officer Smith?*

Questions for Discussion

Answer each of the following questions in a separate response.

1. What makes it difficult for a department to hire the best qualified?

2. Discuss the Negligent Hiring Doctrine recognized in the state in which you live. Interview a law enforcement supervisor or personnel specialist in a law enforcement agency of your choice. Obtain an example of how the negligent hiring doctrine affected the department.

3. Discuss the similarities and differences between 41 USC 1983 and 18 USC 242.

Notes

1. Van Brussel, Adrian. (13 May 2008). Investigator (retired). Cook County (IL) Sheriff's Police. Interview.
2. Anonymous. (16 Sep 2009). Lieutenant of Police (ret). Unnamed police department. State of Washington. Interview.
3. Vargo, Jeffrey, M. (18 Feb 2010). Deputy Chief. Susquehanna Township Police Department, Harrisburg, Pennsylvania. Correspondence.
4. University of Minnesota. Research and Training Center on Community Living. (2008). Generational differences in the workplace. Retrieved from http://rtc.umn.edu/docs/2_18_Gen_diff_workplace.pdf.
5. Ibid.
6. Ibid.
7. Slowik, Donald, W. (1996). Workplace Investigations: A Guidebook for Administrators, Managers, and Investigators. Evergreen Press, Evergreen, CO. p. 29.
8. Ibid.
9. Op-ed. (11 Feb 2007). Screening Police Recruits. *The New York Times*. Retrieved from http://www.nytimes.com/2007/02/11/opinion/nyregionopinions/NJ2police.html?_r=1. Accessed 19 Nov 2009.
10. Ryan, Joe. (28 Feb 2008). Ex-Jersey City cop gets 11 years for fatal crash. The Star-Ledger. Retrieved from http://74.125.95.132/search?q=cache:xRmUUVgOAGcJ:www.nj.com/news/index.ssf/2008/02/a_former_jersey_city_police.html+kevin+freibott&cd=2&hl=en&ct=clnk&gl=us. Accessed 19 Nov 2009.
11. MacIntosh, Jeane. (8 Nov 2010) Death payout: Lawsuit v. MSG settled. *New York Post*. Retrieved from http://www.nypost.com/p/news/local/manhattan/death_payout_3cZGxs4lw9oO8h0KVgcBaI

12. Op-ed. (11 Feb 2007). Screening Police Recruits. The New York Times. Retrieved from http://www.nytimes.com/2007/02/11/opinion/nyregionopinions/NJ2police.html?_r=1. Accessed 19 Nov 2009.
13. Korver, Clinton, D. (2008). The Ethics of Resume Writing. Harvard Business Review. Retrieved from http://blogs.hbr.org/cs/2008/05/the_ethics_of_resume_writing.html#comments.
14. Lydersen, Kari. (18 Jun 2007). Milwaukee Officer Found to Be Illegal Immigrant: Policeman Had Assumed the Identity of a Dead Cousin. *The Washington Post.* Retrieved from http://www.washingtonpost.com/wp-dyn/content/article/2007/06/17/AR2007061701019.html.
15. Castelloe, K.M. (31 Oct 2008). Captain, North Carolina State Patrol. Correspondence.
16. Main, Frank, & Sweeney, Annie. (8 Sep 2008). "Unfit" Stay on Chicago Police Hire List. *Chicago Sun-Times.* Retrieved from http://forums.leoaffairs.com/viewtopic.php?f=104&t=77269.
17. Salkever, Alex. 20 May 2003). An Easy Antidote to Employee Theft: A leading security consultant is urging business owners to take a simple step that will make customers their first line of defense. Bloomberg Businessweek. Retrieved from http://www.businessweek.com/smallbiz/content/may2003/sb20030520_9328_sb018.htm.
18. Association of Certified Fraud Examiners. (2004). 2004 Report to the Nation on Occupational Fraud and Abuse. Retrieved from http://www.acfe.com/documents/2004RttN.pdf.
19. Rosen, Lester, S. (2005). *The Safe Hiring Manual: The Complete Guide to Keeping Criminals, Terrorists, and Imposters out of Your Workplace.* Facts on Demand Press.
20. Americans for Effective Law Enforcement. (Mar 2007). AELE Monthly Law Journal. 2007 (3) AELE Mo. L. J. 201 Employment Law Section - March, 2000. Retrieved from http://www.aele.org/law/2007FPMAR/2007-03MLJ201.pdf.
21. Law Course for Customs Officers. (1999). Office of Chief Counsel, U.S. Customs Service Academy, Glynco, Georgia.
22. Customs Law Handbook. (1995). Office of Chief Counsel, U.S. Customs Service Academy, Glynco, Georgia. Gould Publications, Inc.
23. Slowik, Donald, W. (1996). Workplace Investigations: A Guidebook for Administrators, Managers, and Investigators. Evergreen Press, Evergreen, CO, p. 46.
24. Federal official who will remain anonymous. (12 Jan 2010). Interview.
25. Slowik, Donald, W. (1996). Workplace Investigations: A Guidebook for Administrators, Managers, and Investigators. Evergreen Press, Evergreen, CO, pp. 46–47.
26. U.S. Equal Employment Opportunity Commission, Pre-Employment Inquiries and Arrest & Conviction. Retrieved from http://www.eeoc.gov/laws/practices/inquiries_arrest_conviction.cfm. Accessed 19 Nov 2009.
27. Ibid.
28. Ibid.

29. Ibid.
30. Eggen, Dan. (7 Aug 2007). FBI Bows to Modern Realities, Eases Rules on Past Drug Use: Policy Change Comes As Agency Struggles to Fill Openings. The Washington Post. Retrieved from http://www.washingtonpost.com/wp-dyn/content/article/2007/08/06/AR2007080601260.html.
31. Bureau of Alcohol, Tobacco, Firearms and Explosives. (2011). Special Agent Careers. Retrieved from http://www.atf.gov/careers/special-agents/.
32. Code of Federal Regulations, Title 5, Administrative Personnel, part 731. Retrieved from http://ecfr.gpoaccess.gov/cgi/t/text/text-idx?c=ecfr&sid=ed0c6e726ba90ba579d7277e3024a095&rgn=div8&view=text&node=5:2.0.1.1.7.1.1.1&idno=5. Accessed 19 Nov 2009.
33. Ibid.
34. Ibid.
35. Ibid.
36. Federal official who will remain anonymous. (12 Jan 2010). Interview.
37. Code of Federal Regulations, Title 5, Administrative Personnel, part 732, 736. Retrieved from http://ecfr.gpoaccess.gov/cgi/t/text/text-idx?c=ecfr&sid=ed0c6e726ba90ba579d7277e3024a095&rgn=div8&view=text&node=5:2.0.1.1.7.1.1.1&idno=5. Accessed 19 Nov 2009.
38. Federal official who will remain anonymous. (4 Apr 2009). Interview.
39. Federal official who will remain anonymous. (12 Jan 2010). Interview.
40. Cooley, Robert. Levin, Hillel. (2004). When Corruption Was King: How I Helped the Mob Rule Chicago, Then Brought the Outfit Down. Carroll & Graf Publishers, New York.
41. Fuesel, Robert, former Executive Director, Chicago Crime Commission. (27 Mar 2011). Telephonic interview.
42. Dimond, Diane. (12 Oct 2009). Enforcement Traitors. The Huffington Post. Retrieved from http://www.huffingtonpost.com/diane-dimond/law-enforcement-traitors_b_317494.html.
43. Miller, Judith. (26 Oct 2009). The Mexicanization of American Law Enforcement: The drug cartels extend their corrupting influence northward. City-Journal. vol. 19, no. 4. Retrieved from http://www.city-journal.org/2009/19_4_corruption.html.

Suggested Reading

Slowik, Donald, W. (1996). *Workplace Investigations.* Evergreen, Colorado: The Evergreen Press.

Rosen, Lester, S. (2006). *The Safe Hiring Manual: The Complete Guide to Keeping Criminals, Terrorists, and Imposters Out of Your workplace.* Tempe, AZ: Faces on Demand Press.

Cooley, Robert & Levin, Hillel. (2004). *When Corruption Was King: How I Helped the Mob Rule Chicago, Then Brought the Outfit Down.* New York: Carroll & Graf Publishers.

ASIS International. (2006). Pre-employment Background Screening—Guideline. Alexandra, VA. ASIS International.

CHAPTER SIX
The Investigated

Each personnel category, whether civilian or sworn, has a set of circumstances when interacting with internal affairs. Uniformed officers may have more of a challenge dealing with the public because they usually are the first on the scene when tempers are high, along with making traffic stops, which generate a good share of complaints. Many times detectives are involved in crime after the fact, but whether reactive or proactive, investigators also receive their share of citizen complaints. Federal agents can also receive complaints, ranging from theft or excessive force to entering the wrong domicile while executing a search warrant.

For this publication enforcement officers are described generically. For this purpose a law enforcement officer is one who has the following duties:

1. Carries a firearm
2. Makes arrests
3. Enforces criminal laws

There is such a wide range of jurisdictions and authorities it is difficult to offer a job description of a law enforcement officer. A city officer enforces criminal laws and traffic laws or regulations and city statutes; some may staff a city jail. A deputy sheriff does much the same and can also staff a jail. A deputy also may serve as a court security officer, transport prisoners, serve fugitive warrants, summons and subpoenas, and execute eviction notices. State troopers focus on traffic safety on state highways and interstates, but in some states they can also investigate criminal violations. They all maintain order and prevent crime.

In the federal government, there is a position description group called the "1800 series." The "group includes all classes of positions the duties of which are to advise on, administer, supervise, or perform investigation, inspection, or enforcement work primarily concerned with alleged or suspected offenses against the laws of the United States, or such work primarily concerned with determining compliance with laws and regulations."[1]

Within the 1800 series are the most well-known federal law enforcement officers, which are categorized as 1811s; federal criminal investigators. The 1800 series group also includes many general investigative or inspection positions. Many of these positions do not have traditional law enforcement duties, and may or may not carry a firearm as do the specific 1811 positions, but they may have direct or closely associated duties of enforcing criminal laws.

Federal uniformed police positions can be found in the 0083 series. "The primary mission of police officers in the Federal service is to maintain law and order... Police services are provided in Federal residential areas, parks, reservations, roads and highways, commercial and industrial areas, military installations, Federally owned and leased office buildings, and similar facilities under Federal control."[2]

Whatever the personnel description, federal and local police agencies have a long history of working together. In response to the Wickersham Commission of the 1930s, the FBI National Academy was created to standardize and professionalize law enforcement departments throughout the United States. Training is offered to local, county, state, and other federal agencies.[3] Since entering civilian law enforcement in the early 1970s, I have seen numerous task forces including various combinations of local, county and state officers, along with many federally sponsored combinations. Since September 11, 2001, cooperation has increased exponentially. Therefore, for the purposes of discussing enforcement officers' involvement with the internal affairs function, they are considered a single group.

When speaking of employees of a public organization who are served by an internal affairs unit, many people think of law enforcement officers. Yet a police department or federal law enforcement entity includes many other personnel specialties. Record clerks, human resource specialists, crime scene technicians, computer programmers, and others may make up a large part of many law enforcement departments. In many federal departments with law enforcement authority, the vast majority of employees may not be law enforcement officers, but auditors, project and program managers, fingerprint specialists, social workers, psychologists, lawyers, and other civilians.

Civilian employees, unless unionized, may not have a particular opinion about an internal affairs organization. I have limited experience with unions, but it is no surprise to say that many relationships between unions and management are historically based on mistrust and an adversarial attitude, which brings another dimension to the internal affairs process.

Compared to traditional law enforcement officers, civilian employees may not have the same interaction with the public; therefore, they do not have the same opportunity for disagreements or misconduct. Even with frequent interaction with the public, a civilian employee may not have the type of relationship with the public as does a law enforcement officer and generally would not have the same opportunities to engender complaints. In any department, a civilian employee's contact with an internal affairs investigator will more likely be to supply documents or testimony regarding the actions of an enforcement officer. However, as the subject of an internal investigation, a civilian employee can have direct interaction with an internal investigator because of something done inside the scope of the employee's job description. Supplying documents or information to unauthorized individuals, making summons or reports go away, or the theft of funds or supplies will introduce anyone to the internal affairs function. An internal investigation can also be initiated on a civilian employee because of off-duty activities that could bring unwanted or unfavorable publicity to the department. But typically when the words "internal affairs" are mentioned, they are immediately associated with "the police."

Can't Forget the Auditors

An auditor is another discipline that can be directly involved in enforcing laws and regulations and has authority to conduct official examinations of records rather than the authority of arrest. I worked with many auditors while I was a federal agent. Without audit help, many criminal investigations could end in confusion and much wasted time. I cannot say I understand the audit mind, but I do understand what they can offer: verification, clear focus on criminal wrongdoing, an understanding of a paper trail and complicated financial records, and patience to wade through a myriad of documents. A criminal investigation can play havoc with an audit plan and many auditors may dislike identifying potential criminal activity during an ongoing examination, but many auditors relish working with law enforcement officers.

At times an auditor may cause as much consternation as a law enforcement officer and be the recipient of a complaint. An auditor may also have an equal chance of being the target of bribery. The infamous Al Capone was, in fact, brought to justice not by a traditional badge and gun most people may think; and not by Eliot Ness of the Untouchables fame, but by a Special Agent of the Bureau of Internal Revenue, Intelligence Division (later changed in the 1970s to the Criminal Investigation Division). Frank J. Wilson, a former accountant, with a team of auditors put Big Al in federal prison.

What an Officer Is

In the 1970s, Skolnick identified a "working personality," which helps us understand what makes an enforcement officer tick. What I have seen is a blurred personality, like many working personalities are, with one or more of the following traits:

- → Enjoys excitement
- → Seeks adventure
- → Has a willingness to take responsibility and be in charge
- → Likes that every day can be different than the day before
- → Seeks recognition
- → Seeks danger
- → Enjoys wearing a uniform
- → Desires to carry a firearm
- → Desires to be have authority
- → Seeks respect
- → Seeks job security
- → Does not like sitting at a desk
- → Likes working outdoors
- → Feels comfortable in a military or like style organization
- → Enjoys comradery

Not all officers have the following two traits, some officers shun them:

- → Likes helping people
- → Wants to make a difference and serve the community

A law enforcement officer has many qualities, some qualities are innate, some learned. Some qualities are better than others because of commitment or concern. An officer has a choice to be an ethical officer, an unethical one, or a person somewhere in-between. As does the perception of the internal affairs function, the quality of being ethical or unethical springs from many sources to include the IA process. It certainly can form roots because of leadership or the lack thereof, from elected officials with political agendas, or from outstanding supervisors or ones who fail to perform their duty. A decisive opportunity can also be created by citizens who will entice an officer to make an unwise choice.

Even with optimum leadership support, from experience I found many types of officers, some with a more professional focus than others. Some officers concentrate on service to others while others fixate on crime fighting and become suspicious of the citizens served. Some officers do not know when they are doing something unethical; others, when confronted, admit misconduct, but do not understand why the act is wrong. Other officers have a sense of entitlement, some do as little work as possible, whereas others are proud to carry a badge of a law enforcement officer and conduct themselves and serve citizens as honestly as possible.

In law enforcement I have seen several types of officers with many of the same traits, but with a different life focus.

- → Officers who care about people, who are team players, conduct themselves ethically, and do the best job they can. Their overall conduct is exemplary. They have little contact with internal affairs unless they are assigned to the unit.

- → Officers, who may not be the best, but try to conduct themselves as best they can to serve their department and the public. However, at times they allow themselves to be taken in by other officers who are self-serving, care little about the citizens they serve and generally are considered bad officers. These "followers" may not make the best decisions, either for themselves or the citizens they serve. They may not have a lot of common sense and are led by others, not necessarily their supervisor.

→ Officers with personal problems they cannot control. Alcoholism is the most prevalent, but also included are family and marital problems along with financial difficulties. I include this type because their life focus is confused, their job performance suffers, and others must take up the slack. Because of constant or recurring life difficulties, other officers and supervisors are, at times, brought into the disorder officially and personally.

→ Officers who may care somewhat about others, but are officers because they found job security. They are lazy, at times difficult to work with, and stay on a call longer than necessary to avoid additional work and cannot be counted on. In the federal realm, these officers will find an excuse not to be available when needed and will take longer to prepare for, conduct, and document an interview than an officer who cares to do the best job possible.

→ Officers, who care little, are not team players and who are difficult to work with except for a few close friends who have the same focus in life. Other officers work with them only when it cannot be avoided. Many present and former immediate supervisors know these officers well. Included in this type are bullies who, when told to do something they would rather not, will become belligerent. Many supervisors are reluctant to deal with these officers, and many times they are left to whatever conduct they can get away with while avoiding outside attention.

→ Officers who commit premeditated criminal violations against citizens and the department. They may work alone, with other officers, or may be directly or indirectly associated with traditional, organized crime, street gangs or some type of criminal element outside of the department. I have been told of officers whose law enforcement career is a means to an end; they are motivated to become a law enforcement officer only to

> make it easier to continue stealing cars and burglarizing railroad boxcars. I have heard and read about these officers, but never knowingly met one.

Then there is the perfect cop. "To the Police Chief, the perfect cop is someone who looks sharp, works hard and doesn't expect overtime pay, makes good arrests without offending anyone ...In short, a perfect cop is someone who makes the Chief look good ...To a Prosecuting Attorney, a perfect cop is a meticulous investigator ...To the City Council, a perfect cop is someone who does his job well without making waves ...To the People of the Community, a perfect cop is polite, a friendly person ...He teaches kids right from wrong ...I have been a cop for over 20 years, and have never met a perfect cop. Only a few have even come close, being totally honest and truly caring about people and doing the best job they can ...But all the cops I have ever known are human. They love, laugh, cry, hurt, and sometimes die too young. They try to make it to retirement, although many do not. Divorce is common. Some become alcoholics and some suffer from "police stress," seen in a variety of emotional disorders or heart attacks ...Why do we do it? We don't really know. I hope it's because we simply care about right and wrong."[4]

What an Officer Is Not

Many U.S. military members are acting as peace officers in the sense that they are trying to win over Iraqi and Afghani citizens and are collecting evidence to prosecute terrorists.

Author's Note

At this writing, the Iraqi war has ended and the war in Afghanistan is soon to end.

Some law enforcement officers in the United States view themselves as soldiers in the sense that they also fight terrorists. Is a law enforcement officer a warrior because of participation in the "war on terror"? There is a war on drugs and a war on crime, but these wars are political rhetoric. "War" in this sense is an exaggeration, an exercise in public relations.

The wars on crime or on drugs are not wars, but efforts to control crime and drugs. Historically, a war is a conflict in which arms are used to kill the enemy. I believe any soldier, any true warrior, would say that their main job in a war, in combat, is to kill before being killed, to overwhelm the enemy and to kill quickly. The job of any law enforcement officer, in contrast, is to serve and protect citizens while enforcing the law and maintaining order.

Like soldiers, police officers do move toward the sound of the guns, but to advocate that a law enforcement officer is a warrior may place both the officer and the citizens served in peril. Much time and effort has been placed on the relationship between a law enforcer and a citizen. Community policing, community relations, partnerships between the community and police, alternative police strategy: however you label it, they are all an effort to bring the police and citizens together. These efforts are used to develop and establish a mutual understanding and to decrease crime, to better protect the community, and to decrease conflict between an enforcement officer and a citizen. A patrol car gave officers greater mobility, but less interaction with the people they serve and protect. To reconnect with citizens, departments have introduced bicycle patrols, Segway Transporters and neighborhood substations, fought to keep funding for equestrian units, and reintroduced foot patrols. A warrior mindset will decrease the effectiveness of these strides.

The word "warrior" should never be placed next to the title law enforcement officer. It might be used by the media or by other officers as a gesture of thanks, of pride, or of camaraderie but never officially by the department. I spoke to an Ohio officer who has been in three shootouts in less than 20 years, but I believe the officer's training, rather than the thought he is a warrior assisted in his survival. Professionalism in law enforcement should be identified with education, training and ethical service to citizens.

Although I understand the military has made strides in winning over the hearts and minds of citizens in combat zones, a high crime area in the United States can never be considered a war zone. Soldiers break things in combat; law enforcement officers fix things while maintaining order. In combat zones things happen that should never happen in our country or in our neighborhoods. The rules of engagement in a combat zone are markedly different than the rules of engagement in U.S. policing; the Constitution is the difference. Bravado must be put aside and a law enforcement officer must have the mindset that he is a protector, not a killer, not a warrior. An officer must understand that the citizens served want to live in Mayberry, not Kabul.

Chief White stated "While you often hear that law enforcement is waging a 'war,' I would tend to believe that the label of warrior does not reflect the true mission of law enforcement. While warrior is only a title in name, the connotation would suggest that this type of person would be more likely to approach a problem in a brawn over brain fashion or use a kill'em all and let God sort it out philosophy. The individual traits of the 'warrior' would not be conducive and most likely counter-productive in the community policing organization. This warrior attitude embraces a head-on fight against crime and would tend to alienate the department from the community they serve. At the end of the day, the police officer has to realize that they have been granted their authority only because the public has allowed them to retain this authority. Law enforcement is a team sport, not only with officers and administration, but the public has to be engaged in the battle or the cause is lost."[5]

Many departments have Special Weapons and Tactics Teams (SWAT) or similar units. SWAT training is similar to military training. In fact, some civil and military teams may train together. Tactical team members are proud of what they do, how they are trained, how they dress, and how they are called on when the danger is high. SWAT members do wear their occasional warrior status as a badge of honor. That, however, is where the status of "warrior" must end. What SWAT teams do is sometimes very necessary and brave, but it is an extremely small part of what a police department does and what police work is all about. Fostering the idea within SWAT teams, or in other specialties, that a law enforcement officer is a warrior is a bad idea and only panders to a desire for an over-aggressive image by some members. SWAT team members are already aggressive and fearless when the need arises. However, a like aggressive attitude in other officers will create only a greater divide between officers and citizens. A "warrior mentality" will drag many officers into the internal affair arena. Training focused on "shoot to kill" and aggressive arrest techniques without equal attention to community policing and problem-solving will only aggravate community relations and heighten the potential for misconduct. Officers must understand why a citizen wants a protector, not a soldier.

A warrior attitude brings many officers into direct contact with the internal affairs function. A warrior posture invites noble cause corruption where an officer will do almost anything to obtain a guilty verdict. Warrior status promotes the perception that the internal affairs function is unfair by placing officers in conflict with objective police services. The loss of objectivity creates a sense that an officer is being treated unfairly. Any officer must be reminded to value the rights of an accused.

Rights of Employees Show Fairness

The U.S. Constitution was written to create a federal government for the United States and was finally enacted, after much discussion and consternation, in 1789. Ten amendments to the Constitution were enacted in 1791, to more specifically outline individual rights to prevent the abuse of power. Article V of the ten articles details the right of individuals to life, liberty, and property.

> *"No person shall be held to answer for a capital, or otherwise infamous crime, unless on a presentment or indictment of a Grand Jury ...; nor shall be compelled in any criminal case to be a witness against himself, nor be deprived of life, liberty, or property, without due process of law ..."*[6]

The most widely known protection for an accused is his Fifth Amendment right against self-incrimination. Any law enforcement officer routinely reads or verbally states to an arrestee, a person in custody, his rights. This constitutional right against self-incrimination was affirmed in 1966 by the U.S. Supreme Court in *Miranda v. Arizona,* 384 U.S. 436. Hence, Fifth Amendment constitutional rights are also known as Miranda rights. As a federal agent, I read Miranda rights to many suspects I was about to interview. Many were not in custody, but federal or department procedure, as cautious as it was, required me to read them (I always read it from a card). They had the right to remain silent, anything they said would be used against them, they had the right to consult an attorney, and if they could not afford one, an attorney would be appointed to represent them.

More Employee Protections

In federal internal investigations, a Beckwith warning was also used. The *Beckwith v. U.S.*, 425 U.S. 341 (1976), ruling may be considered a fairness issue to ensure rights to individuals who might be under criminal investigation, but are not under arrest and are not entitled to be read their Miranda rights. The Beckwith warning advises a suspect of the right to remain silent if his response might tend to incriminate him; anything he says could be used in an administrative or criminal proceeding; if he refuses to answer a question that might incriminate him, he could not be fired for remaining silent, but his silence could be used against him in an administrative proceeding. The difference between a Miranda warning and a Beckwith warning is that the accused or the interviewee is not under arrest and is free to end the interview at anytime, therefore not entitled to a rights advisement, but given one nonetheless.

There is also the Weingarten warning. This warning was established from the court case, *National Labor Relations Act (NLRA) v. J. Weingarten, Inc.*, 420 U.S. 215 (1975). It was decided by the U.S. Supreme Court and had no relationship to the public sector, but was later applied to federal employees under 5 USC 7114. As a federal agent I read the Weingarten warning to federal employees. The Weingarten decision actually is similar to other rights advisements but is specifically for union members.

Still another individual protection is the Privacy Act of 1974, 5 United States Code 552a. The act states that no agency shall disclose records maintained on individuals to any person or agency, except upon a written request or with the prior written consent of the individual to whom the record pertains. However, there are several exemptions; among them is a civil or criminal law enforcement activity if the activity is authorized by law. An internal affairs unit is prohibited from disclosing the outcome of an investigation by the Privacy Act of 1974. The only time specifics can be officially disclosed is when it is part of the criminal record in a court of law.

Many law enforcement officers believe they are special. Considering the fact they protect life and have authority to take away someone's freedom confirms that fact. However, that distinction can only go so far. As Chief White stated, officers derive their authority from the people they serve. They enforce laws they are allowed to enforce; they have the authority they are allowed to have.[7] As mentioned in a previous chapter, since 1977, when the California Public Safety Officers Procedural Bill of Rights Act was passed, being special was taken to another dimension. What rights do criminal suspects have that a police officer does not? Every law enforcement officer enjoys many rights and protections in a criminal investigation and trial.

Some of the more familiar to law enforcement officers are the following:

- ***Mapp v. Ohio*** 367 v. 643 (1961)—the decision that created the "exclusionary rule." If evidence is seized in violation of a suspect's constitutional rights, that evidence cannot be used in court.

- ***Gideon v. Wainwright*** 372 U.S. 335 (1963)—the decision which assured that, under the Sixth Amendment, state courts are required to provide the accused in criminal cases assistance of counsel when a defendant cannot afford his own.

- ***Brady v. Maryland*** 373 U.S. (1963), *Giglio v. United States* 405 U.S. 150 (1972), and *United States v. Henthorn* 931 F 2d 29 (1991)—all concern the disclosure to the defense of information favorable to the accused.

- ***Jencks v. U.S.*** 353 U.S. 657 (1957)—the decision held that the government must release to the defense documented statements relied upon by government witnesses in federal criminal proceedings. The Jencks Act further requires the production of police reports, notes, memoranda, and other documents after the witness has testified.

- ***Escobedo v. Illinois*** 378 U.S. 478 (1964)—the decision extended the right of counsel to not only those charged with a crime, but also to those detained for a crime.

- ***Miranda v. Arizona*** 384 U.S. 436 (1966)—the decision required that incriminating statements can be used only at trial if the defendant was aware of his right to counsel and his right against self-incrimination.

- ***Beckwith v. U.S.*** 425 U.S. 341 (1976)—the decision ensured due process by allowing an advice of rights warning to be read to a subject under criminal investigation, but not under arrest and, therefore, not entitled to be read Miranda rights.

- ***Griffin v. California*** 380 v. 609 (1965)—the decision held that the government cannot punish a defendant at trial by inferring to a jury that exercising the right to remain silent is an admission of guilt.

- ***NLRB v. Weingarten*** 420 U.S. 251 (1975)—the Supreme Court upheld a National Labor Relations Board decision that a bargaining unit employee has the right, on request, to union representation during an investigatory interview if the officer reasonably believes he might be subject to disciplinary action. This right is afforded in both administrative and criminal investigations.

- **Privacy Act of 1974, 5 United States Code 552a**—prohibits the disclosure of records without the written consent of the individual to whom the record pertains.

- **The Constitution of the United States**, all of **the Bill of Rights**, but specifically:

  - First Amendment
    - Freedom and privacy of religion

  - Fourth Amendment
    - guards against unreasonable searches and seizures; privacy of one's home

- Fifth Amendment
  - *Ensures that a person is not deprived of life, liberty or property without due process; the government must respect all rights owed to a person according to law*
  - *Arrest for a capital crime must be by indictment of a grand jury.*
  - *A defendant or witness cannot be compelled to incriminate himself; privacy of statements and actions*
  - *Once acquitted a defendant cannot be retried for the same offense.*

- Sixth Amendment
  - *The accused has the right to a public, speedy trial by an impartial jury*
  - *The accused must be informed of the nature and cause of the accusation*
  - *The accused has the right to confront witnesses against him and submit witnesses in his favor*
  - *The accused has the right of a defense counsel to present a defense*

- Eighth Amendment
  - *Protects against excessive bail or fines*
  - *Protects against cruel and unusual punishments*

- Fourteenth Amendment
  - *Ensures due process is provided by states and local governments to ensure fairness*
  - *Requires that states provide equal protection under law to all*

- And the non-right: the Garrity warning.

Garrity Is a Special Non-right

The Garrity decision was discussed in a previous chapter; but because it has caused such controversy in law enforcement it deserves more attention.

An officer is read the Garrity warning when the investigation changes, for that specific officer, from criminal to administrative. *Garrity v. New Jersey* 385 U.S. 463 (1967) held that an officer cannot be compelled to waive a constitutional right in a criminal investigation, so the investigation is changed from criminal to administrative to compel testimony. *Gardner v. Broderick* 392 U.S.273 (1968) reinforced the Garrity decision. After being given the Garrity warning the officer is placed between a rock and a hard place if he admits to criminal activity. After receiving the Garrity warning, if the officer gives truthful responses to questions even if the responses incriminate the officer in criminal activity, the officer will not be prosecuted. That is the protection. The catch is an officer must follow department rules and regulations and give a statement, if a condition of employment, when ordered by a superior officer and, under Garrity, if an officer admits to wrongdoing the officer can face disciplinary action, which can mean termination. That is what some in law enforcement consider the Garrity non-right. In the federal realm the rock and hard place is caused by *Kalkines v. the U.S.* 473 F2d 1391 (1973). The Kalkines warning is freely given when an individual is interviewed during an internal investigation. The warning compels federal employees to cooperate in internal investigations or be fired. It also provides immunity from criminal prosecution.

A Positive Command Presence Shows Fairness

Any officer can be placed under investigation for any number of reasons; some legitimate, others not so legitimate. The public might believe excessive use of force is a clear-cut reason for a complaint and internal investigation. It has been my experience that most allegations are not clear cut, but shaded with gray. There is a strong debate among officers whether excessive force was used on Rodney King. The controversy stems from the media's not showing the full video where King is said to have been violent and uncooperative. In many incidents the shades of gray also originate from the lack of physical evidence or questionable testimony. It has been my experience that eyewitnesses can be highly unreliable for various reasons. One person saw a red car and another who saw the same vehicle will report it was green. A witness may have a dislike for a person that will taint testimony or telling the truth to the police may be contrary to the daily norm. In some situations, witnesses depending on their agenda will report whatever meets their needs.

A good way for department management to show a positive command presence is to support prosecution of individuals making willful false statements or accusations against department personnel. A false statement may be a minor charge depending on the circumstances, but making the effort will go a long way in showing support for the rank and file.

Case Study

Officers Green and Smyth are accused of accepting bribes from motorists to avoid traffic tickets. Both officers have worked together on the same shift for many years. In addition to bribery, Officer Green is also accused of sexually assaulting a female when she did not agree to a payment. Smyth saw the assault take place, but did nothing. Officer Smyth was interviewed by internal affairs investigators and read his Fifth Amendment rights. He was told he was being investigated for bribery and being an accomplice to assault. Smyth invoked his Fifth Amendment right not to incriminate himself. The investigators told Smyth that according to department policy he is required to respond to questions posed by internal affairs investigators, and if he did not answer questions regarding the bribery and assault he would be fired. Smyth declined to answer questions and the interview was terminated.

A few days later Smyth was again approached by internal affairs investigators and read the Garrity warning. The investigators told him if he answered questions even if his responses incriminated him he would not be prosecuted; he answered the investigator's questions. Although Smyth was not prosecuted he was later fired for policy violations.

Case Study Questions

Answer the following questions in one narrative response.

It is appropriate to contact an internal affairs investigator or law enforcement union representative to discuss your response to the following questions:

1. *Did Officer Smyth have the "right" to refuse to answer questions by invoking his constitutional rights?* Explain your response.

2. *If, in fact, there is a departmental policy requiring responses to questions, were the investigators correct in telling Smyth he would be fired if he did not answer questions?* Explain your response.

3. *Because Smyth was apparently unaware of Garrity v. New Jersey, were the investigators required to inform him of his Garrity "rights"?* Explain your response.

4. *Were the investigators correct in telling Smyth he would not be prosecuted if he responded to their questions after being read his Garrity rights?* Explain your response.

Questions for Discussion

Answer each of the following questions in a separate response.

1. Are law enforcement officers "warriors"? Explain your response.

2. Fully discuss the privacy rights of an accused officer.

Notes

1. U.S. Office of Personnel Management. Handbook of Occupational Groups and Families. Retrieved from http://74.125.47.132/search?q=cache:U07XyeGD6KgJ:www.opm.gov/Fedclass/text/GS-1800.htm+group+\includes+all+classes+of+positions+the+duties+of+which+are+to+advice+on,+administer,+supervise,+or+perform+investigation,+inspection,+or+enforcement+work+p

rimarily+concerned+with+alleged+or+suspected+offenses+against+the+laws+against+the+United+States,+or+such+work+primarily+concerned+with+determining+compliance+with+laws+and+regulations&cd=1&hl=en&ct=clnk&gl=us. Accessed October 5, 2009.
2. U.S. Office of Personnel Management. Grade Evaluation Guide for Police and Security Guard Positions in Series, GS-0083/GS-0085 TS-87 April 1988. Retrieved from www.opm.gov/fedclass/gs008385.pdf. Accessed January 26, 2010.
3. Federal Bureau of Investigation. The National Academy. Retrieved from http://74.125.47.132/search?q=cache:QKAXEo7r0ToJ:www.fbi.gov/hq/td/academy/na/na.htm+fbi+national+academy&cd=1&hl=en&ct=clnk&gl=us. Accessed, October 7, 2009.
4. Fraternal Order of Police. Jerrard F. Young, DC Lodge #1. (2006). Miscellany: The Perfect Cop. Simulcast Fall 2006, vol. 24, issue 4.
5. White, Willard, "Neal." (17 Dec 2009). Chief of Police. Police department which will remain anonymous. Electronic interview.
6. Watson, Henry, B. (1996). The Key to the Constitution of the United States. Patriotic Education Incorporated, Rockville, Maryland. p. 38.
7. White, Willard, "Neal." (17 Dec 2009). Chief of Police. Police department that will remain anonymous. Electronic interview.

Suggested Reading

Skolnick, Jerome, H., & Fyfe, James, J. (1993). *Above The Law: Police and the Excessive Use of Force.* New York: The Free Press.

McAlary, Mike. (1987). *Buddy Boys: When Good Cops Turn Bad.* New York: G.P. Putnam's Sons.

Schmidt, Wayne, W. (2004). *Interviews and Interrogations of Public Employees: Beckwith, Garrity, Miranda and Weingarten Rights.* Law Enforcement Executive Forum. Macomb, IL: Illinois Law Enforcement Training and Standards Board.

Smith, Daniel, P. (2008). *On the Job: Behind the Stars of the Chicago Police Department.*

CHAPTER SEVEN
The Investigation

An investigation is an orderly, carefully conducted examination of facts to uncover or determine true times, places, events, relationships, participants, and declarations. Investigative results are presented in an official account or explanation usually titled "Report of Investigation." The goal of an internal affairs investigation is to prove or disprove either a criminal or non-criminal allegation made against an employee, utilizing varied investigative techniques. As in any investigation, investigative techniques vary and their use is based on the allegation, seriousness, complexity, and scope of the investigation.

Lon Eilders stated, "As an IA investigator I soon realized that I had multiple responsibilities and had to meet all of them equally or I would fail.

A good IA investigator [along with the investigation] must:

1. Protect citizens from abusive, overly aggressive, and corrupt officers;
2. Protect officers from false, misleading, vengeful, and malicious complainants;
3. Protect the reputation of the department by maintaining the public trust; and
4. Protect the integrity of the investigation itself.

A failure in any one of these areas is failure in all."[1]

Orlando Winfield Wilson, commonly known as O.W. Wilson, was a well-known and influential police science authority during the mid-twentieth century. As early as 1963, Wilson advocated a certain relationship between internal affairs and the employees served: "...they must understand that the internal investigation unit is as eager to establish innocence as guilt."[2]

For the internal affairs function to be fair, the way an investigation is conducted is important. An investigation must be conducted without taking away a person's dignity while at the same time fostering a culture of respect for what is right to do. Homer Williams believes an employee will readily accept discipline if he believes the discipline is deserved. However, no one wants undeserved discipline or consequences for unsubstantiated actions. Whether an employee is guilty or innocent of an offense, the loss of personal dignity caused by the conduct of an IA investigation is not within the purview of IA to inflict.[3]

Mr. Williams also believes IA must stand above the selfish desires of others, who might want to use IA for their own purposes, in order to consistently do what is right. IA must be above board in all of its decisions and actions to investigate all allegations and ignore none. All allegations must be investigated with integrity, which will give employees a sense of security while not allowing inappropriate investigations to intimidate anyone. To give employees a sense of security, the internal affairs function must not be overly secretive, but should be as open as the investigation, allegations, or law will allow. An investigation can be compartmentalized to allow IA to share as much information as possible with an employee's chain of command and other investigative bodies. This openness will give management and outside investigative bodies (FBI, IG, GAO, Congress, etc.) the control and oversight needed to conduct required operations with enough knowledge of the allegations and investigation to negate or minimize further harm to the organization or its employees.[4] Of course, some corruption is so outrageous and dangerous to investigators that outside coordination during some investigations is problematic.

It is the responsibility of the parent organization and IA leadership, as part of or support to the parent organization, to influence all aspects of the function to ensure open, fair, and unbiased performance. However, the members of the IA process, the media, investigators, rank and file, and others still play a role in the realization of fairness of or the perception of fairness in any internal affairs investigation.

Gary Hillberry believes when an allegation is received by IA, it should first be a routine action for the IA investigator to determine its validity. Many allegations are embarrassing, are a personal disgrace, can cause a financial hardship, and can destroy a career or personal relationship, even when the allegations are ultimately determined to be unfounded. IA must have a professional relationship with the parent agencies' management and have an open dialogue with an employee's supervisor. Supervisors should be told of an employee's indiscretions, if operationally expedient, when they affect the operations or reputation of the organization. However, the allegations should be well-researched prior to an open discussion to avoid making insinuations and innuendos public. Are the allegations provable? Are they possible? Discussing allegations with a supervisor, prior to confirming their validity, may destroy a reputation that may never be repaired.[5]

When possible, the source of the allegation should be interviewed to obtain as much additional information as possible: to determine how the information is known by the source, why the source forwarded the information to authorities and why at the particular time, and what relationship the source has with the suspect employee. If there is a complaint of an officer's action, what witness testimony is available? Is there usable video evidence? Does the source or complainant have an agenda to discredit the employee? A records check should also be conducted to determine if the source has a criminal record or a history of filing allegations against officers. Hillberry also believes "on more serious allegations (criminal allegations that would result in a criminal referral to a prosecuting attorney), the source's motivation must be determined before the investigation continues. As a result the source should be given a polygraph examination to validate his allegations. If the source refuses to take a polygraph, IA management must attempt to validate the allegation by other means without destroying the reputation of the employee. If, after a reasonable and expeditious inquiry, the original source information cannot be validated, the investigation should be closed and made inactive until additional, verifiable information is received. In these instances, IA must notify the employee's management chain to allow management to conduct any necessary 'damage control' to protect the integrity of the employee's work activity."[6]

From my experience and knowledge of polygraph examinations, I believe they should be used as a last resort. Polygraphs should not be offered to every source because many complainants would be discouraged from coming forward. In addition, polygraphs have been shown to be unreliable in many instances, although I do agree with

Hillberry that a polygraph can be used, in certain instances, in an attempt to validate allegations. However, the Associated Press reported that three Alcohol, Tobacco, and Firearms (ATF) Special Agents beat polygraph examinations while undercover with the Mongol motorcycle gang. All three passed while being grossly intimidated with death during the examinations by the Mongols. The ATF agents were trained to pass the test.[7]

The use of a polygraph examination in court and the reliability of its results are still under debate. The American Polygraph Association reportedly believes scientific evidence supports the high validity of polygraph examinations. Conversely, the American Psychological Association reportedly questions whether there is any legitimate way to validate polygraph results. The Supreme Court has never ruled on the admissibility of a polygraph test in court apparently because of the controversy and it is up to a judge to determine if a test can be used. However, the Supreme Court held in *United States v. Scheffer* 523 U.S. 303 (1998) that excluding polygraph results at trial does not deprive a defendant the right to present a defense guaranteed by the Sixth Amendment. Reportedly the likelihood of the results of a polygraph exam being used in court increases if both the prosecution and defense agree to its admissibility before the test is given. The reader can see how the controversy continues by viewing the number of Internet results instructing how to "beat the polygraph."

Case Management

Prior to the conduct of an employee investigation, its seriousness must first be determined. An internal affairs unit is most effective when placed in a position to conduct investigations of only the most serious allegations. Less serious allegations should be handled by the employee's chain of command.

Homer Williams advocates tiered investigations: tier one being the most egregious allegations, tier two lesser allegations still deserving attention by IA, and tier three allegations best reviewed by management. Minor allegations and violations of policy or procedures are not recommended to be addressed by IA. The internal affairs function loses stature, becomes a façade, and is viewed as perfunctory if the IA function is hindered by addressing minor infractions best left to be addressed by management. In addition to the tier concept used by the former U.S. Customs Service, a staff of desk officers reviewed initiation and progress of all investigations worldwide to ensure consistency. This review process took some power and personal influence away from IA field managers and investigators and fostered a sense of consistent application of justice and integrity across agency culture groups. "The portrayal, perception and actual conduct of a fair internal investigation are of the utmost importance."[8]

Some units may conduct preliminary inquiries to:

- determine the seriousness of the allegation
- identify the source if not already known
- re-interview the source for more specific information
- determine the source's involvement, if any
- determine how the source obtained the information
- determine the source's agenda
- identify the violation(s), if any
- determine the provability of the violation(s)
- develop an investigative plan

Tier One—The Most Egregious Violations

As described by Homer Williams, the most serious administrative or criminal misconduct would be identified as a tier one investigation. This category includes allegations of misdemeanor or felony violations of federal, state, and county or city statutes. It also includes serious violations of policy or lack of good judgment, which would be injurious to the department or that would bring unwanted public, media, or political attention which would jeopardize the department's mission.

Tier Two—Less Serious Violations

According to Williams, tier two violations concern allegations that include violations of policy, regulations, or standards of conduct that a department employee must follow. These allegations involve infractions of widely known standards of ethical conduct or accepted practices that would adversely affect the effectiveness or efficiency of the department. When received, the allegation(s) are reviewed by the internal affairs unit to determine a course of action. That action could be the conduct of a preliminary inquiry by internal affairs or a referral to the employee's supervisor to conduct a fact finding mission. Upon completion of fact finding, a response is made to the internal affairs unit to allow for a further determination. Final determination could be for IA to conduct an investigation or for management to adjudicate the information found during the fact-finding mission.

Tier Three—Management Issues

Most issues of employee conduct or misconduct, as described by Williams, may not necessarily reach the level at which internal affairs would take investigative action. As discussed previously it is in the interest of the internal affairs function not to become involved in issues best addressed by an employee's supervisor or management chain of command. Although tier three allegations may not reach the level of IA action, any allegation should be documented and brought to the attention of IA. This will allow the IA unit to enter the information into a system to track repeat offenders and document progressively more-serious violations.

In certain circumstances, however, a supervisor may request an internal affairs inquiry for investigative consideration. Personal relationships, complexity of allegations, and the scope of inquiry may preclude the chain of command from conducting an inquiry. The IA finding should then be provided to the supervisor for review and final action.

I became a Special Agent for the U.S. Department of Transportation in 1979 shortly after the Office of Inspector General (OIG) was created. The office experienced many early growing pains during the early 1980s. When I first arrived, many of the investigations conducted were of a minor nature, but as the office matured, less serious allegations were avoided and more serious allegations become the norm. In hindsight I see that the newly created office had few internal policies and had to overcome many delicate issues with department leadership in order to focus on the most serious concerns.

Use of Discretion

Almost any law enforcement officer has a certain amount of discretion in an investigation. Although a federal officer may have less discretion in enforcing the law, many times city, county, and state officers do have the freedom or flexibility to affect what should or should not be included in an investigation. As retired NYPD IA Detective Joe Gallazzi stated, "in an internal investigation a supervisor wants to be able to speak to the investigator, not to manipulate, but have an ability to reason with the investigator to focus on the allegation(s), and not investigate something unrelated and inconsequential which will only confuse the issue and cause unneeded embarrassment and consternation not only for the employee, but for the organization as well." During an overt internal investigation, it is important for an internal affairs investigator to be approachable by any supervisor. The supervisor can give the investigator a greater understanding of the allegations, of the person under investigation and his background, and of the evidence and witnesses. But, for the investigator to be approachable, he must be trusted. Some issues discussed are not to be disclosed. If a supervisor cannot trust an investigator, subordinate employees will know of the distrust. Even if the process is considered fair, a mistrusted investigator will be conducting an investigation in a vacuum.[9]

This means that the investigative focus is very important, and an officer's supervisor can help. If an investigator is faced with multiple allegations, any seasoned investigator will take each allegation by itself and determine its seriousness and provability. Each allegation should be tiered and have identified levels as does the investigation itself. This tier concept simplifies the investigation to workable parts. After the investigation is concluded, all allegations that do not rise to a level addressed by internal affairs can be referred to the chain of command for attention. Investigative focus will allow the investigator to pick and choose which allegations will most likely be successfully concluded, concluded by either validating the allegation or determining it is unfounded. I believe an unsuccessful investigation is one where the allegation(s) are unsubstantiated, that is, the allegation(s) cannot be proved or disproved.

Investigative discretion and the focus of the investigation can and do go two ways: There are good employees who make bad decisions and there are bad employees. Most employers make every effort to "save" good employees. The cost of hiring and training an applicant to replace a fired employee is enormous. Every effort should be taken to correct an offending employee's actions and to keep him on the payroll. However, there are times when the continued employment of an individual can be detrimental to the department. This is a controversial issue, but continuing personnel issues or numerous confirmed or even unconfirmed complaints against an employee may be cause to expand the focus of the next internal investigation.

Although this investigative technique is a way of protecting the department, it is important not to allow any supervisor to cajole an investigator to expand an investigative focus to satisfy a personal vendetta. To avoid pressure from a supervisor the internal affairs function must have transparency and good communication between human resources, internal affairs, and the parent organization leadership. An expanded focus is a sensitive issue. A wider focus could backfire and cause the entire internal affairs function to be perceived as unfair. The perception of unfairness in an investigation is a serious situation and should not be allowed to take hold.

As mentioned before, Tim Dees believes "There are some police executives that use IA as their own administrative death squad. The IA investigators aren't sent out to kill people, but rather careers." Dees goes on to say, "A disfavored officer or other employee is accused of misconduct, and the IA investigator is told at the outset what the conclusion of his investigation will be. The investigator then starts the evidence collection process, discarding exculpatory information and gathering 'facts' that lay the blame on the target. When the necessary evidence is in short supply, it's not unheard of to construct some, through intimidation of witnesses or outright fraud."[10]

"A variation of this technique is 'package building.' This involves documenting every transgression of the target, real or imagined, while rejecting anything that might tend to redeem the target. Before long, the officer's IA file begins to rival a big-city phone book in volume, and the officer is pecked to death by escalating impositions of discipline, usually starting with documented reprimands and working up to suspensions and termination."[11]

I do not agree with Tim Dees' definition of "package building." From experience, I and other supervisors kept "drop files" of all employees to be used at evaluation time and for disciplinary purposes if the need arose. Any supervisor knows without documentation a wayward employee will continue his actions unless enough information is presented to either file a personnel action or initiate an internal investigation. From experience I know that some employees are "pecked to death" by their own, ongoing misconduct.

Dees also believes "in a criminal investigation, there are safeguards against this sort of railroading. The accused cannot be compelled to give evidence against himself in a criminal case, but if he refuses to cooperate and spill the beans in an internal investigation, he is held to be insubordinate. There is a review by an independent prosecutor before criminal charges are filed, and a second look by a judge to see if there are grounds for the charges. Ultimately, the accused is allowed to have access to all of the evidence against him, to rebut it, to prepare his own defense, and to present it before a disinterested judge or jury."[12]

Dees goes on to say that "unless the accused officer tries to reverse a disciplinary action in civil court, (which usually happens only after the damage [to the officer's reputation] has been done), he enjoys none of these protections, and even then, the rules in a civil case are not the same as with a criminal charge. He may never see the investigative case file, doesn't have the opportunity to cross-examine witnesses or investigators, and may not even know exactly what he is charged with until he is confronted with the disciplinary penalty. The internal investigative process [function] in most law enforcement agencies is not exactly your paradigm of procedural rights."[13]

No One Should Be "Nifonged"

No officer wants to feel he has been treated unfairly; no one wants to feel he has been "Nifonged." Being "Nifonged" is a media-coined word derivation first used during the Duke University lacrosse scandal. Michael Nifong was the Durham County, North Carolina, District Attorney in 2006, when an escort and stripper accused three Duke University lacrosse players of sexually assaulting her. As truth emerged, it was found that Michael Nifong made untrue or misleading statements to the media, inappropriately influenced the police investigation, attempted to manipulate witnesses, ignored evidence potentially favorable to the accused, and created racial tensions.

In October 2008, another example of unfairness occurred when then Alaska Senator Ted Stevens was convicted in federal court "of seven counts of making false statements on financial disclosure forms to hide about $250,000 in gifts and free renovations to his Alaska home."[14] However, during the trial the judge scolded federal prosecutors for various improprieties. On April 1, 2009, newly appointed Attorney General Eric H. Holder, Jr. "asked U.S. District Judge Emmet G. Sullivan to drop the case after learning that prosecutors had failed to turn over notes that contradicted testimony from their key witnesses."[15] One of Stevens' attorneys stated "the conduct of the prosecution was stunning to me. They were hell-bent on convicting a United States senator."[16] A defense attorney on another politically charged prosecution stated, "Too often they [federal prosecutors] are tempted to indict marginal or ambiguous cases."[17] On Tuesday, April 7, 2009, Judge Sullivan dismissed the corruption conviction of Stevens, ordered a criminal investigation of the prosecutors' actions, and stated, "In nearly 25 years on the bench, I've never seen anything approaching the mishandling and misconduct that I've seen in this case."[18]

Timeliness

Timeliness is a controversial issue that is difficult to settle. Timeliness can be a concern for the accused during an overt examination (inquiry, fact finding, and investigation) and to many operations if covert. As previously discussed, an internal affairs investigation can have a detrimental effect on an employee's work product, family life, financial position, reputation, and mental condition. Every effort must be made to conduct an inquiry, fact finding mission, or investigation in a timely manner. However, "timely" means different things to different people for various reasons. The accused wants immediate relief. Many times an investigator will hear, "But I have done nothing wrong!" In fact the investigator may know, because of the circumstances, the accused has done nothing wrong, but immediate adjudication may not be possible. A written process/policy must be followed and there can be no shortcut. Internal affairs investigative policy is or should be in place to competently, correctly, and fairly examine all allegations. A shortcut could be perceived, if discovered, as a cover-up. A cover-up, or the perception of one, can destroy the internal affairs function, or a career, whether civil service or political. Furthermore, many factors are involved directly and indirectly with the internal affairs function over which the investigator has no control. As in any investigation the collection of massive amounts of evidence, reluctant witnesses, or the lack of manpower can affect timeliness. Defense strategy, location of witnesses, or the responsiveness of the prosecutor can all play a role in the timely conclusion of an internal affairs investigation.

Disposition

The disposition of an investigation is a classification designated at its conclusion. From experience, different departments and agencies use different designations, but there are four basic dispositions.

1. "Founded" or "sustained" is used for an investigation that gathered enough evidence to sustain the allegation(s).

2. "Unfounded" is used when the investigation determined the allegation(s) were false.

3. "Unsubstantiated" or "not sustained" is used when there is insufficient evidence to prove or disprove the allegation(s).

4. "Exonerated" is another designation but is controversial. "Exonerated" may be used when the allegation relates to an action by an officer that is determined to be according to policy. This designation is controversial because it depends on the "eye of the beholder." If an allegation involves the use of force, the force may be determined to be allowable according to policy, but seen by witnesses as excessive.

While I was with U.S. Customs there were many intense debates whether an employee should be given an "exoneration letter." I believe the issue was caused by management, not by the Office of Internal Affairs. Management was historically slow in adjudicating findings by internal affairs. In many instances, months would go by after an investigation was concluded, and I or another HQ support officer would receive a phone call from the suspect employee wanting to know the status of the investigation.

I always believed "exonerated" was too strong a word even if the allegation was "unfounded," especially if the allegation had to be re-investigated because of newly found evidence or witness. Also, "unfounded" may be an easier sell to an indignant citizen than "exonerated."

The new train of thought is to offer no disposition designation. Evidence is presented and the reader is left to make a free determination without any outside influences.

Adjudication

Notwithstanding the fact I just discussed disposition classifications on a report of an internal investigation, the internal affairs function should never be part of the decision-making process after an investigation is concluded.

An internal affairs investigative report offers neither prosecutorial decisions nor judgment of guilt or innocence. It makes no difference whether it involves a criminal or administrative investigation. A prosecutor determines if enough evidence is present to prosecute an accused. A judge and jury decide guilt or innocence. In administrative hearings a judge or department manager may adjudicate, but an internal affairs report of investigation never makes suggestions. An internal investigation follows the same process as in any other investigation. An internal affairs investigator gathers facts and documents evidence; the internal affairs function does not determine the outcome of an investigation; the evidence does. The investigative findings will be evaluated by either a prosecutor if criminal charges are warranted, or by parent organization management for any warranted administrative action. This may seem simplistic, but from experience many employees investigated by internal affairs will make a statement like, "look what internal affairs has done to me."

The source of this falsehood could be from supervisors who want to shift responsibility for punishment to another, i.e., to internal affairs. It should be very clear to any employee that adjudication is not in the purview of any internal affairs investigator or unit. If it is, it should not be.

Case Study

Sergeant B. Scout works the midnight shift for a police department in the State of California. He supervises seven officers in a high crime area. Sergeant Scout has a good relationship with all officers except one, Officer Wiseman, who is difficult to supervise. Officer Wiseman has been under investigation several times by internal affairs, but nothing of consequence has ever been found. Wiseman is consistently late for roll call, many times is not in communication to receive calls for service, and in the early morning hours it is difficult for Sergeant Scout to find him in his patrol zone. Wiseman insists he always works zone #3. Other officers on the shift would rather not work with him and consequently he works alone. Because Officer Wiseman is a difficult person to deal with Sergeant Scout has always agreed to his demands, but many times calls for service in his zone must be handled by others.

Recently Sergeant Scout noticed an increase in auto thefts in zone #3. Sergeant Scout has spoken to other officers on the shift and determined Wiseman associates with several men who operate a service station and body shop not far from their assigned district.

The shift lieutenant is a person who does not create waves. When Sergeant Scout approached the lieutenant with his suspicions he said he was late for an appointment and walked away. Sergeant Scout decided to contact internal affairs to ask for their help.

Case Study Questions

Answer the following questions in one narrative response.

1. *Is Sergeant Scout correct in contacting internal affairs? Why or why not?*

2. *Since internal affairs has a tiered system for addressing allegations of wrongdoing, what is the likelihood Scout's suspicion will be investigated?*

3. *What would be a reason for internal affairs not to immediately conduct an investigation into Sergeant Scout's allegations against Wiseman?*

Questions for Discussion

Answer each of the following questions in a separate response.

1. Should an internal affairs investigator have discretion in what allegations are investigated? Is it good policy for an internal affairs investigator to take the supervisor of an accused officer into his confidence and discuss the alleged offense(s); what are the pros and cons of discussing the allegations with a supervisor?

2. During an ongoing investigation, is it good policy for the internal affairs function to expand the investigation by including previously unsubstantiated allegations? Under certain circumstances, is it good policy for the internal affairs function to continue an investigation until sustainable violations are found?

Notes

1. Eidlers, Lon, Sr. (22 Mar 2007). Lieutenant (retired), Manager, Accreditation and Planning, Chattanooga, TN, Police Department. Letter.
2. Wilson, Orlando, Winfield. (1963). Police Administration. McGraw-Hill Book Company, 2nd Edition. pp 121.
3. Williams, Homer, J. (1 Jun 2007). Former Assistant Commissioner, Officer of Internal Affairs, U.S. Customs Service. Interview.
4. Ibid.
5. Hillberry, Gary. (22 Jun 2007). Special Agent in Charge (retired), U.S. Customs Service. Telephonic interview.
6. Ibid.
7. Watkins, Thomas. (28 Oct 2008). Undercover agents beat polygraphs—Armed members of Mongols gang stood behind them. Associated Press. Retrieved from http://www.denverpost.com/obituaries/ci_10831452?source=pkg.
8. Williams, Homer, J. (1 Jun 2007). Former Assistant Commissioner, Officer of Internal Affairs, U.S. Customs Service. Interview.

9. Gallazzi, Joseph. Former Detective, NYPD Internal Affairs Bureau. (30 Oct 2006) Interview.
10. Dees, Tim. (21 Jul 2006). Editorial: The Rat Squad. Officer.com. Retrieved from http://timdees.com/blog/?p=47. Accessed 23 May 2011.
11. Ibid.
12. Ibid.
13. Ibid.
14. Johnson, Carrie, & Wilber, Del Quentin. (2 Apr 2009). Holder Asks Judge to Drop Case Against Ex-Senator, Justice Dept. Cites Prosecutors' Behavior During Stevens Trial. The Washington Post. Retrieved from http://www.washingtonpost.com/wp-dyn/content/article/2009/04/01/AR2009040100763.html.
15. Ibid.
16. Ibid.
17. Ibid.
18. Associated Press. (7Apr 2009). Judge Dismisses Sen. Stevens Conviction. Retrieved from http://www.nypost.com/p/news/national/item_Y5C0LVdMswZiKYhkIoxlMO.

Suggested Reading

Hayes, Read, PhD. ASIS International Foundation Research Council. (2008). CRISP Report: *Strategies to Detect and Prevent Workplace Dishonesty.* Alexandria, VA: ASIS International Foundation, Inc.

CHAPTER EIGHT
The Investigator

Fundamental to the internal affairs function are the actions and integrity of the investigator. The investigator is most often a trained law enforcement officer who should have the critical skills and personal qualities to manage sensitive complaints against employees.

Gary Hillberry believes the caliber and personal integrity of the personnel in an office of internal affairs is most important. The integrity of an IA investigator must be held at the highest level. The professionalism shown must be such to allow the subject of the investigation, a witness, or merely an employee who has knowledge of the investigation, to trust the investigator and to ultimately have trust in the entire internal affairs function. The investigator's competence must be unquestioned, and the investigator must show the utmost respect for the subject being investigated. Above all, the investigator must be unbiased concerning the investigation; if bias exists, the investigator should remove himself from the investigation. This ensures neutrality and reduces conflicts of interest that would jeopardize the finding.[1]

As a player in the internal affairs process, an internal affairs investigator must instill confidence, understanding, and a sense of fairness in the internal affairs function. As does an enforcement officer interacting with citizens, an internal affairs investigator must have a command presence that portrays an attitude that conveys an air of confidence, authority, and respect. The investigator must also impart an impression of impartiality, unbiased thinking, and one with a sense of fair play. A genuine characterization of ethical behavior exhibited by the investigator's command presence will ensure confidence and a perception of fairness in the internal affairs function.

Not Everyone Is Qualified

Additional characteristics should also include undisputed honesty and a background without hint of scandal. An individual known for honesty may be one who respects others, one who witnesses will more likely believe is fair, and with whom they will be more inclined to cooperate. Just as a department applicant's background is scrutinized, all individuals considered for duty with internal affairs should be vetted and their backgrounds examined to determine their aptitude or qualities to be an internal affairs investigator.

The following are characteristics that should be considered desirable for an internal affairs investigator:

- → Outgoing, personable and well liked
- → Honest
- → Concerned for people
- → Sufficiently aggressive
- → Straightforward
- → Approachable
- → Good interviewer and writer
- → Good reputation
- → Known to be fair
- → Sound personal and financial background
- → Follows department policy
- → Team player
- → Unbiased
- → High ethical standards

The following characteristics likely would exclude an internal affairs candidate:

- → Socially inept
- → Not well liked by co-workers
- → Difficult to supervise
- → Has anger issues
- → Holds grudges
- → Biases are evident
- → Reputation for dishonesty
- → History of violence
- → Financial difficulties
- → Addictions
- → Associations with disreputable individuals

In addition, any individual chosen or who wishes to join an internal affairs unit must understand the consequences. It goes without saying that an investigator must always act and speak professionally. I was told early on that on occasion an investigator will be baited to say something that will be regretted later: a statement that an accused can use to discredit the investigator and the investigation. Sometimes the only defense is to attack the investigator. Responding to taunts in an unprofessional manner will give ammunition to the ridiculer. In addition, in organizations lacking senior managers with strong ethical leadership, internal affairs investigators may be insulted or outright shunned and threatened with career-killing actions.

While working as a contractor for the U.S. Department of Homeland Security, I had occasion to meet two lieutenants from the New York Police Department. We had a cordial conversation until I mentioned that I not only worked in New York City in the late 1990s, but that I worked for U.S. Customs Office of Internal Affairs. The friendly conversation was immediately ended when both officers suddenly took an about-face and stopped speaking. It was a very strange but real occurrence.

Another consequence of an internal affairs assignment is an investigator can be placed in a position that may cause difficulties for years to come. Most investigators are usually in the lower ranks of the organization. The seniority or grade level of an investigator is not a discredit, but a fact. The relevance is an investigator may investigate a person of higher rank. Certainly, persons of higher rank may be interviewed during the investigation of disputed or unpopular issues. Being in the forefront of a conflict involving ranking members might diminish career goals.

Loyalty

Homer Williams recalled that up until the 1970s, the Customs Service, Office of Investigations (OI), conducted internal investigations. When the Office of Internal Affairs was created, "old timers" were not especially happy with IA's creation. In some instances, a small number of agents volunteered for and entered IA for ulterior motives: to keep certain people informed of what IA was doing, to determine who was being investigated and to undermine investigations. The Customs Service was a large organization with thousands of investigators, inspectors, and others within many unofficial social groups from various parts of the country. In the Office of Investigations, some groups were unofficially headed by senior managers who informally controlled pockets of special agents by influencing transfers and promotions. These informal groups were not unlike many informal groups in other governmental and private organizations. They made up what is part of a subculture in any organization. Each of these informal groups had members who entered IA to keep their respective group informed. "No one likes someone looking over their shoulder even if they are not doing anything wrong; people just want their way."[2]

Other agents entered IA for other wrong reasons: anger at management or the "system"; having an axe to grind; to "set up" people they did not like; or to intimidate people. Placing the wrong people in internal affairs is one way, among many, to cause a bias of the entire system.[3]

Almost everyone is part of an informal group and most are not influenced where they would improperly impact an internal investigation. In spite of a few employees with ulterior motives who were disciplined, reassigned, or terminated when their motives for inclusion in IA was brought to light, Williams worked with many IA special agents who were not associated with or influenced by an informal group and did what was necessary to place the good of the Customs Service above personal agendas. "Those who were professional IA investigators understood there was no integrity compromise; there was a certain line that was not crossed. However, there was an IA stereotype and 'group think' in the Customs Service regarding those who entered the internal affairs arena. The 'group think' was that if you stepped out of OI as a special agent, you somehow became a disloyal OI employee who became ostracized as a fellow Customs employee. You may not have become a criminal, but if you voluntarily transferred from OI to IA you were seemingly doing something unconscionable. This stereotype is frequently portrayed on television in many law enforcement entertainment dramas. This stereotype was even held by less cynical employees in the Customs Service. At the same time, some employees and other professionals viewed IA investigators as individuals and judged them by their sensitivity shown to employees and whether or not they had an overbearing attitude or professional demeanor during their interactions. [These] employees looked at an IA investigator and judged them by whether the investigator was doing the best for the Customs Service and whether or not justice was being served."[4]

Eventually the Customs Service designed a rotation program where the best and brightest from the Office of Investigations would rotate into the ranks of the Office of Internal Affairs. The program was difficult to implement as seasoned street agents did not want to conduct internal policing. The best and brightest were not always chosen to make the transfer and IA had little recourse. Despite protests, numerous agents were rotated for three-year terms as part of a career-development program, but not all were non-volunteers.

While working for the U.S. Customs Office of Investigations I decided I needed a change. I volunteered for a transfer to the Office of Internal Affairs and was accepted. For me the transfer was an eye opener. I became familiar with many personnel actions I saw only from a distance and expanded my investigative expertise by entering into a new arena. To my amazement I also learned the many thoughtless reasons why a U.S. Customs employee became directly involved in the internal affairs function. In fact, there were a number of employees who could not stay away from the long arm of internal affairs. Out of 20,000 employees there were close to a dozen who seemingly enjoyed the attention of an investigation; when one investigation ended another soon began because of another tactless performance. Although after I made the transfer I was the recipient of several expressions of dislike for the function, I still held the same friends I had before my walk to the dark side.

Sensitivity

The purpose of any public organization is to serve the citizens for which it is responsible. However, for an organization to have a significant and meaningful impact on the service provided, it must be strong and viable. One with inner turmoil will serve less and focus more and more on itself. Therefore, knowing the sensitivity of an internal investigation and showing respect to all employees will create a sense of mutual respect and cooperation.

Whether an investigator is part of the parent organization or from an outside entity, the investigator must show sensitivity when conducting an investigation. During the conduct of an internal investigation, interaction will take place among many parent organizational units: personnel, training, finance, unit(s) of assignment, etc., to gather evidence and obtain statements. Even outside of an investigation or other official duties, there will always be interaction between employees. Interaction between internal affairs and the parent organization employees will routinely occur for personnel issues or because of friendships and organizational activities like holiday parties and summer picnics. To disrespect employees or be ignorant of the sensitivity of an employee investigation can cause turmoil and resentment. Resentment can create a line drawn in the sand; collusion among parent organization employees can fuel a sense of "them and us." During the investigation of a citizen by the detective bureau, if the investigator shows little sensitivity to witnesses, the impact on the department could be minimal. However, if an internal affairs investigator shows insensitivity to fellow employees, the impact could be great. A lack of cooperation could damage the investigation and permeate all that the Office of Internal Affairs does with the parent organization and subordinate units.

While a special agent with U.S. Customs, Office of Internal Affairs, I had the occasion to be interviewed by a special agent from the U.S. Treasury Department, Office of Inspector General (OIG), an OIG investigator with an attitude. I was a potential witness in the unlawful release of confidential information. The agent was cold, impersonal and bureaucratic. And, to my surprise, the agent read me my rights. I was a federal criminal investigator for over 20 years at the time and to say I was shocked, outraged, and insulted would be an understatement. Over time I had given rights advisements to hundreds of people. Now it was my turn and I did not like it, and I let the agent and his partner know it. When I voiced my indignation, he changed his attitude, worked on his rapport, became more sensitive and told me it was merely a procedural requirement, and I should not be offended. He eventually smoothed things over. Although I initially told him I did not wish to speak to him, I did not want to make a potential witness, who actually did not know anything about the allegations, look uncooperative or worse. The point here is that I did not realize when I read suspects their rights, in custody and out, what impact sensitivity and attitude had on an individual.

I.C. Smith, a former FBI Special Agent-in-Charge was contacted as a witness by an investigator from the FBI's Office of Professional Responsibility (OPR): "When the investigator arrived, I was struck by the hostility of his questions ... But I dismissed that as simply a matter of personality (or the absence of personality) ... I provided a sworn statement to the OPR agent and was again struck by his hostility ... I received a draft copy. I was appalled at what I read. It was filled with inaccuracies, some of which even changed the meaning of the statements ... and by omission of facts, failed to convey the true sense of what I had said ... having increased concern for both the competency and objectivity of the OPR agent."[5]

Numerous experts list the best qualities to look for in an effective investigator. Among them are being a self-starter, resourceful, a communicator, of good character, and logical. Little is said about being sensitive while conducting an investigation. An internal affairs investigator cannot be aloof, as many investigators are, or as distant as many uniformed officers are when making a traffic stop. An internal investigator must have a certain understanding of the sensitivity of any employee investigation and the respect that must be afforded the suspect, witnesses, or any employee who is even indirectly involved in the inquiry.

Being sensitive to employees, however, is not to say that an employee who is accused of a criminal offense, i.e., murder, rape, or assault, should be shown the same level of sensitivity as one who is accused of policy or administrative violations or misconduct by a motorist who is unhappy with a traffic ticket.

Understanding the sensitivity of an internal investigation and showing respect for employees by the investigator are as important in an internal investigation as is the respect shown a citizen the parent organization serves. Rapport is important in any investigation during an interview or even in an interrogation. Rapport is the relationship between an investigator and anyone with whom the investigator has interaction. The relationship can be cordial and warm, or hostile and unfriendly, or anywhere in between. Anyone can and does have an understanding with another person or group of people in any situation. A uniformed officer has rapport with citizens or suspects he meets on the street. This rapport can be friendly or it can be heated. The interaction an officer has with an elderly person being assisted crossing a street is different than the interaction an officer most likely would have with a drunk driver the officer pursued for several miles.

An interview or interrogation is much the same except for the rapport established. They are both activities during which an investigator asks questions to obtain evidence. An interview is the questioning of witnesses or someone who has information pertinent to the investigation. An interrogation is an interview, but with a more authoritative attitude or posture shown by the investigator. It is usually reserved for a known suspect, but an interview can turn into an interrogation depending upon the reluctance of a witness. The word "interrogate" has a negative connotation and the word is often used by a defense attorney during a judicial hearing or trial to portray a law enforcement officer as having done something improper. Therefore, many departments or federal agencies no longer use the word "interrogation," but conduct "interviews" on all witnesses or suspects.

Vetting Applicant Backgrounds

To vet an internal affairs candidate, a background investigation similar to that for pre-employment applicants should be conducted. Additional steps should be incorporated in the investigation, however, to determine how the candidate has interacted with citizens as a patrol officer or investigator. This is preceded by a review of internal affairs records to determine whether the candidate has been investigated by internal affairs or whether any complaints have been made against the candidate. Equally important is how personnel of the Office of County Prosecutor or Office of U.S. Attorney portray the candidate. Is the candidate a team player who works well with others? Has the candidate properly documented all evidence, presented himself as a professional and given credible testimony in judicial proceedings? Has the candidate ever withheld or ever been suspected of withholding evidence or misrepresenting the truth?

Personality Traits

Over a number of years, Stephen M. Hennessy conducted a study of police personalities published in *Thinking Cop, Feeling Cop*. The study looked into the inner character of police officers to determine why successful officers may fail under certain circumstances, or why failing officers may succeed in a different situation. Hennessy used the Myers-Briggs Type Indicator (MBTI) determined by the Myers-Briggs multiple choice instrument based on the theories of Carl Jung regarding personality types. Hennessy used it with thousands of police officers and leaders to obtain insight into how police officers function and to understand their preferred ways of absorbing information and making decisions.[6]

"When we consider the course of human life, we see how the fate of one individual is determined more by the objects of his interest, while in another it is determined more by his own inner self, by the subject. Since we all swerve rather more towards one side or the other, we naturally tend to understand everything in terms of our own type."[7]

> Carl Jung identified four functions which make up an individual's personality, as described by Hennessy:[8]
>
> - He believed a person perceives information either through Sensing or Intuition.
> - After an individual digests information, he makes a decision or a conclusion through either Thinking or Feeling.
> - Sensing and Intuition are Perception Functions.
> - Thinking and Feeling are Judgment Functions.
> - Jung concluded there are four possible combinations of Perception and Judgment Functions:
>
>   - Sensing with Thinking (ST)
>   - Sensing with Feeling (SF)
>   - Intuition with Thinking (NT)
>   - Intuition with Feeling (NF)

The Perceptive Functions—Sensing and Intuition

Sensing types prefer to use sight, sound, taste, smell, and touch to digest information. They are practical, realistic, grounded in the present and good at details. They usually are good at details, but may miss the total picture.

Intuition types are generalists and see things more in the macrosense. They are individuals who see things in an abstract, theoretical way, are skilled planners and researchers, and are able to analyze information and come to conclusions. They may see the total picture, but miss detail.[9]

The Judgment Functions—Thinking and Feeling

Thinking types are objective and impartial. They make decisions through pure logic and have skill at impersonal analysis. Thinkers can be somewhat direct and pragmatic and tend to make decisions without necessarily taking into consideration a person's feelings.

Feeling types have an understanding of people, have a desire for harmony, have a warm personality, and tend to be empathic and compassionate. They take people into consideration first.

Working Together

The Perceptive and Judgment Functions work together. Whereas Jung believes one function will always be dominant and one subordinate, others believe the functions work on an equal basis.

Each of the combinations, ST, SF, NT, and NF, portray various behaviors a person exhibits over time.[10]

Personalities Frequently Found in Law Enforcement

According to Hennessy, the Sensing-Thinking (ST) type personality is found in 70% of law enforcement personnel. They ingest information with their senses and use logic and objective reasoning to make decisions. They are systematic and good at details. They enjoy working with clear-cut policy and procedures. They can be less tactful and more straightforward with the truth. They like to organize and control things and are calm in stressful situations. But they may be blunt and insensitive and may not take personal issues of victims into consideration when making decisions.

The Intuitive-Thinking (NT) type personality is found in 14% of law enforcement personnel. They ingest information with their intuition and use logic and objective reasoning to make decisions just like STs. They dislike detail and may neglect routine tasks but are more long-range, futuristic thinkers. Like an ST, an NT tends to be forthright rather than tactful. Because of an NT's inattention to detail, an ST may believe an NT is disorganized. However, STs and NTs both make decisions the same way so an NT does not feel like an outsider. NTs are not people-oriented. STs and NTs "are generally systematic and analytical, often to the point of being or seeming impersonal."[10] The Sensing-Feeling (SF) type personality is found in 11% of law enforcement personnel. They ingest information with their senses like an ST, but make decisions with the feelings of people as their primary concern. The SF type seems to have some of the same characteristics as STs. "However, since they make decisions through feeling, they tend to be more aware of and sensitive to people and their feelings as necessary police work decisions are made. They seem to do very well in law enforcement tasks of community relations, media relations, personnel matters, and anything where people concerns or relations are paramount. They appear to be different than most other officers in law enforcement because of this people orientation. They are best with practical situations that need sound common sense and practical ability in dealing with people ... Because of their preferred decision making style that favors people and human values, they may not seem sufficiently "tough minded" to the rest of the officers ...The SF officers bring a needed balancing dimension to the field of law enforcement, especially if they find themselves in tasks that involve continual relationships with people."[11]

The Intuitive-Feeling (NF) type personality is found in 5% of law enforcement personnel. They ingest information through intuition and make their decision through feeling or social value. Like NTs, NFs dislike detail and may neglect routine tasks, but are more long-range, futuristic thinkers. "They are responsive to people's needs most of all, showing real concern for what others think and want, and they try to handle situations with due regard for other's feelings ...they often stand out from the mainstream of officers as being different ...The majority of these individuals who start in the profession drop out, feeling that the job was not as they expected it to be ...As with SFs, NFs may not seem sufficiently 'tough minded' to the majority of the ST officers ...They, as do the SFs, make excellent people-oriented police representatives that can relate to the community well ...The primary concern of Intuitive-Feeling types while on duty is helping people."[12]

As a Sheriff's Deputy I believe I began as an Intuitive Thinker, but as I matured and gained experience in the job, I realized that exercising more humane approaches, treating people with respect no matter what they were doing, made me more successful in my law enforcement duties than "just the facts, Ma'am" attitude. One does not change their cognitive type, according to Jung's theory, but can learn to use all spectrums of behavior to achieve what they are trying to accomplish. Sometimes a hard, just the facts approach is necessary, but addressing the situation sensibly and with consideration often accomplishes more.

I most likely was an intuitive feeler all along, but was not trained that way. Everyone in the academy appeared to be tough, and I was apprehensive to let anyone know I was different or allow others to know that I could care about people. I initially acted like I thought I was supposed to act. Although I do recall I told the Merit Commission members when interviewed that I wanted to become a deputy because I wanted to help people.

One call on the afternoon shift was a complaint that some boys were playing football on private property. When I arrived, an older woman was upset that a half dozen boys were playing in front of her house: actually a large plot of land across the street. Although I did throw a pass, I soon chased them away. I soon regretted my response and over the years have thought about a missed opportunity to make a difference with a group of black youths. I believe that made me a closet feeler.

Later in my career I received a call of a disturbance in a local bar. A man in his 40's was drunk and causing a disturbance by being loud, obnoxious, and verbally abusive because the bartender would no longer serve him. I responded and was the lone officer at the scene for a short period. When I entered the tavern, he immediately focused his abuse on me. However, I soon found out from a patron that his wife was recently diagnosed with terminal cancer. The man soon approached me and began shouting mostly unintelligible ramblings and began pushing and shoving me. As two other deputies arrived, he began to cry and poke his finger in my chest. One deputy was visibly surprised at my tolerance and told me that we needed to subdue him. I told him to let me handle it. Soon the man's son arrived, and I allowed the son to take his father home. Looking back I put myself in a poor defensive position, but I publicly became a true feeler.

I acknowledged I was a feeler because of the actions of a minority of other deputies, actions that made me realize what type of officer I wanted to be. One deputy was known to start fights, not break them up. One hot, Sunday afternoon I was one of several road deputies who responded to a bar fight. Two of us arrived simultaneously, and soon the situation was under control. When the third deputy arrived shortly after the action was over, I watched him slam a baton across the back of one detainee who was being held, bent over the trunk of a patrol car by another deputy. The feeling he showed for people was not the feeling I cared to show.

Internal Affairs Personality

The analysis of police personalities by Hennessy using theories by Jung and testing by Myers-Briggs includes various strengths and weaknesses of the law enforcement profession. Most people know their strong points and what skills in which they are less successful. A person given a chance to use his natural talents can mean the difference between success and failure, between star quality and less than satisfactory performance. A patrol officer may not do well dealing with certain types of people, such as children or teenagers, but do well dealing with the disabled and the elderly. An investigator may not be successful conducting complex financial investigations, but be more comfortable developing informants and dealing with narcotics dealers and drug users.

According to Hennessy, most internal affairs investigators who took the MBTI were "T's" or thinkers who are more logical and structured, believing more in pragmatic, direct, and impersonal logic. They are naturally drawn to the task in internal affairs. If one, however, can demonstrate more "feeling" in their internal affairs actions, they may be more successful in their investigations. Consequently, conducting an internal affairs investigation may need more of a feeling personality than a thinking one.

The MBTI should not be used to predict behavior, but is an excellent way to explain group behavior in any unit or squad in policing. It should never be used to exclude anyone from any law enforcement task. Rather, these profiles are "to help give applicants better tools to understand their own personal strengths and possible weaknesses ...There are very successful individuals of every type in all occupations."[13]

In addition to personality types, gender can also play a role in identifying the best type of person to conduct internal investigations. Women generally are believed to be more sensitive than men, and "it is generally true ...and many studies indicate, that women do possess better communication skills than men on the whole."[14]

> Hennessey reported that a number of women in law enforcement identified three personality and behavior attributes that are important for law enforcement officers:
>
> → ability to communicate
> → ability to make a quick, sound decision
> → the need for compassion

Another attribute any internal affairs investigator must have is the understanding that they have the power to destroy and they must control that power.

The Importance of Asking the Right Question

> George enjoyed his job with the Border Patrol. He was almost always outdoors, had many friends and Southern California was a great place to live. George had been a U.S. Border Patrol Agent for five years when he observed the beating of a detained illegal alien.
>
> It was a cold night about 2am. George was several hundred yards from the U.S./Mexico border on surveillance watching a known crossing area through a long range telescope. He saw a group of illegal aliens climb through a hole in the flimsy fence and make a dash over the border to a waiting job in the United States.

Before he could radio the position he saw two U.S. Border Patrol vans arrive at the scene and corral the group of ten illegals. As George was watching the action through the scope he saw one of the border agents, a supervisor he knew well, strike one of the illegals with his fist and slam him against a van. Later George discovered the victim suffered a broken nose and was covered with blood.

The assault did not stay unnoticed for long. Hospital personnel notified the Office of Professional Responsibility (OPR) and an internal investigation was begun.

OPR agents interviewed all the illegal aliens, including the victim, but none of those interviewed knew a thing. Next on the list were the Border Patrol Agents involved in the arrest or who were in the sector where the assault took place.

Eventually, George was interviewed by a crack OPR investigator. George had nothing to hide and was ready to identify the supervisor he saw assault the victim.

The investigator asked where were you at 2am the night of the assault? Did you see the arrests? How clearly did you see the aliens and border agents through your scope? George was ready to report the facts, but he was waiting for the question; can you identify the person who assaulted the victim?

How many border agents were present? Did the aliens give the agents any trouble? George was thinking; when is he going to ask me? He was never asked the question and the investigation was closed for lack of evidence.

Asking the right questions is vital in any discipline if you want to discover the facts. Any investigator wants the truth, but without asking the right questions the truth remains evasive. In law enforcement an internal affairs investigator must contend with cynical, cautious, defensive officers who feel they must protect themselves from controversy. An investigator must ask the right questions to reveal the truth.

— *Former U.S. Border Patrol Agent who will remain anonymous.*

Case Study

The Office of Internal Affairs in a large federal agency is looking for one exceptional investigator to complement the investigative function. You are a Supervisory Special Agent with internal affairs and have some input into who is hired.

An Associate Commissioner of Compliance has put forward for consideration an agency investigator who conducts compliance and criminal investigations. The Associate Commissioner, Barbara Jean Johnson, is a neighbor of Special Agent Jack Flack. Johnson has little to no interaction with Flack during work hours, but their families meet regularly with other neighbors in the immediate area. Johnson knows Flack to be a family man and a good father and husband, but he is not very sociable. He is active in his church and coaches his son's little league team. You know Flack slightly through various meetings. He has irritated several people because he puts family issues before work. You know him as an excellent investigator, but his social skills are limited and he has little criminal investigative experience. Flack is noncommittal regarding whether he wants to make the move.

Recently, Special Agent Margaret Schick submitted an application to internal affairs. Special Agent Schick is a criminal investigator with the Office of Criminal Investigations in the same federal agency. She is known as an aggressive investigator. She has always been professional when she has, on occasion, worked with others in the Office of Internal Affairs. She is considered by many to be an outstanding investigator with many investigations resulting in indictments and convictions. Her supervisors like her because she makes their "stats" look good. Schick is divorced with three children and financially stable. She has had some boyfriend problems in the past that caused her to fail to meet work product deadlines. Her responsibilities at home sometimes make business travel impossible.

Case Study Questions

Answer the following questions in one narrative response.

1. The Office Director has asked you for your recommendations about both candidates. Because of budge-

tary considerations only one background investigation can be conducted. In addition, the fiscal year closeout is soon approaching. There is little time to pick "the" candidate for The Office of Internal Affairs.

a. *How would you compare the two candidates?*

b. *What is your thought process? How did you decide who to recommend?*

c. *With so little information is there anything you could do unofficially to hedge your bet?*

Questions for Discussion

Answer each of the following questions in a separate response.

1. What personality type described by Hennessy do you believe would make the best internal affairs investigator? How did you come to your decision?

2. Define and discuss sensitivity and rapport in an investigation. Give an example from personal experience how the two qualities affected your relationship with a law enforcement officer, a teacher, a friend, or a counselor.

Notes

1. Hillberry, Gary. U.S. Customs Service, Special Agent-in-Charge (retired). (30 May 2007). Telephonic interview.
2. Williams, Homer, J. Former Assistant Commissioner, Office of Internal Affairs, U.S. Customs Service. (1 Jun 2007) Interview.
3. Ibid.
4. Ibid.
5. Smith, I.C. (2004). Inside: A top G-Man Exposes Spies, Lies, and Bureaucratic Bungling Inside the FBI. Nelson Current, Nashville, TN.
6. Hennessy, Stephen M. (1999). Thinking Cop, Feeling Cop—A Study in Police Personalities, Third Edition. Center for Applications for Psychological Type, Inc.
7. Hull, R.F.C. [revision by Hull] from translation by Baynes, H.G. (1976). Psychological Types. First Princeton/Bollingen paperback printing with corrections.

8. Hennessy, Stephen M. (1999). Thinking Cop, Feeling Cop—A Study in Police Personalities, Third Edition. Center for Applications for Psychological Type, Inc.
9. Ibid.
10. Ibid.
11. Ibid.
12. Ibid.
13. Ibid.
14. Ibid.

Suggested Reading

Hennessy, Stephen, M. (1999). *Thinking Cop, Feeling Cop: A Study in Police Personalities*. Gainesville, FL: Center for Applications of Psychological Type, Inc.

CHAPTER NINE
The Asset

Are Good Officers Afraid of the Bad?

Edmund Burke, an eighteenth-century British statesman and philosopher, stated, "The only thing necessary for the triumph of evil is for good men to do nothing."

No matter how hard an employer tries to hire good, upstanding, ethical employees, inevitably someone will violate criminal law or department policy in a fit of anger or a willful act and make a poor decision that may be regretted. Good people make mistakes: ordained ministers, teachers, doctors. However, it is naïve to say that an offending employee will admit an egregious mistake, take punishment, and move on. Some may, but they would be in a minority.

Not all misconduct is equal. Some misconduct is willful, some is not. Some offenders have remorse, others do not. Some misconduct is a one-time individual act; some misconduct is repeated or committed with others. Some leave an indelible mark on an individual or society. Some leave no lasting effect. Often misconduct is disregarded, but there are some incidents of misconduct that should never be overlooked. Minor mistakes, lapses of judgment, or policy violations may be overlooked, but the most egregious violations of criminal law should never be ignored.

Then there are the good men and women who want to serve, help, protect, who stay out of trouble, and do the best job they can. They are the "assets."

Assets

Anyone can be an asset. Anyone who is fed up with corruption, misconduct, inaction, or looking the other way can supply information to improve his life and follow his conscience. Federal, state, county, township, or city officers as well as directors, chiefs, captains, lieutenants, group supervisors, and special agents can supply information on mayors, chiefs, and directors on down.

A supervisor, especially a newly promoted one, can be placed in a situation where subordinates are unruly and uncontrollable to the point that the supervisor faced with an unsupportive chain of command can do nothing. Assaults, theft, and other misconduct may be so ingrained that a supervisor who cares will not have much, if any, impact without outside help. Just like anything else in life, the asset must know the rules of the game.

To Report or Not to Report

I do not advocate that an employee report every violation to internal affairs, a supervisor, or an entity outside the organizational chain of command. I do, however, strongly encourage employees to report violations that are so grievous, outrageous, and contrary to the rule of law that they are against all that a law enforcement officer represents. Other violations an officer should report are ones that may implicate the reporting officer in the wrongdoing. The only way to void the misconduct is to report it.

There are several reasons why I add more controversy to the internal affairs function by not encouraging officers to report all misconduct. Supervisors must be allowed to supervise. Managers must be allowed to manage. Leaders must be allowed to lead. Management should be given a chance to handle the situation. In other words, pick your fight; let minor misconduct take its course. However, if the misconduct is not addressed and is intolerable, it should be reported to the entity or person who can address the allegations.

For most people, reporting wrongdoing is a painful experience. Since childhood most are taught not to be a tattletale. Everyone wants to be accepted by his peers and coworkers. A police organization deals with informants on a daily basis, but an employee who informs on a fellow employee is now in a different category. To become known as an informer may have a detrimental effect on one's life. Many supervisors will peg an informer as a troublemaker because information that may have been known but never officially discussed or never documented is now in the open. Even if it was not known, it is now and must be dealt with along with other administrative situations that are always present. "Not on my watch," meaning not while I am here or not on my shift, has been coined by many leaders. An individual giving police information on a bank robbery they observed is a witness. A criminal giving information on another criminal is an informant, less objectively described as a rat, a snitch, stool pigeon, stoolie, a snake. To many, the employee is the informer, the rat, the snitch, a whistleblower. He may now be despised by many of his co-workers as well as distrusted by them.

A whistleblower is one who reports unethical conduct. "Whistleblowers' actions may save lives or billions of dollars. But rather than receive praise for their integrity, they are often targeted for retaliatory investigations, harassment, intimidation, demotion, or dismissal and blacklisting."[1] However, "[w]ith the truth on their side, individuals can make a difference. Whistleblowers are the Achilles heel of organizational misconduct, if they bear witness when it counts."[2]

Reporting Misconduct Is Not Disloyalty

Coleen Rowley was an FBI special agent who wrote a memo to FBI Director Robert Mueller informing him how FBI HQ ignored information about Zacarias Moussaoui, a September 11th coconspirator. She not only hand-carried the memo to Director Mueller's office in May 2002, but she also gave copies of the memo to two U.S. Senators who were members of the Senate Intelligence Oversight Committee.

In the memo Agent Rowley mentioned the importance of the FBI's response, or failure to respond, to evidence of terrorist activity and that the issue involved was one of integrity. Although she attempted to temper her words, she not only suggested an FBI failure but also that the director and others at the highest levels of management slanted facts regarding the September 11th attacks. After the memo became public, Rowley was vilified by both active and retired FBI agents. She was compared to Robert Hanssen, an agent who was convicted of giving highly classified information to the Russians. Reportedly, a discussion was held at FBI HQ regarding possible criminal charges against her.

Rowley was condemned by many for being disloyal. Rowley stated, "Loyalty to whoever you work for is extremely important. The only problem is, it's not the most important thing.

And when it comes to not admitting mistakes, or covering up or not rectifying things only to save face, that's a problem."[3]

The Outside Man Looking In

> *"Frank Serpico! The first police officer not only in the history of the New York Police Department, but in the history of any police department in the whole United States, to step forward to report and subsequently testify openly about widespread, systematic cop corruption—payoffs amounting to millions of dollars."*[4]
>
> — Peter Maas, author of the biography *Serpico*

In New Yorker Magazine 25th Anniversary Issue

Francisco Vincent Serpico was a New York City Police Officer from early 1960 until 1972. In the mid-1960s, he was assigned as a plainclothes officer. During his time in plainclothes, he encountered widespread police corruption in which he declined to take part. He reported this corruption but was met with many bureaucratic roadblocks and received many death threats for his efforts. In 1971, during a narcotics "buy and bust," he was shot in the face. There is much controversy surrounding the shooting. Arguably, Serpico was placed in danger by other police officers. Apparently no assistance was given him by his partners immediately after the shooting. A neighbor in the building in which the operation took place assisted him until help arrived. You can learn more about the life of Frank Serpico in the book *Serpico* by Peter Mass published in 1973 or in the movie, *Serpico*, released in 1974.

"I became a police officer because I wanted to serve the people of New York City and while an officer I wanted to do the right thing. Because I always did the right thing I was never afraid of the Internal Affairs Bureau." However, he was readily accepted as a "cousin," an officer on the take, by many corrupt officers, because of, he believes, "the way I looked while I was plainclothes." He had long hair and a beard which was unusual for any police officer in the 1960s, even one who worked undercover. Earlier in his career, while in uniform, he was also accepted as a cousin. During a traffic stop with a training officer, a motorist offered Serpico a $35.00 bribe.

When informed, the training officer interceded and accepted the bribe. When Serpico declined to accept his "share," the training officer was happy to keep the entire proceeds. Since Serpico did not raise the bribe as an issue, he was considered "safe" by the corrupt officer and others. While in plainclothes, he also witnessed many officers who accepted payoffs from drug dealers.[5]

Over time Serpico could no longer ignore the corruption that surrounded him. "I believed what I was told in the police academy and I was a cop 24 hours a day. As an officer I was inspired and knew that there was a thin line between what I did and the wrong side of the law, especially while an undercover plainclothes officer, but I knew I could never cross that line. The ethics I lived as an officer was up to me, it was up to the individual."[6]

"After it became public that I exposed widespread corruption I personally saw many people in the department who tried to mitigate what I disclosed and who made many attempts to discount my allegations. I was viewed as an informer, a rat, a traitor to the blue uniform. Other officers avoided me and did not want to work with me. Police executives stated that I did not have first-hand information of corruption and that I exaggerated minor discrepancies. Whether they were corrupt or not, many officers, especially high ranking ones, did not want my allegations to tarnish the department or their careers. These ranking officers were probably involved in the corruption or at least were when they were on the street."[7]

Frank Serpico was shot on February 3, 1971. The shooting is controversial in that the circumstances surrounding the shooting are in dispute. Also in dispute is whether law enforcement officers place their lives at risk if they violate their department's unwritten code of silence. "Frequently used in support of this theory [of risking your life] is the movie version of Frank Serpico's efforts to get action on his allegations of police corruption. The film begins with an incident where Serpico is shot in circumstances that make it appear that he was set up by his colleagues to be killed. The evidence does not support this interpretation."[8]

Skolnick and Fyfe "... agree with Patrick V. Murphy, New York's Police Commissioner at the time Serpico was shot. Murphy writes: I do not believe Serpico was set up, and, even more, I do not believe that Detective Serpico believes it either. Further, although it probably has occurred at some point in American police history, we know of no other cases in which police have punished those who betrayed the code of silence with anything as extreme as a shooting. Instead, the code—and there is a code—typically is enforced by the threat of shunning, by fear that informing will lead to exposure of one's own derelictions, and by fear that colleagues' assistance may be withheld in emergencies."[9]

I understand Frank Serpico's version of the shooting; he was shot by a drug dealer and given little or no help by his follow officers. Serpico was not shot by an officer, but by a drug dealer. I agree with Patrick Murphy's statement that Serpico was not set up. I also agree with Skolnick and Fyfe that there is a code, and that code was imposed on Frank Serpico, if the correct facts are known, in that his "colleagues assistance" was "withheld" in an emergency.

Author's Note

Published in 2012, *They Wished They Were Honest,* by Michael F. Armstrong reveals, "Rumors and speculation have suggested that Frank was set up by the cops in an attempt to exact revenge for his turning on his comrades. Frank never made any such claim. He faulted the cops who were with him for not being quicker in coming to his aid, but he firmly denied the suggestion, made in the later book and movie about his exploits, that he had been deliberately put in harm's way." Book footnote: "At that time, Frank generally groused about the minor inaccuracies he said abounded, particularly in the movie."

According to Lon Eilders, "Frank Serpico is not an aberration. If you do not go along, you may be alone and no one will come to your aid when you need it. When an officer is asked about corruption in an open forum it would benefit the officer to say, 'I did not hear it,' 'I did not see it,' 'I was not looking that way,' 'I have no clear recollection.' An officer's safety may depend upon the answer to a question. Any officer wants to know if another can be trusted."[10]

"... a code of silence is not unique to the police. In every identifiable group, there exists an unspoken understanding that one reports on members' misconduct only at some risk."[11]

"... any member of any group who considers becoming a whistleblower must know that, however laudable one's motives doing so will forever change one's own life and status in the group."[12]

A retired Chicago officer, who will remain anonymous, stated: "Most police officers are fearful to speak out on wrongful acts because they would feel like a 'rat' and some officers will say you cannot to be trusted. Many officers will not say a word against another officer unless they are placed in a corner. However, it is important from the beginning to set the ground rules. When you are a new arrival at a station, officers test you; they talk amongst themselves and feel you out. I used to teach new officers that if you don't stand up for yourself, the bad officers will own you. All you have to do is stand up for yourself the first time and they will not bother you again. They will talk bad about you and many cops won't ride with you, but I never cared because I always hung around the officers who cared about the job and would do the right thing. Everyone I worked with knew that I would not tolerate any type of misconduct. Bad officers knew that and would not show up on calls when they knew I was there. They just didn't have much to do with me. I have always felt comfortable about how I conducted myself, I always associated with officers who thought like me, who wanted to do the right thing and I never had to personally worry about corruption or misconduct."[13]

The Inside Man Getting out

Robert Leuci was a respected New York City Police Officer who became entangled in a web of corruption. Frank Serpico cannot be compared with Robert Leuci "whose testimony eventually put his whole squad and about seventy other New York City narcotics detectives behind bars."[14]

However, Skolnick and Fyfe, along with Leuci himself, portray him [Leuci] as a stand-up guy, his actions as something heroic, and downplay the fact that he was a corrupt officer. "I'm not going to implicate any one close to us ... I want to end this life I have been living."[15]

Leuci's wife states, "I know you feel guilty. Other people are responsible, not you. They are guiltier than you are ... I know you. It's going to kill you. They [the prosecutors] will force you to hurt friends, people who have done no harm to you, only good." [16]

Skolnick and Fyfe state that Leuci "anticipated—correctly—that none of the people he 'hurt' would try forcibly to silence him or to avenge his turnaround ... In the end ... he could never be what he once was: 'Prince of the City,' the hotshot member of the most envied and prestigious detective unit [Special Investigations Unit] in the biggest police department in the country." [17] The authors also discuss and give examples of the cohesiveness of the unit, that Leuci is still welcome in the circle of convicted felons and what he did is just "water under the bridge."

However, I have never met, and I suggest no other law enforcement officer has either, an informant who has told the entire, naked truth. Leuci stated he was not going to implicate people close to him. Leuci gave testimony and dozens of officers were convicted, lost their jobs, their pensions, their financial security, their reputations, and some may have lost their families. There are lifelong hatreds among officers because of bungled investigations, failed backup attempts, union differences, conflicting testimony and extra marital affairs. "YOU SCREWED ME, YOU BASTARD, AND I WILL NEVER FORGET IT." How many times has that been heard? If what Leuci did is just shrugged off by many, then he lived up to his word and there are others who were not prosecuted.

Leuci was once a respected police officer who crossed the line. If all the facts were reported correctly, he along with other officers took bribes from the lowest of the criminal element. Leuci was an unindicted coconspirator who informed on criminals. There is a difference between an officer who brings corruption to the surface to do the right thing and an officer who is forced to testify about criminal activity in which he and others are involved. I find no honest comparison between Leuci and Serpico. Leuci was an officer who voluntarily took part in criminal activity; Serpico was an officer who could no longer tolerate crime, in which he took no part. If there is any comparison between Leuci and Serpico, it is that they are both surrounded by controversy.

The Risk Taker

I previously stated I advocate law enforcement officers to supply information on others when the crime is such that the reporting officer cannot tolerate the violation. I may be an advocate, but only one person can make the decision to bring corruption to the surface: the officer who takes the risk. Therefore, before any overt action is taken, an officer must consider all the consequences if he is going to approach a supervisor or other authority. The officer and his family may be vilified, shunned, intimidated or disenfranchised professionally and socially if his action becomes public. "Good" assignments may disappear, promotions may never come and favors from friends may be hard to find. The officer may be placed under investigation to take the spotlight off the real problem. An offense is a good defense. The code of silence is strong in many departments, and many officers may be unhappy that one dared to inform on another. However, when supplying information, an officer must consider himself an asset to the department and to the citizens it serves. He is not an informant, but an asset. He is not a criminal who is being forced to testify against other officers to reduce his sentence, but an officer who is doing the right thing for the right reasons. In deciding whether an officer will supply information, he must be honest with himself and decide whether to take responsibility others avoid. Realistically, many will think about it, but few will take the step. Without the first step, sexual assaults, protection payments by restaurant and bar owners, theft of narcotics, and other crimes will continue.

Consider What You Are Gaining

Officers can and do become embroiled in allegations of misconduct because they work with or associate with those who commit misconduct. Guilt by association is an injustice, but it can happen to any officer. This association may be present because the officer is merely assigned to a certain location or shift. An officer may not have committed any violation, but perception is sometimes as bad as reality. Furthermore, following the leader can be worse than guilt by association. Leadership can be official or unofficial. Sometimes the unofficial leadership can be stronger than the real supervisor's ability to control it. A weak supervisor may allow others to become involved in misconduct or ignore misconduct because of an informal but stronger leader. Some personalities are stronger than others, but leaders, whether recognized or rogue, inspire. Appropriately, misconduct is contrary to most officers' ethical values and is against what they believe. Most officers want to do the right thing; that is why they entered the law enforcement field. They want to protect and do good. Becoming a department asset may preclude unintentional involvement in misconduct. It enables an officer to protect himself and others.

It was the experience of a Chicago officer that "most police officers in the faster [busier] districts have a greater potential for misconduct. Officers in the faster districts do not seem to care as much about lawful arrests, community relations, and doing the right thing as much as an officer who works in a slower district who must hunt for a felony arrest or a good case. Officers in fast districts seem to think it is OK to wander off the path a little because their duty is so dangerous. Transferring into a busy district I found other officer's attitudes surprisingly unethical and it seemed to run rampant throughout the station. I found myself arguing with other officers and transferred out shortly after arriving because I did not like the things I was seeing nightly."[18]

To protect himself, an officer must have a command presence when dealing with the public that conveys an air of confidence, authority, and respect. The Chicago officer presented another type of command presence to protect himself from other officers. The command presence shown other officers was one of confidence which said, "I respect myself and others."

Keep It to Yourself

> *"To sin by silence when they should protect makes cowards of men."*
>
> — Abraham Lincoln (1809–1865)
> 16th U.S. President

There is a good chance the supervisor and the chain of command of the offending officer know the officer has problems and may also know of the specific violation you want to report. Do not be surprised if this is the case. You may be reporting a violation that is widely known but has never been documented or addressed. This brings up something that is as important as deciding to become an asset.

If you value your career and personal life, I strongly suggest you become and remain forever an anonymous asset. As shown previously, you can become an outcast if you violate the code of silence. If your identity is known, you will become the officer who caused problems from the sergeant to the chief and from the chief to the mayor. Stay anonymous. Do not discuss your actions with your wife or husband, best friend, or partner. Take advice from ones who know.

Deep Throat

On August 8, 1974, Richard M. Nixon resigned as the president of the United States. President Nixon's resignation was caused by many things: lying about his complicity in a politically motivated burglary and then lying to cover up the crime; but those things were kept in the public eye by one person with the help of the *Washington Post.* From 1972 until 2005, that one person was known only by the moniker "Deep Throat." After more than 30 years, it was revealed "Deep Throat" was W. Mark Felt, the second in command of the Federal Bureau of Investigation in the early 1970s. "The identity of Deep Throat is [was] modern journalism's greatest unsolved mystery. It has been said that he may be the most famous anonymous person in U.S. history. But, regardless of his notoriety, American society today owes a considerable debt to the government official who decided, at great personal risk, to help Woodward and Bernstein as they pursued the hidden truths of Watergate."[19]

Actually, "Felt was adamant about remaining silent on the subject—until his death—thinking his past disclosures somehow dishonorable." Felt believed that he might be fired or criminally charged for his actions. During the Watergate scandal, many times he was accused and certainly suspected of being Deep Throat. He always denied the allegation. Yet, on the other hand, later in life he revealed to several close friends and associates he was, in fact, Deep Throat. It is anyone's guess what would have happened to Mr. Felt if he confirmed during or soon after Watergate that he released law enforcement sensitive or higher information to unauthorized individuals.[20]

But there are others who took the risk.

The Man with Few Regrets

Thomas M. Tamm would not have to guess what would happen when he overtly released classified U.S. Justice Department information. While an attorney in a Justice Department unit managing "wiretaps of suspected terrorist and spies," he found "[t]he unit had special rules that appeared to be hiding the NSA [National Security Agency] activities from a panel of federal judges who are required to approve such surveillance." Another unit member revealed to him that "the program" was "probably illegal." Reportedly Tamm has a "passion for justice."[21]

Tamm eventually called *The New York Times*, which reported 18 months later "that President George W. Bush had secretly authorized NSA to intercept phone calls and emails of individuals inside the United States without judicial warrants."[22] *The New York Times* won a Pulitzer Prize and the FBI opened a criminal investigation of Mr. Tamm's activities. "Tamm is haunted by the consequences of what he did—and what could happen to him"[23]... I [Tamm] didn't think through what this could do to my family..."[24]

"Tamm's story is in part a cautionary tale about the perils that can face all whistleblowers ... Some Americans will view him as a hero ... Others ... will deride Tamm as a renegade who took the law into his own hands and violated solemn obligations to protect the nation's secrets ... Tamm understands some will see his conduct as 'treasonous.' But still, he says he has few regrets ..." After becoming aware that "the program" was illegal, "Tamm says his immediate thought was, 'I'm a law enforcement officer and I'm participating in something that is illegal?' "[25]

The Man with Many Regrets

I knew the officer for about ten years when he was shot and the shooter was killed. When recovering from the incident the officer re-evaluated his life and, in his words, "allowed the Lord to enter my life." He was part of an undercover operation where he saw many policy and alleged criminal violations committed by other officers. There were suspicious operational financial transactions, questionable funds accountability, misuse of operational assets, misuse of personnel, and the flagrant disregard of court instructions.[26]

He approached his supervisor with the allegations. The supervisor assured the officer his concerns would be addressed. Months later he discovered his allegations were ignored and he contacted a second-level supervisor. The officer was told to go along to get along. He contacted internal affairs because no one in authority would listen to him.[27]

Prior to his contact with internal affairs, he was considered an outstanding individual, professionally and personally. I knew him as a hard charger, a cut above others. After contacting internal affairs, the officer was reassigned and was given a fitness-for-duty medical exam.[28]

Subsequently, internal affairs and the prosecutor's office received numerous, anonymous allegations against him. Former confidential informants were interviewed to determine if the officer shared source payments when he paid them for information. After passing the fitness for duty exam, he was again reassigned. Reportedly, he was denied a promotion and choice assignments. He finally was transferred to a distant location where life was good until another officer involved in the allegations was reassigned to the same location and identified him as a "rat." Allegations against him again began to surface and he was transferred to a third location. The strain, all along difficult to sustain, finally caused him to retire prematurely when diagnosed with post-traumatic stress disorder and depression resulting from the shooting incident. "I now live day to day and regret ever going to Internal Affairs as it changed my life forever." [29]

> *"The world is a dangerous place, not because of those who do evil, but because of those who don't do anything about it."*
>
> — Albert Einstein

Remember Your Training

When reporting any incident, just as taught in law enforcement training, the officer must obtain as much information as possible before going forward. The officer may never get another chance at offering the information or may not want to take the chance again, so the information must be as complete and credible as possible. Collect dates, times, locations, license numbers, persons present, everything anyone would want to know about the misconduct. Merely stating that Officer Doe sexually assaulted a motorist during a traffic stop does not offer credibility or enough information for action. In addition, unspecific anonymous information may not be taken seriously even if the information is known to be true. Many supervisors, including some internal affairs supervisors who work for management—don't forget IA is a key part of department management—will take every opportunity to avoid controversy, to deny knowledge.

I once reported, anonymously, a hostile work environment and a profoundly unprofessional encounter with a senior executive. I was a witness to the executive's intimidating, degrading, and browbeating of an individual to the point I feared for the individual's safety. If it had not been such a violent encounter, and if I had not determined it had happened numerous times before to others, I would not have reported it. While shouting, the executive was nose to nose, save a centimeter, to his subject of wrath. The shouting, which could be heard several hundred feet away through a closed door, was about a violation of a personal preference rather than of department policy. Although reported anonymously, I was listed as a witness. Eventually two witnesses were interviewed, both of whom denied knowledge. I and others were never interviewed, and the situation was quietly covered up.

If an officer acting as an asset values his career, the information must not be attributable to him. Because of circumstances, the asset and others might be interviewed by an investigator, but to single himself out as the only witness is equivalent to shooting himself in the foot. However, if the asset is involved but wants to avoid criminal charges or other discipline, overtly offering information may be the only option. But if the asset is one of several unwitting witnesses and wants to forward information, the information can and should be anonymous. Submitting a list of witnesses, including the asset, would be appropriate.

Whether you remain anonymous or decide to go public, there are a few things you must always remember no matter what is said about you or how you are treated. If you are reporting information anonymously, suspicion may still surround you. You may be approached to confirm the suspicions. Always stay professional, anything you say or do can and will be used against you. If you are unprofessional your credibility will be questioned. If your credibility is questioned the credibility of the information you submit may be questioned. Further, "[a]lways be on guard not to embellish your charges. This is essential to maintaining your credibility. It is far better to understate than to overstate your case, because your employers can leap at every slight exaggeration and use it to discredit you."[30]

I became aware of anonymous allegations of improper bid procedures with powerful political consequences. It involved a government contract, a disagreement between two businessmen, one the winning contractor, one the losing. Both had Senatorial backing from opposing political parties. The allegations were many and revolved around the way a long-standing vendor lost the contract. The response to the allegations was immediate because of the congressional interest and disrupted the lives of dozens of investigators, auditors, inspectors, program managers, and subject-matter experts. After months of investigation and thousands of hours, it was determined that one disgruntled employee had embellished minor policy errors, reintroduced previously reviewed and adjudicated personnel matters, and added fictitious details to innocuous personal and official financial transactions to cause problems for a supervisor. Every one of the allegations was thoroughly investigated and discounted. During the investigation, the anonymous source was identified. Although no credible information was found, this source not only discredited himself but everyone at the work location because of uncovered personal problems between coworkers.

Pick Your Fight

As I said before, pick your fight. I would like to say reporting egregious corruption most likely will occur once in your career. Realistically it may depend on the department or agency in which you work. If you feel you must supply information more than once over a 30-year career, you are either in the wrong job or your department may need new leadership.

Some information you report may never be acted on or you may never know the outcome, so do not look for justice, vindication, or satisfaction. Some information will be difficult to prove no matter how much detail you supply. There still is the code of silence to deal with; witnesses with bad memories, or a victim's reluctance to testify against a police officer or other authority figure.

I previously said to keep your identity anonymous. There are dozens of federal and state whistle-blower laws that purportedly protect individuals who are publicly identified as ones who report criminal violations or waste, fraud, and abuse to authorities or others. In principle, these state and federal laws are supposed to protect individuals from retaliation. "All too often, however, employees who choose to exercise these rights on the job find that their rights exist on paper only ... Federal employees often are confined to defending their rights before an administrative judge who lacks the bureaucratic independence to rule against powerful interests without risking reprisal themselves ... these whistle-blower laws provide only second-class rights, hardly the foundation for first-class public service. Perhaps most frustrating, the law provides little to deter those who retaliate."[31]

> *"History will have to record that the greatest tragedy of this period of social transition was not the strident clamor of the bad people, but the appalling silence of the good people."*
>
> — Martin Luther King, Jr.

Know Who Can Act On the Information

After deciding to report an incident, you must decide how to do it and to whom it should be reported. There are only two ways to document information, verbally or in writing, but there are numerous ways to forward information: telephone, in person, electronic message, U.S. mail or other private mail service. If you go public with your information, it may not matter how you forward it. However, if you wish to remain anonymous, the transmission of the information must be in a way that cannot be traced back to you. If you use the U.S. mail or a private carrier, you should mail the envelope as far from your home as possible. If you are acting at the local level, a change of zip code might be best, but on a national level, I would travel to another city or state to hide your identity. Typed, not handwritten, documentation from an unassociated computer printer is the best way to proceed. When using the mail, an asset must be aware of compromising DNA (saliva and oils) on the envelope and stamp and, of course, fingerprints. Anonymity requires a lot of thought. Other forms of anonymous communication will be discussed below.

Just as stressful as protecting yourself is determining to whom or to what organization the information should be sent: to hotline personnel, to the news media, prosecutor's office, political activist organization, a governor's office, internal affairs unit or inspector general. There are a wide variety of recipients depending upon the government entity: city, township, county, state, or federal.

The choice may be a simple one because of the circumstances, but you still must pick the recipient carefully. Or, the choice may be more difficult depending upon the information, timing, and political ramifications.

> You must do research to determine the best avenue and approach.
>
> → Is a newspaper or television station conducting an expose of actions of which you are intimately aware? Are your allegations enticing enough for a local or national newspaper or television station to become interested? "But sometimes owners or key institutional stockholders may be tied in some way to the targets of your whistleblower disclosure, or even be implicated directly ... [or] ... the owners and managers of newspapers and television stations may feel political and monetary pressures."[32]
>
> → Would a congressional representative or senator act on the information because of a special interest? Would a congressional staff merely forward a letter to the appropriate constituent, which may lead back to the wrongdoer?
>
> → Would a county prosecutor or the Office of the U.S. Attorney be your best choice because of past prosecutions or recent media statements? However, remember local and federal prosecutors are either elected or appointed government officials. Some are more political than others.

- → Advocacy groups like the Government Accountability Project (GAP) (http://www.whistleblower.org) can give you advice regarding disclosures. GAP promotes corporate and government accountability by, among other things, protecting whistleblowers.
- → A citizen review board (CRB) can be an excellent avenue to pursue, but again research is a must. Some CRBs have authority to investigate wrongdoing and can subpoena witnesses; others have less power.

Conspicuously absent from the list are an Office of Inspector General, Internal Affairs Bureau, Office of Professional Responsibility, or other internal organization. All these offices are management tools. Some may be passionate and will vigorously investigate allegations. Others may be politically controlled by the parent organization and find an excuse to avoid a fair look at allegations that may embarrass the organization.

Early in my career I received allegations of theft by employees of a federally funded railroad. It was obvious from the start that the railroad police officer I contacted was more concerned with protecting the railroad from me, an outsider, than with investigating theft by employees. The allegations were never pursued because of the lack of cooperation and other more credible allegations.

Late in my career I was the lead investigator on a politically charged investigation that was adjudicated in favor of the government. During the course of the investigation, I briefed several high-level executives. Discussions after each briefing always included how to mitigate the impact of the findings on the organization.

If you want your information to be acted on with more honesty, find an interested party outside your organization. In addition, information of misconduct or corruption may be timely within a narrow window, due to politics, even with an outside party. Do not be surprised if you discover no one is interested in the information. Politics makes the world go around.

Crime Stoppers

Crime Stoppers USA is a nonprofit organization of citizens against crime. The organization operates secure tip lines throughout the U.S. through community programs in all 50 states. Similar community programs also operate in Canada and various other countries around the world. Citizens with information of criminal activity contact Crime Stoppers to supply information which is forwarded to various police agencies. "Many U.S. Crime Stoppers affiliates use TipSoft, a technology which incorporates double-encryption of email and internet–web messages." TipSoft technology allows for anonymous contact with Crime Stoppers.[33]

Not all Crime Stoppers affiliates use TipSoft. TipSoft is a two-way communications security software for email, text messages, and telephone contact, but users must be aware of each affiliate's capability by asking questions before giving information. When sending email, text messages, or making contact by telephone, the communication is first forwarded to a secure server in Canada, where the contact information is encrypted and assigned an alias. The Canadian server retains only the minimum information required, and the text message itself is not retained. The message is then sent to the TipSoft server in the United States where a second alias is assigned before the message is forwarded to the appropriate Crime Stoppers affiliate. The same encryption and alias procedure is used when replies are sent back to the originator.[34]

"Anonymity is also guaranteed when using land-line or cell phones through 'informer's privilege' "[35]

Author's note

"Informer's privilege" is a right derived from a U.S. Supreme Court decision, *McCray v. Illinois,* 386 U.S. 300 (1967), which is supplemented by statutes in many states. The privilege is the government's right to keep confidential in a suppression hearing the identity of persons who supply information to law enforcement officers. The privilege recognizes public interest in effective law enforcement by preserving the anonymity of persons who report violations of law. However, in *Roviaro v. United States,* 353 U.S. 53 (1957) the Supreme Court ruled that the privilege may not continue at trial if the informer's identify is necessary to ensure fairness. The way around identifying a source is by the TipSoft software keeping no identifying information.

"Not only are Crime Stoppers' communications confidential and privileged, but no identifying information is ever gathered which makes it impossible for the disclosure of a person's identity. Crime Stoppers has been subjected to subpoenas duces tecum to produce information, but none have been successful since no information is possessed to produce."[36]

"After receipt by Crime Stoppers the appropriate law enforcement agency is forwarded the information. If a supplier of information requests it be forwarded to a certain person or organization, that request will be honored. Crime Stoppers understands the sensitivity of corruption, the importance of anonymity of an officer, and the fact some information must be forwarded to an entity more prone to properly and completely investigate allegations."[37]

Code of Silence or Not

It is difficult to discuss the internal affairs function or ethics in a law enforcement organization without mention of the "blue wall of silence." The "blue wall" is an unofficial show of unity or loyalty by officers when another is accused of misconduct. In my years in law enforcement I have seen little of the code of silence but I believe the code is different in every department or agency. As reported by criminologist Carl B. Klockars, "[e]ven with assurances of confidentiality, police officers are unlikely to be willing to report their own or another officer's corrupt activities." However, Klockars also discovered "that the more serious a particular behavior was considered by police officers, the more severely they thought it should and would be punished, and the more willing they were to report it."[38] Criminologist David Weisburd found there is "the possibility of a large gap between attitudes and behavior. That is, even though officers do not believe in protecting wrongdoers, they often do not turn them in ... More than 80 percent of police surveyed reported that they do not accept the 'code of silence' (i.e., keeping quiet in the face of misconduct by others) as an essential part of the mutual trust necessary to good policing ... However, about one-quarter (24.9 percent) of the sample agreed or strongly agreed that whistleblowing is not worth it, more than two-thirds (67.4 percent) reported that police officers who report incidents of misconduct are likely to be given a 'cold shoulder' by fellow officers, and a majority (52.4 percent) agreed or strongly agreed that it is not unusual for police officers to 'turn a blind eye' to other officers' improper conduct ... A surprising 6 in 10 (61 percent) indicated that police officers do not always report even serious criminal violations that involve the abuse of authority by fellow officers."[39]

Law enforcement officers' bias against management, politicians, the media, citizens, and internal affairs: all of this causes what is called the "blue wall of silence," the unspoken code. "I saw nothing, I heard nothing, I did nothing illegal." The question is "Why should I expose an act of corruption when management will not stand behind me, my fellow officers will not support me, the politicians will deny they knew any corruption occurred, and I will be portrayed as a disgruntled employee?" The code of silence is an ingrained feature of some police department's culture, but not all.

While a law enforcement officer, I saw little of the deep-seated, inherent code that prohibited an honest officer from reporting misconduct. But, I believe there is a code and that the code is practiced by two separate and distinct groups of officers. One group consists of corrupt officers who protect other corrupt officers. No matter what the misconduct, the officer is protected by an unwritten rule that an officer will not report transgressions. However, the other group consists of honest, hard-working officers. They do not want to get involved in corruption, but they practice the code because they do not want to be identified by management as troublemakers. More importantly, they are afraid of the corrupt officers, the bullies who may physically and mentally assault an officer who reports corruption or misconduct of any type. No matter which groups practicing the "code of silence," all are corrupt if they do not report violations of the law.

Case Study

Officer Brown is a newly hired officer for a medium-sized police department. He did extremely well in police training, scoring first or second in firearms training, academics, and physical fitness. He is well liked and does well in all areas of patrol work. Older officers like him because he is one of the younger generations who actually listens to constructive criticism, with one exception.

The one exception is that Brown is beginning to irritate everyone. He has discussed with you, his training officer, and most of the midnight shift whether it is ethical for officers, while in uniform, to receive a 50% discount on food at most fast food restaurants in the precinct. Brown believes there is only right and wrong and receiving the food discount is wrong. He believes that while officers are congregating at one or two restaurants other businesses or neighborhoods are being given less police service. He also believes that the business owners who give special treatment to police officers are indirectly and sometimes directly asking for special service in return.

Case Study Questions

Answer the following questions in one narrative response.

1. *As a young, newly hired officer is Brown approaching the situation correctly? Why or why not?*

2. *You consider yourself an ethical officer and serve the public as best as you can. You have never given the discount a second thought. What advice would you give your trainee?*

3. *Should Brown inform internal affairs of his concern? Why or why not?*

4. *Should the chain of command be informed? Why or why not?*

If you do not have law enforcement experience it is appropriate to interview and discuss the case study with a sworn officer.

Questions for Discussion

Answer each of the following questions in a separate response.

1. Is reporting corruption or misconduct an act of disloyalty to your employer? Why or why not? Would you report all wrongdoing? How would you report ethical lapses?

2. If you became personally aware of an officer sexually assaulting female motorists, would you report the information? Why or why not? If you decided to report the information, to whom would you report the crime? What factors would you consider prior to taking action?

Notes

1. Devine, Tom. (1997). The Whistleblower's Survival Guide—Courage Without Martyrdom. Government Accountability Project, the Fund for Constitutional Government, Washington, DC.
2. Ibid.
3. Ripley, Amanda, & Sieger, Maggie. (30 Dec 2002). Colleen Rowley: The Special Agent. Time Magazine: Persons of the Year. Retrieved from http://www.time.com/time/magazine/article/0,9171,1003988,00.html.
4. Maas, Peter. (19 Apr 1993). Serpico Testifies 1971. *New York Magazine 25th Anniversary Issue.* pp. 132.
5. Serpico, Frank. (12 Sep 2007). Telephonic interview.
6. Ibid.
7. Ibid.
8. Skolnick, Jerome, H. & Fyfe, James, J. (1993). *Above the Law—Police and the Excessive Use of Force.* The Free Press. p. 110.
9. Ibid., p. 110.
10. Eilders, Lon, Sr. (6 Sep 2007). Lieutenant (retired), Manager, Accreditation and Planning, Chattanooga, TN Police Department. Interview.
11. Skolnick, Jerome, H. & Fyfe, James, J. (1993). *Above the Law—Police and the Excessive Use of Force.* The Free Press. p. 110.
12. Ibid., pp. 111.
13. Chicago Police Officer (retired) who will remain anonymous. (6 Jul 2009). Electronic interview.
14. Skolnick, Jerome, H. & Fyfe, James, J. (1993). *Above the Law—Police and the Excessive Use of Force.* The Free Press. p. 111.
15. Ibid., p. 112.
16. Ibid., p. 112.
17. Ibid., p. 112.

18. Chicago Police Officer (retired) who will remain anonymous. (24 Jun 2009). Interview.
19. O'Connor, John, D. (Jul 2005). *The Deep Throat Revelation: "I'm the Guy They Called Deep Throat."* Vanity Fair. Retrieved from http://www.vanityfair.com/politics/features/2005/07/deepthroat200507.
20. Ibid.
21. Isikoff, Michael. (13 Dec 2008). The Fed Who Blew The Whistle: Is he a hero or a criminal? *Newsweek.* vol. CLII, no. 25.
22. Ibid.
23. Ibid.
24. Ibid.
25. Ibid.
26. Law enforcement officer who will remain anonymous. (11 Dec 2008). Email and telephonic interview.
27. Ibid.
28. Ibid.
29. Ibid.
30. Devine, Tom. (1997). *The Whistleblower's Survival Guide—Courage Without Martyrdom.* Government Accountability Project, the Fund for Constitutional Government, Washington, DC.
31. Ibid.
32. Ibid.
33. Carter, Richard, W. Judge (retired). (28 Jan 2009). Director of Legal Service, Crime Stoppers of the United States of America, Inc. Electronic interview.
34. Anderson, Kevin. (9 Feb 2009). Anderson, Anderson Software. Telephone & electronic interview.
35. Carter, Richard, W. Judge (retired). (28 Jan 2009). Director of Legal Service, Crime Stoppers of the United States of America, Inc. Electronic interview.
36. Ibid.
37. Ibid.
38. Klockars, Carl, B., Ivkovich, Sanja, Kutnjak, Harver, William, E., & Haverfeld, Maria, R. (May 2000). The Measurement of Police Integrity, National Institute of Justice.
39. Weisburd, David, Greenspan, Rosann, with Hamilton, Edwin, E., Williams, Hubert, & Bryant, Kellie, A. (May 2000). Police Attitudes Toward Abuse of Authority: Findings From a National Study. National Institute of Justice.

Suggested Reading

Armstrong, Michael F. (2012). *They Wished They Were Honest.* New York: Columbia University Press.

Government Accountability Project. (1997). The Whistleblower's Survival Guide, Courage without Martyrdom, Washington, DC, Fund for Constitutional Government.

Maas, Peter. (1973). Serpico: The Classic Story of the Cop Who Couldn't Be Bought. New York: Perennial.

CHAPTER TEN
Openness

"Cooperation, it's the grease that makes
the world go 'round'." [1]

We have examined the fact that the perception of unfairness in the internal affairs function can be created by organizational leadership, the rank and file, or by an internal affairs investigator, among others. Unfairness also can be created by innuendo or by contentious rather than professional operations. Departmental culture also plays a key role in how the internal affairs function is perceived or accepted.

To avoid the perception of unfairness and to promote an aboveboard, even-handed, and honest internal affairs investigation, I encourage opening up the entire internal affairs function. Open up the function as much as the law allows to both departmental personnel and the public. Privacy laws may prohibit much information from being made public. Unofficially, however, information at times is discussed by personnel not involved in an investigation, and many times what is discussed is inaccurate gossip. The spread of hearsay information or rumor is a disservice to the organization and especially to the person under investigation. Open up the function and give employees all the information the law allows without compromising the investigation. The internal affairs function should not be part of a secret culture within any department. The better the understanding employees have of the function, the more likely they are to accept it. It all comes down to communication. Communication will foster trust.

Each Office of Inspector General (OIG) in the federal government periodically issues a report to Congress. As an example, the Inspector General for the U.S. Postal Service issues a Semi-annual Report to Congress outlining the conduct and supervision of audits, reviews, and investigations. Dozens of closed investigations are discussed to illustrate the successes by the OIG and the results of poor decisions by employees and others. Numerous general descriptions are presented discussing mail theft, financial embezzlement, theft of property, and narcotics use by employees, and contract fraud by vendors.

Another example of openness is the Annual Report of the Commission to Combat Police Corruption in the City of New York. Established in 1994, the Commission is mandated to monitor efforts by NYPD to gather information, to investigate allegations, and to implement policy designed to deter corruption. A way the Commission achieves its mandate is by reviewing the Internal Affairs Bureau's (IAB) pending and closed investigations. Although specific information is not presented, the Commission Report illustrates not only what criminal or policy violations can get an officer into trouble, but that someone other than the IAB is looking at the actions of officers.

"The devil you know is preferable to the devil you don't." [2]

Tell Your Customers What to Expect

A way to be open is to let any officer who cares to know what will happen if a certain violation is committed. A table of offenses and penalties will inform employees of the likely punishment for a listed violation. Some may argue a table of penalties is too restrictive and may not allow the adjudication authority to weigh knowledge, intent, and willfulness and may not allow consideration of all factors that should be reviewed before discipline is imposed.

In my experience a table of offenses and penalties is used as a wake-up tool for the few employees who need many things spelled out. "This may happen to you if you do this!" The table is a broad guide; it can never include all possible offenses. The table merely gives a range of penalties for an offense and, in at least federal employment, "Douglas Factors" are always considered.

Douglas Factors are the result of a 1981 United States Merit System Protection Board (MSPB) opinion in *Douglas v. Veterans Administration* (5 MSPR 280). The MSPB developed an administrative process in personnel issues involving adversarial actions against federal employees.[3]

The following are the 12 Douglas Factors which are considered when deciding the penalty in a disciplinary action of federal employees:

1. The nature and seriousness of the offense, and its relation to the employee's duties, position, and responsibilities, including whether the offense was intentional or technical or inadvertent, or was committed maliciously or for gain, or was frequently repeated;

2. The employee's job level and type of employment, including supervisory or fiduciary (level of trust, power, and/or confidence placed in a person) role, contacts with the public, and prominence of the position;

3. The employee's past disciplinary record;

4. The employee's past work record, including length of service, performance on the job, ability to get along with fellow workers, and dependability;

5. The effect of the offense on the employee's ability to perform at a satisfactory level and its effect on supervisors' confidence in the employee's ability to perform assigned duties;

6. Consistency of the penalty with those imposed on other employees for the same or similar offenses;

7. The consistency of the penalty with any applicable agency table of penalties;

8. The notoriety of the offense or its impact on the reputation of the agency;

9. The clarity with which the employee was on notice of any rules that were violated in committing the offense, or had been warned about the conduct in question;

10. Potential for the employee's rehabilitation;

11. Mitigating circumstances surrounding the offense such as unusual job tensions, personality problems, mental impairment, harassment, or bad faith, malice or provocation on the part of others involved in the matter; and

12. The adequacy and effectiveness of alternative sanctions to deter such conduct in the future by the employee or others.

Serving Taxpaying Customers

Disclosure and openness can work in a law enforcement organization. In many departments it does work. In 2005 the Charlotte-Mecklenburg, NC Police Department published *A Guidebook for the Public and Our Employees On What We Do and Why We Do It.*[4] The publication was the result of responses from both the public and department employees and was intended to foster and reinforce trust in the department. The guidebook was designed to define how the department addresses accountability issues and why the process is conducted in a certain way. Although I believe the guidebook is a great way to be open I understand when police leadership changed, the guide was put aside for more traditional policing. Other departments have identified the citizens they serve as "customers," customers from whom the departments seek trust, feedback and satisfaction. If citizens are departments' customers, any employee can be an internal affairs customer. Anyone can be an internal affairs' customer not in the sense that an employee is being investigated for wrongdoing, but in the sense that the customer is an employee who is being protected from corruption that would threaten the department's integrity and the employee's job or job satisfaction. Identifying a citizen as a customer has caused some controversy in law enforcement. Although accepting the word "customer" caused me to change my attitude while an investigator some in law enforcement believe identifying a citizen as a customer is somehow over reacting to political pressures.

While a Special Agent for the U.S. Department of Transportation, Office of Inspector General (OIG), most of my time was spent investigating federal funds funneled through various state programs to contractors. The funds were used to maintain highways, build bridges, re-manufacture transit buses, improve highway safety, build airport runways, and a variety of other uses. Although I supported department employees in protecting their programs, I believe the employees would say I was looking over their shoulder, something they did not appreciate. In the early 1980s, the OIG began calling departmental administrations and employees "customers." That word was new to me and others. At first I did not understand the concept. I was an investigator conducting criminal investigations and I did not serve customers. I interviewed suspects and witnesses, conducted grand jury investigations, and obtained information from various sources. I was not a bulldog, but a professional investigator trained to obtain physical evidence and witness statements. I may have been considered aloof because I stayed at a distance from many department employees. After a period of time, I better understood the concept and became more agreeable and I accepted and adapted to the new idea. Rather than "take" information from sources with little collaboration from me, I began to share information. I shared as much information as I could considering the sensitivity of a criminal or administrative investigation. I shared information with the other administrations in the department, the FAA, Federal Highway Administration, and others. The transformation was amazing. Interactions became congenial and cooperative rather than sometimes antagonistic. I obtained more pertinent information from more sources faster. The word "customer" opened my eyes and opened communication between the OIG and department administrations.

The word "customer" also changed my attitude about how I conducted any type of investigation. My attitude changed from not speaking freely and staying at a distance to sharing as much information as I could without jeopardizing the investigation. My approach became matter of fact when I spoke to a subject of investigation. "This is who I am; this is what I do. A complaint has been made and I am here to gather the facts."

Service to the Community Is Not Forced

In some departments disclosure and openness are forced. Some departments are poorly led and are mismanaged. Some are a closed society not serving the public in the most sincere, earnest way, but in a way more common in past decades. Less progressive departments allow officers to provide service with contempt and disrespect, are reactive rather than proactive, have little interaction with citizens served, and bestow little value to desired outcomes. "Several police departments in the United States are or have been under federal consent decrees to initiate reforms in their respective agencies. Police departments in Pittsburgh, Pennsylvania; Steubenville, Ohio; Los Angeles, California; Detroit, Michigan; and the New Jersey State Police (NJSP) are or were signatories to separate decrees with the United States Department of Justice (USDOJ) and supervised by federal district courts." [5] In Steubenville "The United States alleges that officers of the Steubenville Police Department have engaged in a pattern or practice of conduct that deprives persons of rights, privileges, or immunities secured and protected by the Constitution and the laws of the United States." [6]

The 1997 decree continues:

→ The City shall develop and implement a training policy for all SPD officers.

→ The City shall develop and implement use of force policies that comply with applicable law and current professional standards.

→ The City shall develop, and require all officers to complete, a written report each time an SPD officer performs a search without a warrant (excluding searches incident to arrests, frisks, and pat downs), seizes any property without a warrant (excluding towing vehicles), or conducts a traffic stop, or an investigative stop based on suspicion of criminal activity (a stop authorized by *Terry v. Ohio*, 392 U.S. 1 (1968)).

Author's Note

Terry v. Ohio is a U.S. Supreme Court decision that held a police officer can stop a suspect on the street and frisk him without probable cause to arrest if the officer has reasonable suspicion the person has committed, is committing or is about to commit a crime and has a reasonable belief the person may be armed and dangerous. The decision held that the Fourth Amendment prohibition of unreasonable search and seizure is not violated.

→ SPD officers shall give detainees warnings required by *Miranda v. Arizona*, 384 U.S. 436 (1966), on taking a suspect into custody, without delay. The City shall randomly audit compliance with this requirement.

→ The City shall develop and implement an Internal Affairs policy and manual for the SPD, detailing policies and investigative procedures.

→ The City, by and through its officials, agents, employees, and successors, has an affirmative obligation to supervise, monitor, and discipline its officers.

→ The City shall develop a plan for maintaining information necessary for supervision and management of the SPD. Prior to implementation, the plan must be reviewed by the independent auditor and approved by the United States.

→ The City shall develop and implement a performance evaluation policy for officers.

→ Within 60 days after the entry of this Decree, the City and the United States shall together select an independent auditor who shall report on a quarterly basis the City's compliance with each provision of this Decree.

→ The City shall immediately provide copies of, and explain the terms of this Decree to all current and future officers and employees, and all City officials with oversight or responsibility for SPD operations, in order to ensure that they understand the requirements of this Decree and the necessity for strict compliance.

There are actually ninety-nine (99) stipulations under numerous categories, and as you can see from the few listed above, the City of Steubenville had to be told by the federal government many things of common knowledge. Be open and honest or you will be told to be.

Federal departments are not immune from mismanagement. Unrelated to law enforcement, but the most public example of failure in recent history, was the FEMA failure of a timely response in New Orleans in August 2005, immediately after Hurricane Katrina. If the facts were reported correctly, miscommunication and inaction were issues for both state and federal officials, but most federal failures are not as publicized or are blamed on warring politicians, not on conniving, self-centered, uninspired bureaucrats. Neither are federal agents immune from making dumb mistakes or committing criminal actions. However, federal agents do not have the same level of public interactions as local officers continually do and public scrutiny is not as intense.

Another Way to Use Community Policing to Protect Citizens

Techniques used to fight crime in the community can be and are used by a department or agency to fight internal misconduct. Techniques like problem-oriented policing have proven to be very effective.

"Problem-oriented policing is an approach to policing in which discrete pieces of police business (each consisting of a cluster of similar incidents, whether crime or acts of disorder, that the police are expected to handle) are subject to microscopic examination (drawing on the especially honed skills of crime analysts and the accumulated experience of operating field personnel) in hopes that what is freshly learned about each problem will lead to discovering a new and more effective strategy for dealing with it."[7]

"Problem-oriented policing places a high value on new responses that are preventive in nature, that are not dependent on the use of the criminal justice system, and that engage other public agencies, the community and the private sector, when their involvement has the potential for significantly contributing to the reduction of the problem."[8]

"Problem-oriented policing carries a commitment to implementing the new strategy, rigorously evaluating its effectiveness, and subsequently, reporting the results in ways that will benefit other police agencies and that will ultimately contribute to building a body of knowledge that supports the further professionalization of the police."[9]

In the internal affairs realm a technique similar to problem-oriented policing examines clusters of similar incidents of misconduct. These incidents are analyzed by experienced IA investigators and/or skilled intelligence analysts with experience in IA investigations. This analysis gives a fresh look at recurring problems that might lead to increased insight into a more effective approach to addressing misconduct. Like problem-oriented policing this strategy is preventative and engages supervisors, educators, policy makers, ethics trainers, and others to reduce misconduct. The strategy is periodically re-evaluated to make improvements and to increase the professionalism of all officers.

Several companies have been marketing computerized programs to analyze reports and activities to uncover anomalies. Many departments now use computerized data mining as an early warning or proactive system to identify misconduct.

Other Ways to Be Open

Broken Windows

Like problem-oriented policing, other techniques known and understood by officers can be or are used to control misconduct. The controversial but reportedly successful "broken windows" theory is an early warning system for community crime. The theory proposes a well-ordered urban environment that may prevent vandalism and crime. Similarly, a well-ordered department atmosphere and high standards may prevent misconduct and corruption. "One unrepaired broken window is a signal no one cares." [10] ***One unaddressed lapse of ethics is a signal no one cares.*** "We suggest that "untended" behavior also leads to the breakdown of community controls." [11] ***Untended behavior also leads to the breakdown of department policy and the rule of law.*** "...serious street crime flourishes in areas in which disorderly behavior goes unchecked. The unchecked panhandler is, in effect, the first broken window." [12] ***Serious misconduct flourishes in departments or agencies in which disorderly behavior goes unchecked. The unchecked minor policy violation is the first broken window.*** [Bold italics added by the author]. Therefore, the smallest policy violation should be enforced to control greater violations. The broken windows theory is controversial because it is more of a thought than a theory and some believe a department can be too zealous in enforcing the law, making order maintenance unrealistic. Unrealistic expectations cannot be placed on a law enforcement officer, although some departments or precincts/districts in a department may need a greater emphasis on ethics than others. Although a department with zero tolerance for crime may create an advantage in protecting the citizens it serves, I am talking out of both sides of my mouth when I say some misconduct will always be present because certain neighborhoods seek a strong effort by police to maintain order. Some misconduct will be overlooked because some citizens want protection that skirts the law only because street justice may be the only way to get justice.[13]

Citizen Satisfaction Survey

Along with community policing/problem-oriented policing and broken windows, a form of citizen surveys can also be used in the internal affairs realm. To some the following is controversial, maybe as controversial as other policing techniques, but it is a proactive measure to counter police misconduct. Many departments already use surveys to determine the quality of services provided to citizens. The survey I suggest may be similar but is focused on officer conduct.

Community policing is a partnership between the police and the citizens they serve. There is no one definition and community policing and practices vary. Over time police strategy and tactics in some departments changed to serve the needs of different communities. Citizen groups became more involved with police activities, and the police reached out to the community with, among other things, meetings and citizen volunteers, usually with a change of patrol techniques.

Officer misconduct can mean many things. Whatever the misconduct is, community leaders, business people, church ministers, social workers, and others know much about police activities. To identify covert misconduct, someone needs to be asked about it. For example:

Starting in the early 1980s, while an agent for DOT/OIG, I began conducting a bid rigging investigation involving contracts on federally funded highway projects. I say "investigation" but it was actually a survey because there were no concrete allegations, just a suspicion that a crime was being committed. Bid rigging is an act of collusion between two or more contractors-competitors, to determine among themselves who will be awarded a construction contract. In price fixing contractors agree what amount each will bid so one will not only be awarded a contract but at a higher price than the contract would normally be if each proposal was honestly submitted. In market allocation a contractor wins all contracts in a certain area.

At the time I was given the assignment, I was surprised to find I would not be working with an Assistant U.S. Attorney and federal grand jury, but alone, sometimes with a partner from the department or a state attorney general's office. I wondered without grand jury subpoenas who would speak to me about their involvement in potential criminal activity?

After preparing a two-page structured interview, I traveled among other investigations off and on over a five-year period to four Midwestern states. My efforts were successful only in one state, but the information I and others obtained by cold calling more than 100 construction contractors was amazing. Few contractors told the truth about their involvement in criminal actions, but enough information was gathered to successfully prosecute numerous cases. Other information gathered was stale, and prosecution was not possible. However, during interviews it was discovered, among many other revelations, that one contractor was assaulted in a state office building and his bid package stolen to eliminate his company from the competition. Other contractors secretly agreed to allow each company to take a turn at winning a contract while the others submitted complementary higher bids.

The point here is that if you ask, someone will tell you, eventually.

This type of inquiry will work in the internal affairs realm only with the cooperation of department or agency leadership along with the concurrence of elected officials. When you seek, you will find, and you had better be prepared for what you find. If there is not a chief with moral conviction or an elected official with an open agenda, plausible deniability will win the day. No questions asked, no information gained.

Some may find this survey a stretch and one that is not realistic in some areas with certain cultures. However, I agree with General George S. Patton, Jr., the famed World War II commander who said, "If everybody is thinking alike, then somebody isn't thinking." [14]

The Way You Ask the Question Makes the Difference

Anyone can ask survey questions, but in a community street environment, I suggest civilians or retired officers not associated with the department surveyed will be more effective. In fact many officers, even those assigned to internal affairs, may not want to get involved. But when all is said and done, extensive interview experience and professionalism are the most important requirements.

The scenario might be different in the federal realm. In most federal agencies, the clients contacted may have little to do with law enforcement officers, and the interaction will be different. Although not always true, the people contacted by federal agents are more likely to be business people or benefit recipients, the interactions focusing more on audits or white-collar crime than police actions relating to street crime. However, depending on the federal program, many interviewees can be street-smart individuals where different interview techniques will be required.

A structured interview must be specialized and focused on each specific audience and the information you hope to obtain. Remember, a survey is seeking to either substantiate or disprove rumors or suspicions. I used a structured interview to scrutinize the actions of a specific industry in various states. I am reluctant to use the word "allegation" because there was no specific knowledge of wrongdoing by any one person or business. The survey was a tool to determine what was going on in a specific industry that might warrant an investigation. Are there suspicions that bar owners are making payments to officers for special services or protection against liquor laws? Are cab drivers suspected of paying officers to avoid traffic or regulatory fines? Are recipients of Medicare payments suspected of collusion with medical professionals? Each interview is constructed with a slightly different focus, but each has the same objective.

Whatever the focus, the interview is at the person's home or place of business, not a so-called interrogation held at a police facility. It is a survey with a cordial reception and conduct, at least at the start. You are conducting a survey, not a criminal investigation, at least not yet. The people interviewed are in their own environment; they are not under arrest; they are free to leave or ask you to leave at anytime. After an introduction, an explanation of what the survey hopes to accomplish is appropriate. For a police department, the purpose of the survey is to ask citizens how they rate the service provided by the department. After the introduction, to put the person at ease, I always discussed the business, which allowed the interviewee to brag. From my experience with highway contractors, business owners appreciate and open up while discussing their success in the business world.

Remember there are no secrets in the department whose officers will surely know about the survey in the initial stages and for the business people the officers will interview. Even if specifics are not known, business owners and community leaders will shortly know what this survey is about after the first few interviews. Hundreds of interviews may be conducted with little or no concrete results, or many leads may be found that can lead to a successful investigation and prosecution. This survey may take months with no results, but then you just might find someone who will give you solid information. Even if no concrete information is obtained, there is still something called "voluntary compliance." The telephone lines will be burning, nerves will be rattled, and business as usual will stop; at least while the heat is on, the temperature will stay high as long as needed by the ones who care. The few who need the heat will get the point.

What Would Any Department or Agency Expect to Find from a Survey?

Not all departments may want to risk conducting the type of survey I suggest. Many will consider it a "fishing expedition" that could uncover unknown and unwanted revelations. I did not conduct a scientific survey to determine what types of misconduct could be found. However, I suggest a citizen satisfaction survey be conducted because of what I learned while in the law enforcement field and what I learned while conducting interviews for this book. Anyone in law enforcement or who follows the profession has heard many stories of misconduct.

These are a few of the more interesting relayed to me, certainly not an all inclusive list:

- An officer once traveled to a Midwestern department to pick up a prisoner. He was directed to the supervisor's office where he found the lieutenant with what appeared to be thousands of dollars on his desk in rows of neat piles. The lieutenant was not taken aback by an officer from another department seeing the loot, but merely gave an off-handed comment that it was a Friday night and the bagman was busy, the payments from area bars had just arrived.

- Officers, in uniform, accepting alcoholic drinks while on duty.

- Officers, on a day off and in uniform, accepting meal discounts for themselves and their family.

→ Officers, while on duty, conducting smash and grabs. Officers breaking a store window and walking away with the cash register.

→ Officers "spinning" a drunk: taking anything of value while literally spinning a drunken person.

→ Officers delivering bodies to certain funeral homes for a fee.

→ Officers going on "treasure hunts" when responding to the death of a person; looking through the descendant's property to find things of value.

→ Officers paying a supervisor for the privilege of using the traffic radar equipment. The fee is recovered the first hour and the next 7 hours of use is profit.

Private Industry Example of Openness

Johnson & Johnson Tells It Like It Is

In the late 1800s, Robert Wood Johnson together with his two brothers founded the well-known company, Johnson & Johnson, the medical supply giant. From the beginning, Johnson believed in saving and improving the lives of anyone he could by manufacturing products to confront disease and advance public health. In the mid-1930s Johnson published a pamphlet, *Try Reality: A Discussion of Hours, Wages and the Industrial Future.* In the publication Johnson urged other capitalists to join in his efforts to create a new sense of corporate responsibility. Johnson believed not only his corporation but all business had a responsibility to customers, employees, the community, and stockholders.[15]

Then in 1943, Johnson published the corporate credo, a one-page document outlining his beliefs in responsibility to others. Johnson directed his staff to make the credo part of their daily business life. The Johnson & Johnson Credo is a value system that serves as a moral design to guide daily decisions made by management and employees. The credo places the needs and welfare of the people served, their customers, above all else. "It also speaks to the responsibilities we have to our employees, to the communities in which we live and work and the world community, and to our shareholders. We believe our Credo is a blueprint for long-term growth and sustainability that's as relevant today as when it was written." [16]

The Johnson & Johnson Policy on Business Conduct goes even further. The Policy on Business Conduct outlines the responsibilities of managers and employees and defines the conduct that is expected of each employee. Discussed are conflicts of interest and compliance with numerous state and federal laws and regulations. The policy discusses compliance with antitrust, environmental, consumer products, labor and security laws, the sensitivity of political activities and contributions, respect for trade secrets and confidential information, and the importance of company funds, assets, information, and complete documentation and accurate maintenance of books and records.[17]

To enforce the policy outlined is the responsibility of managers and employees.

- → "All managers shall be responsible for the enforcement of and compliance with this Policy ...
- → Appropriate managers will periodically be required to certify compliance with this Policy.
- → All employees are responsible for complying with this Policy. Any employee having information concerning any prohibited or unlawful act shall promptly report such matter to ...
- → Employees can write to ... anonymously at the Company's Headquarters ...
- → Employees should be advised of this reporting obligation and encouraged to report any prohibited or unlawful activities of which they are aware ...
- → The Corporate Internal Audit Department has audit programs with procedures to assist in monitoring compliance with this Policy." [18]

The key to the Policy on Business Conduct is disclosure. "Any employee who has a question about whether any situation in which he or she is involved amounts to a conflict of interest or the appearance of one should disclose the pertinent details, preferably in writing, to his or her supervisor ... The end result of the process of disclosure, discussion and consultation may well be approval of certain relationships or transactions on the ground that, despite appearances, they are not harmful to the Company. But all conflicts and appearances of conflict of interest are prohibited, even if they do not harm the Company, unless they have gone through this process."[19]

Finally, The Johnson & Johnson document *The Right Course, Everyday Compliance—An Introductory Guide For Our Employees* outlines how decision-making can be safeguarded "from both the appearance and the fact of undue and improper financial influence." The guide discusses how single acts of misconduct can result in multiple issues of civil and criminal sanctions and the devastating results such conduct can have on an organization and its mission. Nothing is left to chance.[20]

The Proof Is in the Pudding

In the fall of 1982, seven people in the Chicago area died when they ingested Extra-Strength Tylenol capsules. It was later found that poison-laced bottles were placed in seven Chicago area stores. In response to the situation rather than deny, deny, deny, Johnson & Johnson issued a nationwide alert, recalled 31 million Tylenol bottles, which reportedly cost the company $125 million, inspected all factories and established a crisis hotline.

A retired corporate executive employed by Johnson & Johnson for over 25 years acknowledged the company Credo was a part of day-to-day culture. Many difficult business decisions were made by referring to the Credo of integrity. Assessments of employee compliance to Credo values were ongoing. Failures were corrected; the Credo is a guiding beacon with a tough management philosophy as a guide.[21]

Case Study

You are an investigator for an Office of Inspector General (OIG) in a department of the federal government. Over an extended period the OIG has received rumors that security officers at a distant department location have been stealing the contents of boxcars in a railroad yard outside the facility. Specific facts have never been received, and an initial covert review has not developed any actionable information.

You were recently told by your supervisor a review of the department will take place in the near future by the Government Accountability Office (GAO). The first areas to be reviewed include the facility close to where the boxcar thefts are taking place. The results of a recent citizen satisfaction survey indicated several mayors of communities surrounding the facility have concerns about environmental safety and the heavy-handed actions of some security officers when patrolling the outside perimeter of the facility.

The chief of the security force has held numerous meetings and discussions with all personnel to express the seriousness of ethical lapses along with the seriousness of the upcoming review. The chief discussed his expectations and the penalties for criminal and policy violations.

The security chief wants everything in the open so the community leaders will know the department is doing all it can to work well with the surrounding communities. When you tell the chief and facility manager that the OIG does not investigate unsubstantiated rumors, you receive a telephone call from your supervisor instructing you to immediately open an investigation.

Shortly after you open up an investigation on the rumors, the FBI indicts three security officers for theft of interstate shipments. The indictments confirm the rumors. One officer who was involved was not indicted and is testifying against the three indicted officers.

You open an investigation on the one unindicted officer, Hugh Dumass, and find he was an unwitting conspirator. He gave the FBI items stolen from railroad shipments saying he did not realize they were stolen property. You understand Officer Dumass made a statement to no one in particular, "now I am going to be rolled over the coals by the OIG."

Case Study Questions

Answer the following questions in one narrative response.

1. *What is a table of offenses and penalties and how can the table help leadership express ethical standards and show fairness by the internal affairs function?*

2. *Discuss the Douglas Factors. How can they help or hurt a federal employee when deciding disciplinary action? How do the factors show fairness?*

3. *What is a citizen satisfaction survey? How can it uncover community concerns of officer wrong doing?*

Questions for Discussion

Answer each of the following questions in a separate response.

1. Analyze the broken windows theory as it could be used with police personnel. Give the pros and cons.

2. Discuss ways the Johnson & Johnson Company influences and impresses upon employees the importance of ethics.

Notes

1. Briscoe, Lennie played by Orback, Jerry. (10 Feb 1999.] TV drama *Law & Order*, Episode "Hunters" 9-194. *Law & Order* Alphabetical Episode Guide with Memorable Quotes.
2. Sides, Hampton. (May 2002). *Ghost Soldiers.* Anchor Books. p. 238.
3. Engells, Thomas, E. (Jan/Feb 2001). Defensible punitive discipline: The application of the Douglas Factors. *Campus Law Enforcement Journal.* Hartford: vol. 31, Iss. 1; pg. 17. Retrieved from ProQuest.
4. Geller, Bill, & Charlotte-Mecklenburg Police Department. (2005). *The Pursuit of Excellence—Employee Conduct: Investigations & Discipline, A Guidebook for the Public and Our Employees On What We Do and Why We Do It.* U.S. Department of Justice, Office of Community Oriented Policing Services. Grant # 2002-HSWX-0020.
5. LaSalle, Gerard, Ph.D. Complying with a Consent Decree. Retrieved July 7, 2009, from CALEA.org/online/newsletter/N091/ consent decree.htm.
6. United States Department of Justice. (1997). Consent Decree. In the United States District Court for the Southern District of Ohio,

Eastern Division; *United States of America, plaintiff v. City of Steubenville, Steubenville Police Department, Steubenville City Manager, in his capacity as director of public safety, and Steubenville Civil Service Commission, defendants.* Retrieved from http://www.justice.gov/crt/about/spl/documents/steubensa.php.

7. Goldstein, Herman. (2001). Center for Problem-Oriented Policing. http://www.popcenter.org/about/?p=whatiscpop.
8. Ibid.
9. Ibid.
10. Kelling, George, L., & Wilson, James, Q. (Mar 1982). Broken Windows, The police and neighborhood safety. The Atlantic Online. Retrieved from http://www.theatlantic.com/magazine/archive/1982/03/broken-windows/4465/.
11. Ibid.
12. Ibid.
13. Ibid.
14. Patton, George S., Jr. General George S. Patton Quotes. Retrieved from wwwlgeneralpatton.com/quotes.
15. Gurowitz, Margaret. (16 Mar 2009). The Story of Johnson & Johnson and Its People: Try Reality. Johnson & Johnson Services, Inc. Retrieved from http://www.kilmerhouse.com/2009/03/try-reality/.
16. Johnson & Johnson Services, Inc. Our Management Approach. Our Credo: Our Guiding Philosophy. Retrieved from http://www.jnj.com/connect/about-jnj/management-approach/.
17. Johnson & Johnson Services, Inc. Policy On Business Conduct. Retrieved from http://www.investor.jnj.com/governance/conduct.cfm.
18. Ibid.
19. Ibid.
20. Johnson & Johnson Services, Inc. The Right Course, Everyday Compliance - An Introductory Guide For Our Employees. Retrieved from http://www.jnj.com/wps/wcm/connect/13445d804f5568a4a06ea41bb31559c7/the-right-course.pdf?MOD=AJPERES.
21. Corporate executive (retired) who will remain anonymous. (15 Oct 2010). Johnson & Johnson Services, Inc. Interview.

CHAPTER ELEVEN
The Future Outlook of the Internal Affairs Function

No one early in my lifetime could have predicted the remarkable advancements in technology that have taken law enforcement from pencil reports to computers in patrol cars. As electronics become more sophisticated, the potential for communication and identification capabilities seems to be unlimited. Currently both federal and state governments are pressing for radio frequency identification tags (RFID) and various other forms of high-tech IDs. We already have electronic passports, and other e-cards are on the horizon.[1] But changes in law enforcement, in internal investigations, or management techniques will certainly include other electronic developments for surveillance, identification, and training.

The future of the internal affairs function will also be affected by generational differences, the further breakdown of gender bias, ethnic diversity, media attention, and the presence of politically sensitive subjects. What might be a more difficult evolution will be positive changes in the internal affairs process. How will interactions among the players in the process; departmental and community leaders, unions, the rank and file and others; change when future generations have a more open and united agenda?

It would be naïve to say misconduct can be eradicated. But misconduct can be reduced or regulated by enhanced technology, improved ethics, strong leaders, proactive measures by management and the internal affairs function, parallel programs with private industry, and newly empowered citizens. Improved initiatives and strong management support throughout the chain of command will improve attitudes and foster cultural change where change is needed. New attitudes will change how the law enforcement community currently pulls on the heart strings of the public when an officer is harmed, but at the same time ponders how citizens suffer from officers' misconduct.

One also should consider current attitudes on Wall Street, in the U.S. Congress, the banking industry, and other institutions where greed and self-interest rage. Excess in politics and corporate boardrooms is eroding the safety and happiness of the common man while enhancing the enrichment of a few. U.S. law enforcement is decentralized but focused on a universal goal: service to and protection of citizens. The reform of policing in America must continue to develop through training, technology and ideology. Professional law enforcement officers must influence the future social order even more than their predecessors. Historically police have resisted ethical changes and always seem to be behind the power curve. Police ethics seem to improve only after society demands it. The players in the internal affairs process must work together to demand true ethical reform, not just cyclical makeshift changes. A culture must be created that makes any law enforcement officer who violates ethical boundaries to ask himself "what is wrong with me?" The culture shift may not affect all officers, but officers who care to be the best they can be will feel supported.

The Role of Diversity

Ethics also must take a greater role in law enforcement because of the increase in diversity. The all-male force was forever changed in 1972, when Congress passed an amendment to Title VII of the Civil Rights Act of 1964 prohibiting state and local agencies from job discrimination based on gender. I have seen no effect on officer ethics because of the increase in female law officers other than I understand a female officer is less likely to be accused of misconduct. However, I believe the increase in foreign-born officers, and officers born U.S citizens but with foreign-born parents who are entering the law enforcement profession in greater numbers may have an effect on the level of personal and departmental ethics. I mentioned previously that many parts of the world have cultures whose ethics include a greater emphasis on personal success, profits, and self-aggrandizement. Multiculturalism and diversity must be appreciated, but at the same time a training regimen must be in place to bind all into an accepted ethical standard.

In addition, American "citizenship" in the twenty-first century has taken on a new significance. The *Washington Post* reported in 2010 that there are dozens of consulting firms in the United States that cater to Chinese expectant mothers. While pregnant, the mothers travel to the U.S. long enough to give birth.[2] The Fourteenth Amendment to the U.S. Constitution gives citizenship to anyone born in the United States. Reportedly the point of the travel and U.S. birth, other than to circumvent China's one child per family rule, is to obtain American citizenship and a U.S. passport in order to, later in life, take advantage of, among other things, free or affordable education in the United States. Apparently, loyalty to the United States has little to do with the economic advantages of being a U.S. citizen. Other world players are surely taking advantage of the opportunity and more sinister reasons may also be part of the birthing paradox.

The hiring of more ethnically diverse officers also will necessitate expanded background investigations. Merely investigating U.S. domestic activities of a foreign-born applicant or a U.S. born applicant who is an international traveler may only scratch the surface of due diligence requirements. Since September 11, 2001, the importance of due diligence in an applicant's background is essential to national security

Generational Diversity

Generation Y is defined as individuals born sometime after 1974. They are stereotyped as being loyal to themselves, but not necessarily to their employers. Those entering public service, on the other hand, may not be as self-serving as the generation is portrayed. However, new officers may ask, "what can you do for me?" rather than what I and other baby boomers asked, which was, "how can I help?"

Then there are members of the Net Generation, described as individuals born after 1982. They were introduced to computers at a young age, many at home, and others the first day at kinder care. Talking to each other, some total strangers, is more technological communication rather than the typical face to face or telephonic discussions engaged in by their parents. They speak a new language with ease that is foreign to older generations. Their global world is smaller than previous generations. They multitask; blogging, texting to the person sitting next to them, telling friends and strangers their inner most thoughts and how they saved by buying their clothes on the Internet.

Reportedly a breakdown of camaraderie is occurring in some departments because of the new generation. Some younger officers are shunning social interactions; participation in after-hour retirement farewells is for the older generations. In one department an officer was injured on the job and was sent to the hospital, unaccompanied, and was alone until his family arrived. Hours later a supervisory officer showed up for just minutes and left. The new generations may not be as loyal to each other as was the boomer generation. An environment must be created that motivates overlapping "new generations" to follow policy, be loyal to their organization and most importantly be loyal to the public they serve.

In addition, a law enforcement organization must get past "the way it always has been" mentality. Many departments and agencies are striving to move into the twenty-first century, but during my research I encountered several local departments still living culturally in the 1970s. Furthermore, while driving extensively through the U.S. during the summer and fall of 2008, I saw numerous billboards announcing FBI and Border Patrol vacancies. I suppose there is still a place for advertising familiar to the grandparents and even great grandparents of the newest generation, but venues of advertising familiar to the new generation need to be put in place. Of course, many departments, including the FBI and the Border Patrol have entered the twenty-first century and are actively participating in various Internet settings. However, electronic advertising may still be foreign to some in authority. In the twenty-first century some attracted to employment by static advertising may not have the skills needed for the position advertised.

Training

The vast majority of law enforcement officers are good people; they want to do well, but many are viewed by the public with a sense of suspicion because of the actions and attitudes of a few. Some administrators will look the other way to avoid confronting misconduct for various reasons. Cosmetic changes are made to an organization to appease cynical officers and suspicious citizens, but training and leadership are the keys to prevent misconduct and citizen complaints. Training always must teach service to citizens as the officer's primary duty.

However, the training of officers to instill the highest level of ethical conduct, to focus on controlling emotions, and to instill the realization that "To Serve and Protect" is not just a logo on the side of a patrol car may not receive the same emphasis as officer safety. Over time, police culture has changed from a culture of unchallenged authority and unchecked corruption to what we have today: individual misconduct or corruption usually confined to a few. In the short term the impact of the law enforcement community policing itself must be accelerated. The law enforcement profession cannot wait for another negative media event before additional strides in ethical reform are taken. The internal affairs function cannot wait for the players in the internal affairs process to agree on a reform agenda. There never will be total agreement. The players have too much at stake; too many political and personal agendas to reach a consensus.

Personal v. Impersonal Training

I received ethics training, often called integrity training, numerous times over my career. However, in the mid-1990s, I began receiving computerized ethics training that was less than effective. I was reminded of my obligations through reading and then answering multiple-choice questions, but ethics training became a chore, not something I spent much time thinking about. A computerized test was taken after reading pages of what was correct, legal, or appropriate, and what was improper or against policy or criminal law. Often after someone took the test, the answers were passed around to avoid wasting time; there were more important things to accomplish. The attitude was "get it done"; the importance of the training was secondary.

We are in the computer age and computerized training has its place, but ethics training must be given the same importance as SWAT, firearms, and self-defense training. It should mirror instruction of other police disciplines by adding role-playing and simulated situations. Along with personal instruction, ethics training should also educate; officers must be taught to perform their duties ethically while at the same time learn why performance must be a certain way.

In the twenty-first century with technologically savvy young people entering law enforcement computerization will take a bigger role in ethics training. Computerized training has taken large strides in the first decade of the century. Computer games are recruiting and training many professions. A massively multiplayer online role playing game (MMORPG) is a type of video game where a large number of people interact with one another in a virtual, persistent game world. Each player assumes a character role and controls the actions of that character which interacts with other characters assumed and controlled by other real world players. A virtual world in an MMORPG is an online community that exists through a computer based online environment that persists even after a player leaves the game. The world is a 24/7 environment where a player can join any number of others in an environment that continues to exist and change even when all players are not present. In one popular MMORPG, World of Warcraft®, millions of players worldwide take on the role of heroes in a medieval fantasy world, organizing into large groups called guilds to battle powerful monsters and each other.

A similar platform but less costly is the multiplayer online game. Unlike the MMORPG the multiplayer online game does not have a persistent world and does not require the administrative expense. The United States Army sponsors the multiplayer online game "America's Army," which "provides players with the most authentic military experience available, from exploring the development of Soldiers in individual and collective training to their deployment in simulated missions in the War on Terror." [3]

Science Applications International Corporation's (SAIC) OLIVE online interactive virtual environment products provide "private, virtual worlds [which] allow your organization to practice, rehearse, and operate in safe, realistic environments that replicate the real ones in your world. This enables organizations to learn from mistakes in the security and safety of the virtual world, so they can avoid them in the real one."[4] Using a similar design, a multiplayer game and simulated environment can be hosted by a law enforcement department or more likely by a contract supplier who can create, control, and evolve a game world with the goal of training officers. In a law enforcement environment a player could simulate patrolling streets, the conduct of investigations, interactions with citizens and other role players, make arrests and testify in court all along being exposed to ethical dilemmas, difficult public/community exchanges, compromising circumstances, and tempting situations. These online scenarios could provide virtual world, authentic experiences for basic and advanced training.

A field training officer, one with good work habits and street experience, is a good choice for developing ethics training. In my experience ethics training is developed by well-meaning people with no first-hand knowledge of the actual work performed or temptations encountered.

Technology—Someone Is Always Watching

Technology always is evolving, with some improvements and new systems developing more rapidly than others. Dashboard cameras have protected officers from wrongful complaints for at least a decade. The cameras have also protected citizens from overzealous officers. Video is becoming more and more a part of security and law enforcement. Neighborhood watch cameras, store security cameras, ATM cameras, pistol cameras, cameras carried on various parts of the uniform, and videos of the executions of search and arrest warrants all are part of the way enhanced technology can help decrease misconduct and unjust complaints. Do not forget the impact of the media and citizens with video and cell phone cameras. "Videophones let citizen reporters provide information from an incident before first responders are on scene and perimeters are established." [5] The term "crowd sourcing" means the act of taking a job customarily held by an employee and outsourcing the job to a large group of people in the form of an open call. In the law enforcement sense, crowd sourcing might mean another form of community policing where citizens take videos of police misconduct and report it to Internal Affairs or another similar organization. In many cities and states, however, it is illegal for a citizen to video police in action and arrests have been made. On the other hand, reportedly courts have generally decided against police and have held that it is legal to record public police activity.

To that end, because of new and emerging technology, it is important that officers be reminded they are being watched.

They always have been watched, but new technology is recording actions for instant replay. In addition, new technology lets citizens feel more empowered and less afraid of reporting misconduct by law enforcement officers.

Camera awareness should be part of ethics training because it is apparent some officers need to be told someone is watching. On July 2, 2009, the Associated Press reported that the police chief of an Ohio township retired after a dashboard camera from a police cruiser was viewed. It was discovered that the chief and a female officer were kissing and caressing in the cruiser while a prisoner sat in the back seat.[6]

In early 2009, a Hollywood, Florida, police officer rear-ended a female driver. It was determined the driver was drunk and was arrested. However, it was discovered five months later in July 2009 that the arresting officer, along with others, conspired to frame the woman for the accident the officer caused. "Saying she was hammered anyway, one of the arrogant, brick-headed defenders of justice (that is a descriptive quote from the news article, not this author's comment) is heard saying how he will do a little Walt Disney with his accident report and put the wreck in the woman's lap." The amazing part of this story is that several officers were heard "very clearly laughing and conspiring within earshot" of a patrol car dashboard camera.[7]

James Howe said, "I believe police officers can also be affected when their work is being watched, and they know they are being observed. For example, when my department goes through their accreditation process with CALEA [Commission on Accreditation for Law Enforcement Agencies, Inc.], everyone is on pins and needles due to the amount of pressure and oversight present, both from CALEA and the department itself. Officers increase production (not necessarily arresting more people, but they finish reports in a timely manner and follow the rules to the letter) and spend a little more time ensuring they are doing things the right way the first time. Another example is about five years ago my department went to a supervisor review program, which required all supervisors to review arrest reports for accuracy, probable cause, and general spelling and grammar mistakes. A healthy portion of the officers began taking classes to improve their grammar, spelling, and overall writing abilities, and the prosecutor's office reported an increase in convictions and better plea deals after the program's implementation. Civil suits against officers and the department also decreased during the time frame. The officers knew they were being observed, and they had no desire to be called to [on] the carpet for a bad arrest report. The illumination on the reports was what it took to turn the problem around, and the officers responded by writing better reports and were recognized for their efforts." [8]

Although officers should be taught that someone is always watching, officers should not be taught to act ethically just because of the possibility of surveillance or "being caught." Ethics must be taught, learned, and embraced as a way of life.

Tracking Behavior by Computer

The Air Force Institute of Technology (AFIT) has developed technology that can help in identifying problem employees by analyzing email activity. Although originally developed to identify insider threats and recognize security violations, intelligence lapses, and subversion, the technology can also be used as an early warning system in law enforcement.

Dr. Gilbert Peterson, PhD, an AFIT Associate Professor, believes the information "extracted may be useful for identifying misconduct or corruption. Although the analysis is not intended to be used as a decision-making or end-all-be-all tool, it can be used by management as a data indicator of an individual who may need help, guidance, or just attention. The information indicator can have a lot of meanings, from this person may be at risk for committing suicide to having behavior that is potentially improper. This technology could fit fairly well into any organization's personnel management process, whether it is human resources, direct supervisor interaction, or internal affairs activities." [9]

According to Dr. Peterson, the software performs text mining and builds graphs that connect individuals who send emails about the same and similar topics. A second graph of direct emails between individuals is also built. For example, the first graph could show that both individuals are interested in a certain personnel issue; the second graph could show that both have sent emails between each other that mention the same issue. In other words, if there is a topic of concern, the graphs could be analyzed to confirm or refute suspicions.

If an individual emails about a topic, but isn't directly emailing individuals in the organization about the topic, then there may be a concern that they are leaking information. For example, if an individual is emailing about narcotics but isn't on the narcotics squad and isn't emailing individuals on the narcotics squad, then the behavior may be of concern. Of course, it could all be part of a case they are working on as well, therefore the technology is not an end-all be-all tool or signal. The technology is statistically based, and can only be an indicator for further investigation, and should not be considered as evidence.[10]

"In addition, we overlap this information with topics on general hobbies and outside interests. If an individual is not emailing others about their hobbies, they may be being ostracized (either their doing or their coworkers doing). This can be a general indicator of a lack of connection to the organization and possibly disgruntlement. At the furthest end, disconnecting from social contacts is a signal of potential suicide risk. In terms of insider threat and organizational risk, disgruntled individuals are less likely to act in the organizations best interests."[11]

Departments and agencies will continue to proactively use the intelligence profession to collect and analyze information with the focus on suspicious activities of officers. In addition, more departments and agencies will compare information already available in various data bases, such as information collected on the date, time, and location of crimes, and time, attendance, and location of officers, to identify suspicious anomalies.

The Media

The media will continue to take a role in reporting police misconduct. How the media report the news has changed rapidly along with how the media gather the news. My children, all in their early 30s, do not read many newspapers or magazines. When they want to know the latest news, they search the Internet on their iPad for the information of interest. High school and college students are even more attuned to electronic communication. "... people under 20 generally don't get their news from daily newspapers or TV stations, not even from AM or FM radio. If they're interested in what's happening, they find out from Google, Yahoo, YouTube and other service providers." [12] Since 2008, reports have increased regarding the bankruptcy or demise of various well-known metropolitan newspapers. Opening a newspaper still published, you may find your favorite columnist or comic strip no longer available. Local television news is now competing with numerous 24-hour cable news outlets. Progressive departments will continue to focus on electronic communication as a major avenue in information collection and the hiring process.

"Innovative communicators have long recognized the need to get their messages out using the newest technology. While *The New York Times* and *The Washington Post* struggle with falling circulation and loss of advertisers, new communicators are moving ahead in leaps and bounds ... The U.S. Army uses the Internet as a recruiting tool with its amazing successful game, America's Army ... In Vancouver, the city police department created a virtual-life site as part of its recruiting campaign to hire 'cyber-cops.'[13] It successfully attracted young men and women to the possibility of a career in policing who wouldn't have been interested in the traditional methods of going to job fairs with a booth, some pamphlets and uniformed personnel." [14]

Crime reporting is also going through a metamorphosis as mentioned in the technology discussion. "Governments can't control the public's view of incidents the way they once did as the official voice of authority." [15] Many times citizens are doing the reporting to the media before 911 receives the information. Allowing the media inside the outer perimeter at an incident location, but outside the inner perimeter may be problematic because the media are now multifaceted. But there are still things reported by electronic media that will never change.

Media Characterization of Internal Affairs

As police officials learned in the twentieth century, especially during civil rights protests, the media can be a friend or foe to a police agency. As the twenty-first century matures police leaders will deepen their embrace of the media for assistance in reporting and solving crimes, and to publish accurate information. Leaders will use the media to champion police actions and budgets. A leader who supports a strong internal affairs function and one who wants to defeat a negative perception of the function will use the media to portray the function at its best.

Hoping to generate some interest in portraying the function in a positive, rather than negative way in film media I sent the following letter to the Writer's Guild of America – West.

September 25, 2009

Writer's Guild of America – West
7000 West Third Street
Los Angeles, CA
ATTN: Mr. Patric M. Verrone, President

Dear Mr. Verrone,

I am an adjunct professor of criminal justice for American Military University. I am writing a diary of my experiences regarding employee investigations and conducting research into the internal affairs process [function] in law enforcement. During my career and while doing research I have developed concerns over how the process [function] is perceived by law enforcement officers and how it is portrayed in the media.

The purpose for writing you is to ask that my concerns be brought to the attention of your members in the hope that a more level position be taken regarding the characterization of the internal affairs process [function] and the professional investigators who conduct employee investigations. Over the years television and film have portrayed law enforcement officers from keystone cops to scientific genius. It is common knowledge the media plays a role in today's society affecting the thoughts and actions of many. Over time the media has portrayed law enforcement officers as professionals, but has continued to brand the investigation of wrongdoing as flawed and internal investigators as scoundrels. As president of the Writer's Guild of America – West, I hope you can bring about a more unbiased portrayal of the entire scope of the internal affairs process [function].

During my 30 plus years in the security and law enforcement fields, I, like most of my contemporaries, disliked internal affairs "types" only because they had the authority to investigate other law enforcement officers. My eyes and attitude were opened when I first began conducting employee investigations. However, many of my contemporaries without the experience of conducting internal investigations, continued to view the internal investigative process [function] as unfair and internal investigators as back stabbers and incompetents. Among several reasons for the overall opinion is the highly visible, biased portrayal of the internal affairs process [function] in film media.

Although I have over 10 years experience conducting and supervising employee investigations, during my research even I was surprised at some of the information I found. Although there is strong difference of opinion, many law enforcement officers do not believe in the "code of silence" and studies have shown a strong propensity or willingness of many officers to report others for engaging in misconduct. It was reported in THE POLICE CHIEF magazine in 2003, that contrary to Hollywood portrayals, a significant number of police officers will neither tolerate nor ignore serious misconduct within their department. During a study of the Houston Police Department records between 1992 and 2002, of the 11 years examined it was found in seven years more than 50 percent of complaints investigated were made by fellow officers rather than citizens. Similar statistics were found in seven other departments across the nation. Further, the Charlotte-Mecklenburg, NC, Police Department reported that in 2003, 62% of department internal investigations were self-initiated.

In 1994, the Mollen Commission issued a report regarding how the New York City Police Department addressed corruption. The report indicated many department members considered the Internal Affairs Bureau as a "white socks" operation; one that harassed hardworking members for minor violations rather than focusing on those officers involved in serious misconduct. The Commission also found that many members of NYPD were distrustful of internal affairs personnel because of perceived incompetence and the belief internal affairs investigators were out of touch with reality.

After the commission interviewed a number of investigators who were compelled to work in internal affairs, an entire new story emerged. In hindsight the officers believed they were better for the experience. For the most part, their fear of an incompetent work environment was unfounded. Many of the officers found internal investigative methods and resources to be sophisticated compared to other bureaus in which they had worked. They also found that most of the people working in internal affairs were skilled members of the department rather than outcasts that they had been expecting to encounter.

There are numerous opinions on this subject matter; as many opinions as there are police officers or federal agents. Although there are many opinions, not all are as biased as portrayed in the media. Many believe the perception portrayed in the media is the reality. I suggest when a law enforcement advisor is used, an officer with internal affairs experience be employed to give a more realistic angle especially when employee misconduct is included.

I appreciate your time and consideration of my concerns. I would appreciate an acknowledgment or rebuttal. I can be reached at insideinternalaffairs@gmail.com.

Sincerely,

John F. Hein
Adjunct Professor
American Military University
Criminal Justice Programs

As much as I hoped, I did not receive a reply. I did show the letter and discuss my concerns with a ranking member of the NYPD. "You must understand that a television program or feature film is not a documentary. Even though technical advisors educate television and film makers on proper procedure, there are times when entertainment trumps accuracy. They are in the entertainment business and if more people are going to watch the show by making Internal Affairs vicious or incompetent that is what they are going to write."[16]

Lon Eilders stated, "I served in IA for four years in the early 1990s and came to some conclusions about the process [function] from both an accused officer's position and an IA investigator's perspective. Much of what we see portrayed on TV is for dramatic effect and has little to do with how IA actually operates. If I had tried to conduct myself in the same manner as television IA investigators, someone would have probably knocked my head off. That aggressive posturing works on the tube, but not in real life." [17]

I am sure medical and other professionals as well as law enforcement officers find fault with media portrayals. The portrayal of an internal affairs investigator may enhance drama as does some criminal portrayals. In portrayals on television, officers arrive at a crime scene and arrest a subject who is then prosecuted and sentenced all in an hour's time. Real-life juries have found defendants in criminal trials not guilty when overwhelming evidence indicates otherwise. But, one must understand the jury members may have relied on their vast knowledge of evidentiary value and forensic science learned during their many hours watching *CSI: Miami.* I have always marveled at Detective John Munch in *Law & Order, Special Victims Unit,* as he obtains mud sheets (telephone records) or financial documents in record time (don't forget the suspect must be sentenced by the end of the program) when in reality these records may take days, weeks, and even months to obtain. I marvel, but I have always enjoyed watching the program even though at times I roll my eyes. Entertainment or self-interest always seems to triumph reality.

Although not a law enforcement officer, in July 2010, the media portrayed Shirley Sherrod, a U.S. Department of Agriculture official as a racist. Ms. Sherrod, a black woman, was made to appear as a racist when a video appeared on the Internet. She was subsequently forced to resign her high-level position.

After the video excerpt was broadcast worldwide, it was discovered the out-of-context video only showed part of a speech given by Ms. Sherrod. The full video told a different story of Ms. Sherrod explaining her thought process and how she understood that race was less important than other things in life. After the truth became known apologies came from all corners to include one along with a job offer from the Obama administration.[18]

Discipline

I have seen how positive discipline is used to "save" an employee and save the federal government a considerable amount of time and money going through the firing process, and if successful, hiring and training a replacement. More and more departments and agencies will take the high road, which will not only save time and money, but instill more trust among all parties.

I did not always experience positive discipline in the federal government. While I was a special agent with the Internal Revenue Service in Chicago, everyone ran for cover when a mistake was made. I recall little positive feedback when a policy was violated. IRS policy, like the tax code, could fill Yankee Stadium. A counseling session was a dreaded experience with a hardheaded group manager, or worse yet, a no-holds-barred division chief who took great pride in scolding and belittling an agent for a minor, but important policy violation. Slicing a pound of flesh was the norm. Trust between an agent and supervisor was earned after hours, out of earshot of others and rarely known outside a select few.

The Los Angeles Police Department (LAPD) decided in 2008 that positive, rather than negative discipline is better received by officers and also more effective. Less punitive punishment requires officers to recognize areas of improvement, which causes an adult to learn. LAPD is moving toward being more thoughtful regarding discipline and is shifting away from inflexibility.

I have found, as I stated before, when decisions are made, the questions asked should include "what is best for the department, what is best for the citizens served?" Now in the twenty-first century add, "What is best for the employee?"

Department Culture and the Economy

The economy has wreaked havoc with public sector budgets for several years. Unemployment and stagnant economic growth have brought a downturn in real estate and retail sales tax revenues. Cities, counties, and states are laying off public employees to help balance uncertain budgets. In Oakland, CA, "In the wake of the city's laying off 80 police officers last month, Chinatown is leading a new trend in the crime-ridden city: an increase in privately financed public safety. [The Chinatown Chamber of Commerce] has asked every business owner to install a street-facing camera. A new Chinatown security force, perhaps staffed by armed guards, could be on the streets as soon as next month ... The layoffs, which helped close a budget deficit of more than $30 million, eliminated a community-policing program that assigned officers to walk their beats and attend neighborhood meetings. Now some residents are pooling resources to restore a law-enforcement presence. The affluent Montclair District in the Oakland Hills and the Kings Estates neighborhood in East Oakland are also looking into private patrols."[19]

"Oakland's budget deficit is expected to grow for the next five years. Its crime rate is among the highest in the state. The City Council hopes to put a $360-per-household parcel tax on the November ballot to restore the officers, avoid more layoffs and balance the budget. But Mr. Chan indicated the residents of Chinatown might prefer to put that money into a private program. [But] 'After paying taxes, it should be the job of the city to provide sufficient police services to each community,' he said." [20]

It has been my experience that sworn law enforcement officers generally have a disdain for private security guards. I always have seen reluctance by many to work with or get close to a "rent a cop." However, this strained relationship will change as budgets shrink and sworn and private officers are compelled to work closely. Depending upon the department culture and the hiring practices of citizen and business groups and the due diligence of private security firms, this closeness may create ethics violations. As the two occupations interact, the ethics of one will affect the other. The better trained may increase the professionalism of the less trained, but the less scrutinized may decrease ethical practices.

Economic circumstances will temper the strain between public police and private security by bringing the two occupations closer together. Experienced officers will continue working past normal retirement because of the economic downturn. Others will retire and become supervisors and managers in the private security sector. Younger officers, the ones most likely to be laid off, will become temporary private security officers until the economy recovers. This scenario demands that all public law enforcement officers embrace ethics as a way of life.

Another factor is "Budget cuts are forcing police around the country to stop responding to fraud, burglary and theft calls as officers focus limited resources on violent crime. Cutbacks ... have forced police to tell residents to file their own reports—online or in writing—for break-ins and other lesser crimes."[21]

"We've been doing policing more or less the same way for a couple hundred years," said Barry Krisberg, a criminologist at the Center for Criminal Justice at the University of California, Berkeley. "We've reached a point financially where we have to start exploring new ways to deliver law enforcement." [22]

City budget cuts are affecting public police service quality while limited community budgets affect private security quantity. Additional stresses will cause increased ethical lapses. Uniformed officers will take the wrath of citizen frustration. But patrol officers will not be the only recipients of citizen discontent as investigators, crime scene technicians, report clerks, community outreach officers and administrators receive comments and complaints. Increased parking fees and fines and a push to write more traffic tickets and make more DUI arrests to enhance falling tax revenues will play havoc with small business people and reduce other police services. Police will receive less support from the citizens they serve, and the stress will increase the interactions with the internal affairs function.

There is another culture, a culture cultivated by the suppliers of law enforcement equipment and others who promote weapons, ammunition and equipment of all types for wide distribution. I do not see the economy having much effect on this culture, what I do see is the potential for escalating violence affecting the conduct of officers. At the same time organizations advocate the right of every citizen to own a weapon of almost any type, suppliers of law enforcement equipment promote weapons to defend against the very citizens who have the right to own the weapons. From an internal affairs standpoint this interaction among gun owners, law enforcement, and weapons manufacturers militarizes law enforcement organizations and places both citizens and law enforcement officers in danger. As I mentioned previously, militarization places a divide between law enforcement officers and citizens and is contrary to efforts made for decades to bring a better understanding between officers and the citizens served. In addition, because of diminishing revenues, as weapons proliferate, the number of law enforcement officers decline.

More on the Economy

Robert W. Weber, a retired federal executive with extensive internal affairs experience, told me "there are hundreds of police agencies currently using or contemplating professional standards software to have computers do basic legwork in early detection of anomalies or vulnerability trends. Early detection would save investigative hours and, of course, dollars. Early detection also saves money by avoiding the conduct of later complex investigations. To save further dollars, computer-based training [CBT] is also strongly in use at an expense far less than personal training sessions. Whether CBT is as effective as personal training is certainly up for debate, but a poor instructor can be more expensive and less effective than a computer program, so human interaction is not necessarily the better way to go if a clear, solid anti-corruption message is the end point of the training." [23]

"I don't see a strong movement towards privatization of IA units because there is a need for a full understanding of the tactics, techniques, principles, and policies of any given department. Only those who have experienced living under such rules and regulations can have a full understanding of them. There is also the cost factor; hiring contractors to do IA work is a line-item expense that can be absorbed by department staff. Additionally, I believe there is a mindset within departments that they can best police themselves, and there is a pride in that position which would be lost if "outsiders" got into the nitty-gritty of police business. I believe citizen oversight groups will always be there, but principally in those departments that have experienced high profile integrity problems, especially when mandated by judicial decree. As long as departments can show that they are effectively policing themselves and the message shows this to be the case, citizen groups become unnecessary. The FBI taking over routine misconduct investigations [aside from public corruption cases impacting departments], either mandated by congress or otherwise, is a non-starter in my opinion. Again, there are resource issues to be considered, and except for high profile, criminal corruption cases involving LEO's (law enforcement officers) on which the bureau has initiated a federal investigation, departmental misconduct should truly be the role and responsibility of individual departments, and could also include high profile cases.[24]

There is a move by some IA units to discontinue providing substantiated/unsubstantiated/unfounded designations at the conclusion of the investigative report. New thought is that the report would outline and document all of the investigative findings by the IA officer, but the deciding official would make the decision regarding discipline, without being swayed or forced toward a certain decision by virtue of an IA "finding." In the best of cases, a "finding" is an assessment of the totality of the investigation by the case agent, so the thought is to let the deciding official make that call.[25]

More Culture Change Is Coming

As I mentioned in a previous chapter I have experienced many cultures in a law enforcement setting: a culture of an entire organization, of a few officers on a scheduled work shift or of a number of agents in an enforcement group. A culture can be formed over hundreds of years but can also be shaped in a short period of time through rapid hiring on a grand scale. I have also found it only takes one person or one directive to change a culture whether in an organization of thousands or in a small group of five.

For a time while a federal agent, I was assigned to a small group, all federal criminal investigators. Initially, the culture was one of content and cooperation but as agents came and went, the culture gradually changed to one of distrust and obstruction. One agent who found one aspect of his position was not to his liking, voiced his opinion to new hires and soured the work environment for others. All others initially accepted the duties as part of the job, but over time the unhappy agent convinced others that certain assignments were ones to complain about. This change caused by the persistence of one had a negative effect on the entire office operation. In another organization with thousands of employees, I watched as one person in authority poisoned every action a certain office took no matter how genuine the effort.

I had another experience of cultural change in the late 1980s while I was detailed from the U.S. Customs Office of Enforcement in Miami to the Florida Joint Task Group (FJTG). FJTG was a Drug Enforcement Administration (DEA) specialized unit of DEA and Customs special agents that combated narcotics smuggling in South Florida. The organizational culture was one of working hard for long hours and then playing hard. Many unit members would meet after work at one of many bars and drink for hours. When I first arrived I was welcomed by many, but not all unit members. Some were wary of a new arrival, especially experienced DEA special agents of a newly hired untested Customs agent. I was tested by DEA my first week when I was assigned to drive a tow truck, which was the "crash" vehicle to take down the front door of a drug smuggler's home. Actually, the hook or tow device was connected to the security gate and I was to drive away with the gate when directed. I sat in the driver's seat while others took cover. The situation ended without incident. After the test, successfully working with others, and getting to know all while socializing, in a few months I felt I was a fully fledged member of the group. Actually, I believe socializing by drinking with fellow agents gave all of us a better understanding of each other and fostered a trust that would have taken longer during work hours. After-hours drinking gave everyone the opportunity to let go and to take down barriers that were present during times when machismo took precedence. I certainly am not saying drinking with a weapon or two, with a government car waiting to take you home was the right thing, but getting to know your many partners was something that was of great importance. Socializing after hours was the fastest way to do it. After a time I realized there were a few people who I had difficulty determining whether they were "Customs" or "DEA," the acceptance was that great, at least for me.

That acceptance turned 180 degrees sometime in 1987–88 when a new DEA Administrator enforced a long-ignored policy that forbade using a government-issued vehicle for unofficial business. Almost daily social events stopped and grumbling started. The entire culture of playing hard changed overnight. As new agents arrived, it was difficult to know them unless I made a special effort. I was not the only one who felt this way. As one DEA agent told me, "going over to a co-worker's house to lay sod, plant a tree, or even celebrate Thanksgiving or Christmas with each other are pretty much gone ... I have neither been to nor know where my GS's (group supervisor) home is. I have been to one agent's house for one party in the

10 years that I have been in my current post of duty. I know where two other agents live but have never set foot in their houses. It just ain't like it used to be ... you know what I mean?" [26]

In 2002, elements of the U.S. Customs Service and the Immigration and Naturalization Service (INS) were separated from the U.S. Treasury and Justice Departments. They were merged into two distinct organizations: Customs and Border Protection (CBP) and Immigration and Customs Enforcement (ICE), both part of the newly created Department of Homeland Security. The U.S. Customs Office of Investigations, from which I retired, was merged with criminal investigators from INS, and ICE was formed. "The two agencies were merged from recommendations of individuals with little knowledge of either organization. Customs was a strong enforcement organization, conducting smuggling investigations of narcotics, U.S. currency, child pornography and other criminal violations which were supported and embraced by federal prosecutors. Immigration criminal violations, many documented by multi-jurisdictional, multi-lingual investigations were often avoided by U.S. Attorneys because of the complexities involved to include the language barrier. U.S. Attorneys would decline immigration criminal cases and refer them for administrative sanctions. When the merge took place, immigration agents were promoted into managerial positions with limited knowledge of U.S. Customs criminal investigations. Many former Customs special agents are now embarrassed to identify themselves as ICE agents, and some ICE offices have identification showing only that the office is part of the Department of Homeland Security." [27]

Author's Note

ICE special agents have since been placed into a new ICE directorate titled Homeland Security Investigations (HSI).

"At the same time, U.S. Customs agents did not understand immigration law and policy. Many Customs agents, depending upon the situation, stopped work at 5pm and held evidence until the next working day. On the other hand, when called to make arrests Immigration agents were obligated to work until all individuals were processed. Immigration policy dictated that all individuals illegally in the country had to be processed and given summons directing them to appear in court to answer for their illegal status. Immigration agents know full well that most illegal immigrants would not appear in court, but the paper work had to be completed; legacy Customs agents would not accept the bureaucratic reality. Additional rivalry was caused by the fact that some federal judicial districts readily accepted immigration cases for prosecution while others avoided them because of other, more pressing issues. Legacy Customs agents felt they had more important investigations to conduct, but were forced by legacy immigration supervisors to spend time on matters never to be prosecuted."[28] Two organizations with long histories of success were thrown together in October 2002, causing an immediate culture change that will take a generation to unite in harmony.

My experiences have made me believe that a culture can be changed for good or bad, either over time or in a short period by a strong personality or policy change. Any law enforcement organization can be changed and can be focused in another direction by a bold leader with clear, firm objectives. But it is not easy. Loyalty must be instilled in all employees of any organization. As I mentioned before, any organization, whether public or private, has splinter social groups with many interests and those interests may not necessarily be those of the organization. I worked with many outstanding individuals, one of whom told me and others many times that "attitude is everything." The new generations along with their attitudes will change the playing field. Some change will be for the better, some not. It all depends upon the leadership of today and the future guiding and focusing the newer generations with their attitudes to the point where they believe service to others and trust are complements to attitude.

Without strong leadership and explicit ethical training, behavior may not be in the forefront of an officer's mind. Most officers do not plan on acting unethically, but in the heat of conflict may fixate on an arrest, rather than how to lawfully make the arrest. Other officers who are consciously unethical can be given a wake-up call or rooted out by a strong leadership commitment. The U.S. Department of Justice, along with many police departments, has made strides in the struggle to control misconduct. Studies have been conducted and strategies formulated to serve the public with honor. Even with strong leadership, the mystery of the subconscious of street-level officers, the lieutenants, sergeants, patrol officers, detectives, and special agents has not been mastered. Proactive measures like integrity control officers, field associates, audits, and inspections may complement leadership but may also be considered a supplement for poor supervision. But if management does not act in the best interest of the department, its officers, and the citizens served, someone else may take the initiative.

The Trump Card

Barack Hussein Obama was elected the 44th president of the United States on November 4, 2008. Barack Obama was touted as a reformer, an idealist, one who inspires hope in others and one who wants to change the future. He believes in responsibility. The theme of his presidential campaign was "change we can believe in." Ninety-five percent of Black voters supported him, 69% of first-time voters along with 66% of voters under 30, 73% of voters with incomes under $15,000, and 63% of urban voters supported him.[29] His election made people cry. He has been compared to Abraham Lincoln.

He is one who looks for noble causes; he wants things to be as they should be, not as they are. He believes in public service; he purportedly advocates transparency in government. He was a community organizer, he worked with churches to improve communities, and he directed a voter registration drive. As a Harvard-educated attorney, he worked with a law firm that specialized in civil rights litigation. The United States has entered a new era where the election of the first Black president swept "away the last racial barrier in American politics." [30]

"If there is anyone out there who still doubts that America is a place where all things are possible, who still wonders if the dream of our founders is alive in our time, who still questions the power of our democracy, tonight is your answer." [31]

On January 20, 2009, President Barack Obama gave his inaugural address. He discussed the economy and other domestic issues that concerned him most: world peace and international issues. He called for the nation to make hard choices and to prepare for a "new age": "... we gather because we have chosen hope over fear, unity of purpose over conflict and discord."[32] No mention was made of law enforcement, no mention of police misconduct. He did mention, however, "what free men and women can achieve when imagination is joined to common purpose, and necessity to courage ... What the cynics fail to understand is that the ground has shifted beneath them ... Those of us who manage the public's dollars will be held to account—to spend wisely, to reform bad habits, and do our business in the light of day—because only then can we restore the vital trust between a people and their government."[33]

"What is required of us now is a new era of responsibility—a recognition, on the part of every American, that we have duties to ourselves, our nation, and the world, duties that we do not grudgingly accept but rather seize gladly, firm in the knowledge that there is nothing so satisfying to the spirit, so defining of our character, than giving our all to a difficult task. This is the price and the promise of citizenship."[34]

Months and years after the election, there is much controversy, but some voters seem to still be optimistic ... cautious, but optimistic ... that their hopes will be realized for the many promised changes President Obama will make. He is a dreamer, and many still believe in him. He may be naïve when he proselytizes before Congress to abandon pork barrel politics, but he is an activist and he empowers people.

In early 2009, he attacked with dollars, whether rightly or wrongly, the downward spiral of the economy with strength, resolution, and confidence. His plans are, among others, to have a multi focus on improving the economy, along with legislation for energy and education initiatives and tax changes. He was successful in passing national health care legislation. We may not know the success or failure of his efforts for years to come but the naysayers will always be present, whether a Democrat or Republican is president. However, if failure looms, other initiatives will rise to the forefront and President Obama will look for people and things he is comfortable with. He will look to community activists.

President Obama confronts situations others may not, things like pork barrel politics, excessive corporate compensation, and Congressional excesses. He connects with voters in a way most politicians do not. When there is another outrageous episode of police misconduct, one word from a community leader about police excesses will bring the weight of the current president and his administration on police behavior.

In the summer of 2009, a Black Harvard University professor was arrested by the Cambridge, MA, police for disorderly conduct. Charges were made against the police that the arrest was an example of racial profiling. President Obama clearly demonstrated his desire to be involved in grassroots issues when he unexpectedly commented on a purely local, but racially charged incident. Historically, presidents have weighed in on racial issues when they affected masses of people. However, Barack Obama, the community activist, rose to the occasion on this local issue and, arguably, added fuel to the already stoked flames of a singular controversy. Admittedly not having all the facts, he insulted the Cambridge, MA police, specifically, and all law enforcement generally by calling the actions of the police stupid and raising historically poor relations between minority groups and U.S. law enforcement. Two weeks after the incident all parties met at the White House, for the so-called "beer summit," where the professor and arresting officer discussed the situation. President Obama's conviction is clear; he is not reluctant to champion local issues; issues regarding perceived police misconduct.

Another grassroots issue the community activist has championed is the killing, some say murder, of Trayvon Martin. Martin a young, Sanford, FL, high school student was shot and killed by George Zimmerman, reportedly a self-appointed neighborhood watch captain. Because of issues clouded by Florida law Zimmerman was not initially arrested for the shooting because he claimed self-defense. Apparently, because of national attention and racially charged mass protests President Obama, cautious not to interfere with an ongoing federal investigation, commented on the shooting by saying that "If I had a son he would look like Trayvon."[35]

Another example of the President's mindset is that "President Obama endorsed new protections for national security officers who blow the whistle on abusive, corrupt or illegal behavior, by offering them the right to sue for damages and challenge denials of their security clearances."[36] His Republican-appointed defense secretary opposed the change, but wants a more open and accountable government.

There Will Be Other Efforts

It may take only one more Abner Louima or Rodney King to make a section of society rise up because they are fed up, whether or not the community leader is the president of the United States.

On May 5, 2010, "The new mayor of New Orleans has asked the Justice Department to review the city's embattled police department ... Mayor Mitch Landrieu asked Attorney General Eric Holder to assign a team from the department's civil rights division to help the city address and prevent police misconduct. 'I have inherited a police force that has been described by many as one of the worst police departments in the country,' Landrieu says in the letter. 'It is clear that nothing short of a complete transformation is necessary and essential to ensure safety for the citizens of New Orleans ... The police force, the community, our citizens are desperate for positive change...' The mayor said in his letter that most officers 'honor their commitment to protect and serve each day,' but an independent investigation must evaluate the department' ... Investigations of city police by the Justice Department are not uncommon, but cities themselves rarely initiate them, according to Merrick Bobb, executive director of the Police Assessment Resource Center in Los Angeles ... Peter Scharf, a criminology professor at Tulane University said, 'People are more afraid of the police than they are of the criminals, and we have really scary criminals,' ... The mayor said, 'This is about examining patterns and practices, thinking about excessive force, dealing with internal affairs and basically to engage in what I would consider to be transformational, systemic reform' ..." [37]

On July 25, 2012, the Huffington Post reported that the U.S. Justice Department entered into a consent decree with the City of New Orleans. [Attorney General Eric] "Holder said the agreement is the most wide-ranging in the Justice Department's history and resolves allegations that New Orleans police officers have engaged in a pattern of discriminatory and unconstitutional activity. The decree offers a list of requirements to improve the department's policies and procedures and it is anticipated will fundamentally change the culture of the New Orleans Police Department. Although the U.S. Justice Department has reached similar agreements with numerous other departments... "the scope of the New Orleans consent decree is billed as the broadest of its kind and includes requirements that no other department has had to implement.[38]

For instance, the agreement requires officers to respect that bystanders have a constitutional right to observe and record their conduct in public places. Its "bias-free policing" provisions, which call for creating a policy to guide officers' interactions with gay, lesbian, bisexual and transgender residents, also are believed to be unprecedented for a police department's consent decree."[39]

The decree is expected to last at least four years but is viewed skeptically as a permanent end to historical problems.

In Conclusion

Command presence is a key to many situations faced in the law enforcement profession. The desires, actions, and interactions of an officer can either cool or inflame tempers during a call for service. In the same way, a positive or negative command presence by members of the internal affairs process can affect an officer's attitude while responding to a citizen's call for service or create a sense of unfairness or injustice in the internal affairs function. The display of a negative command presence in any circumstance by anyone in authority or anyone perceived to have influence over an officer's life, can add to the cynicism many officers already exhibit.

A strong desire presented by a few can change the culture and the perceptions of many. The internal affairs process made up of many influential people can and does play a direct role in building trust between the internal affairs function and all who are affected by it. A positive command presence by department leaders is key to not only providing ethical police services, but supporting a professional and fair internal affairs operation. Opening department activities to public scrutiny as much as the law allows, leaders honestly confronting rather than avoiding emotionally charged situations, and addressing perceptions or the reality of unfairness and wrongdoing by the internal affairs function, will create a command presence of fair and impartial service to both the citizens served and the officers who serve them.

Although the ultimate duty of the internal affairs investigator is to uncover the truth many players in the process may vilify and portray the investigator or the entire function as one which undermines good policing by acting markedly unfair. Many members of the process will revel in the bait-and-switch game by presenting true ethical standards, but at the same time, overlooking officer transgressions and scolding the internal affairs investigator for doing his job.

There will always be controversy associated with the internal affairs function because the function deals with controversial issues and divergent agendas of the process members. Many members pursue agendas not necessarily for the good of the citizens served or officers involved. Department, political, union, or community leaders who interfere with investigations, under fund an office, or make misleading statements to obscure the truth can create a perception or the reality that the internal affairs function is unfair. Some media portrayals make drama a reality.

Department leaders will never have much control over the players in the internal affairs process, but without a strong sense of fairness, a leader can lose control of the investigative function. The fact that an officer chose to report wrongdoing to an outside entity is a sign of lack of control. Leaders must take every opportunity to challenge opposing agendas that conflict with reality or help create a negative perception of internal investigations. Successfully controlling the internal affairs function will present a positive image of the entire department.

In the twenty-first century the ongoing use of advances in technology, training techniques, and management methods will foster positive perceptions and realities. Higher education, community oriented leaders, committed operational supervisors, and hiring practices aimed at the recruitment of the best without political interference can eventually support a culture change in many departments where willful misconduct will be an anomaly.

In the future, fewer managers will ask when corruption is uncovered, "how could he do that; how stupid can he be?" Rather the questions asked will be, "how could I allow that to happen; how stupid could I be?" IA will have little effect, as it does now, on misconduct or corruption, but change will take place because of management practices, training, and the hiring process. Management commitment and sincere ethical training and behavior will never rid a department of misconduct or corruption but will continue to minimize it.

Case Study

On November 5, 2009, U.S. Army Major Nidal Malik Hasan, a U.S. born Muslim carried out a shooting spree at Fort Hood, Texas, killing 13 and wounding 32. Prior to the shooting, the U.S Army and the Federal Bureau of Investigation knew of Hasan's extremist views. Although Hasan's emails with a known terrorist were monitored, prior to the shootings authorities determined that the emails did not present a threat. As an internal affairs investigator for a large sheriff's department in the State of Texas you begin thinking the internal affairs function has just entered into the twenty-first century.

Case Study Questions

Answer the following questions in one narrative response.

1. *Do constitutional protections, like freedom of religion and the right to privacy, along with the current trend of political correctness make it difficult for law enforcement agencies to focus on and identify likely terror suspects? Explain your position.*

2. *How can a department's internal affairs function protect the United States from a law enforcement officer with intentions similar to Hasan's?*

Questions for Discussion

Answer each of the following questions in a separate response.

1. How can technology assist to maintain or improve ethics in law enforcement?

2. Contact a local, county, state, federal, or military law enforcement department. Interview an administrator, personnel specialist, or law enforcement officer and discuss and report the types of discipline used in the department. What effect, if any, has positive discipline, if used in the department, had on an officer's attitude and performance? If you are not in a position to contact a department, discuss positive and negative discipline, their differences and similarities. Give examples.

3. Conduct online or traditional library research and discuss the Hawthorne Studies. From experience, do you believe if you are being watched, you will be more ethical in any situation? During your discussion consider youthful learning experiences.

Notes

1. Lewan, Todd, Associated Press. (12 Jul 2009). New IDs raise privacy concerns: Built-in chips allow tracking at a distance. *The Tennessean.* vol. 105, no. 193.
2. Richburg, Keith B. (19 July 2010). Consultants sell "birth tourism" to expectant Chinese mothers. *Washington Post.* Retrieved from http://www.chron.com/news/article/Consultants-sell-birth-tourism-to-expectant-1702744.php
3. FreeMMOGamer.com. (8 Mar 2012). Retrieved from http://www.freemmogamer.com/2008/09/americas-army.html)
4. Science Applications International Corporation (SAIC). (9 Mar 2012). Retrieved from http://www.saic.com/products/simulation/olive/
5. Stanton, Jim. (26 Sep 2008). Web 2.0 Challenges Traditional Government Communications. Government Technology Magazine. Retrieved from http://www.govtech.com/featured/Web-20-Challenges-Traditional-Government-Communications.html.
6. Associated Press. (2 July 2009). Ohio Police Chief retires after Video Shows Him Kissing Female Officer in Cruiser. Retrieved from http://www.foxnews.com/story/0,2933,529844,00.html.
7. Brochu, Nicole. (31 Jul 2009). Ugliness echoes from Hollywood cops' creative writing exercise. *South Florida Sun-Sentinel.* Sun-Sentinel.com. Retrieved from http://www.sun-sentinel.com/news/opinion/todaysbuzz/friday/sfl-hollywood-police-cover-up-buzz-brochu-m073109,0,2460841.story
8. Howe, James. (24 Aug 2009). Detective from police department which will remain anonymous. Electronic interview.
9. Peterson, Gilbert, Dr. (25 Jun 2009). Air Force Institute of Technology. Telephonic interview.
10. Peterson, Gilbert, Dr. (3 May 2011). Air Force Institute of Technology. Electronic interview.

11. Ibid.
12. Stanton, Jim. (26 Sep 2008). Web 2.0 Challenges Traditional Government Communications. Government Technology Magazine. Retrieved from http://www.govtech.com/featured/Web-20-Challenges-Traditional-Government-Communications.html.
13. Ibid.
14. Ibid.
15. Ibid.
16. Police Officer who will remain anonymous. (30 Sep 2009). City of New York Police Department. Electronic interview.
17. Eilders, Lon, Sr. (22 Mar 2007). Lieutenant (retired), Manager, Accreditation and Planning, Chattanooga, TN Police Department. Letter.
18. Fox News. (20 Jul 2010). Video Shows USDA Official Saying She Didn't Give "Full Force" of Help to White Farmer. Retrieved from http://www.foxnews.com/politics/2010/07/19/clip-shows-usda-official-admitting-withheld-help-white-farmer/. Accessed September 7, 2010.
19. Parks, Richard. (13 Aug 2010). In Oakland, CA, Private Force May Be Hired for Security—Chinatown is leading a new trend in the crime-ridden city: privately financed public safety, Los Angeles Community Policing. *The New York Times*. Retrieved from http://www.lacp.org/2010-Articles-Main/081310-OaklandPrivate ForceMayBeHired4Security.htm. Accessed August 21, 2010.
20. Ibid.
21. Johnson, Kevin. (25 Aug 2010). Home burglarized? Fill out a form—Budget cuts force police to curtail calls for lesser crimes. *USA TODAY*. Retrieved from http://www.usatoday.com/print edition/news/20100825/1albottomxx.htm.
22. Parks, Richard. (13 Aug 2010). In Oakland, CA, Private Force May Be Hired for Security—Chinatown is leading a new trend in the crime-ridden city: privately financed public safety, Los Angeles Community Policing. *The New York Times*. Retrieved from http://www.lacp.org/2010-Articles-Main/081310-OaklandPrivate ForceMayBeHired4Security.htm. Accessed August 21, 2010.
23. Robert W. Weber, former director, Office of Professional Responsibility Immigration and Customs Enforcement; Deputy Assistant Director (retired), Homeland Security Investigations; Department of Homeland Security; President, Robert Weber Consulting. (28 Oct 2010) Electronic interview.
24. Ibid.
25. Ibid.
26. Drug Enforcement Administration Special Agent who will remain anonymous. (15 May 15 2009). Electronic interview.
27. Immigration and Customs Enforcement Special Agent, legacy U.S. Customs, who will remain anonymous. (16 May 2009). Telephonic interview.
28. Immigration and Naturalization Service Special Agent (retired) who will remain anonymous. (16 May 2009). Telephonic interview.
29. CNN Election Center 2008. CNNPolitics.com. Retrieved from http://www.cnn.com/ELECTION/2008/results/polls/#USP00p1.

30. Nagourney, Adam. (5 Nov 2008). Obama Elected President as Racial Barrier Falls. *The New York Times*. Retrieved from http://www.nytimes.com/2008/11/05/us/politics/05elect.html.
31. Ibid.
32. Associated Press. (21 Jan 2009). Inaugural address of Barack Obama, 44th President of the United States. *The Tennessean*. vol. 105. No. 21.
33. Ibid.
34. Ibid.
35. ABC News. (23 Mar 2012). Trayvon Martin Case: Timeline of Events. Retrieved from http://abcnews.go.com/blogs/headlines/2012/03/trayvon-martin-case-timeline-of-events/j
36. Smith, R., Jeffrey., & Warrick, Joby. (18 Feb 2009). Obama, Gates at Odds Over New Whistleblower Protections. *The Washington Post*. Retrieved from http://www.washingtonpost.com/wp-dyn/content/article/2009/02/17/AR2009021703006.html.
37. Shoichet, Catherine, E. (6 May 2010). New Orleans Mayor Wants Feds to Probe Police. CNN Justice. Retrieved from http://articles.cnn.com/2010-05-06/justice/new.orleans.police.mayor_1_police-officers-police-force-new-orleans-police-department?_s=PM:CRIME
38. McGill, Kevin & Kunzelman, Michael (25 July 2012). New Orleans Police Department Reforms: Plan Aims to Excise Corruption, Discrimination and Frequent Use of Deadly Force. The Huffington Post. Retrieved from http://www.huffingtonpost.com/2012/07/25/new-orleans-police-department-reforms_n_1700960.html
39. Ibid.

Suggested Reading

Manis, Jennifer, Archbold, Carol, A, & Hassell, Kimberly, D. (2008). Exploring the impact of police officer education level on allegations of police misconduct. *International Journal of Police Science & Management*, vol. 10, no. 4, pp. 509–523, DOI: 10.1350/ijps.2008.10.4.102. Retrieved from https://www.ncjrs.gov/App/publications/Abstract.aspx?id=248508

Friedrich, Roman, Peterson, Michael, & Koster, Alex. (2011). The Rise of Generation C: How to prepare for the Connected Generation's transformation of the consumer and business landscape. *Strategy+Business magazine*, Booz & Company, Inc. New York. issue 62, Spring 2011. Retrieved from http://www.strategy-business.com/media/file/sb62_11110.pdf

Index

Notes

Notes